S.E.B.G.

NEW ORLEANS ARCHITECTURE

VOLUME III

The Cemeteries

NEW ORLEANS ARCHITECTURE

VOLUME III

The Cemeteries

Edited by
MARY LOUISE CHRISTOVICH

Authors:
LEONARD V. HUBER
PEGGY McDOWELL
MARY LOUISE CHRISTOVICH

Photographs by
BETSY SWANSON

Drawings by
DOYLE GERTJEJANSEN

PELICAN PUBLISHING COMPANY
GRETNA 1974

Library of Congress Catalog Card Number: 72-1722-72
International Standard Book Number: 0-88289-020-4
First printing: April, 1974

Published by Pelican Publishing Company, Inc.
630 Burmaster Street, Gretna, Louisiana 70053
Manufactured in the United States of America
Printed by The TJM Corporation, Baton Rouge, Louisiana
Designed by J. Barney McKee

Library of Congress Cataloging in Publication Data
Huber, Leonard V., etc.
     New Orleans Architecture, Vol. III
     The Cemeteries
Gretna, Louisiana   Pelican Publishing Co.
April, 1974
(New Orleans Architecture)

CONTENTS

FOREWORD

During the two decades since The Friends of the Cabildo was founded as a volunteer auxiliary to the Louisiana State Museum the organization has played a vital role in historic preservation.

Among its major efforts, The Friends obtained the funds necessary to restore three historic New Orleans structures: the Cabildo, the Presbytere, and, most recently, Madame John's Legacy. It also has presented eighteen exhibits in the Museum and sponsored hundreds of lectures on Louisiana's colorful history. Through its leadership, artifacts valued at more than one hundred thousand dollars have been donated to the Museum. The five thousand members of The Friends can be proud of their organization's efforts toward making the Museum one of America's finest.

It is with equal pride that we present this third volume in the *New Orleans Architecture* series, *The Cemeteries*. It is particularly noteworthy that this volume is published at a time when many cemeteries merit the kind of attention attracted to other areas of historic New Orleans by the previous two volumes. Hopefully, this attention will stimulate efforts for the care and preservation of this unique New Orleans art form.

The impact of the first two volumes of this series, *The Lower Garden District* and *The American Sector,* has been profound. More than three million dollars in private funds have been invested in the Lower Garden District, the area covered in Volume I, since its publication in 1971. Additionally, a number of studies currently are being conducted relating to the preservation of many commercial structures featured in the American Sector, the subject of Volume II. The adaptation of these buildings for twentieth-century needs and commercial usages has proved both feasible and profitable.

I want to express appreciation to those many members whose efforts have been instrumental in the preparation of Volume III. Only dedication — in many cases, total dedication — has made this work possible.

A special word of appreciation must go to three particular individuals:

Leonard V. Huber, author, historian, and immediate past president of The Friends, who has compiled a brief history of the cemeteries;

Mrs. Peggy McDowell, a native of Memphis, Tennessee, and assistant professor of art history at Louisiana State University in New Orleans, who spent three years researching architectural styles and interpreting nineteenth-century tombs; and

Mrs. Mary Louise Christovich, a past president of The Friends and former member of the Louisiana State Museum Board who provided editorial direction for the entire volume and conducted an extensive survey on which the section on cemetery ironwork is based. She also was a major contributor to and driving force in the preparation of the two previous volumes.

FOREWORD

As in the compilation of the preceding volumes of this series, a great many institutions and individuals have rendered invaluable assistance. Much of the research material for this book is the result of the diligent efforts of Mrs. Aline Morris and Miss Rose Lambert of the Louisiana State Museum Library. Through their generous contributions of time and effort a vast amount of material was made available to the authors.

Boyd Cruise, Director of the Historic New Orleans Collection, uncovered heretofore unknown facts concerning the early cemeteries of the city. His tireless pursuit of historical data added to this volume a dimension that otherwise would have been impossible to achieve. A particular word of appreciation is due the Board of Trustees for granting permission to reprint the de Pouilly and Waud drawings and other pertinent material.

Collin B. Hamer, Head of the Louisiana Room of the New Orleans Public Library, and members of his staff, particularly Miss Jean M. Jones, made available statistical data from their excellent newspaper files and directories. Clive Hardy and Ken Owens, staff members of the Louisiana Collection, Earl Long Library, Louisiana State University in New Orleans, served as research consultants and gathered lists of bibliographical information. Ralph Hogan and Ken Barlow, photographers for the LSUNO Audio Visual Center, supplied many study photographs.

The Special Collections Division of the Tulane University Library, under the able direction of Mrs. Connie Griffith, was the source of many important illustrations. Miss Elizabeth G. Lockett and Mrs. Faye M. Swanson of the Tulane Library furnished excellent source materials.

A special note of gratitude is due Henry Alcus, whose patience and expertise produced the technical, and much of the historical, information on cemetery ironwork. Guy F. Bernard, who has photographed and catalogued cemetery ironwork for the past forty years, and Stanley Diefenthal, who braved the summer heat to make on-the-scene analyses of many iron enclosures, merit special thanks. Manuel C. De Lerno and Mrs. Abbye A. Gorin also provided many photographs.

The Reverend Monsignor Henry C. Bezou, pastor of St. Francis Xavier Church in Metairie, Leonard E. Gately, Sidney L. Villeré, and Mrs. William Loevy, temple administrator of the Gates of Prayer Congregation, contributed photographs and historical data. The Reverend Monsignor Raymond A. Wegmann, director of the New Orleans Archdiocesan Cemeteries, extended every courtesy and made available maps and burial records of the Catholic cemeteries. Mrs. Ella LeBourgeois and Charles Gagliano of the St. Louis III Cemetery office were particularly generous with their time and files.

The authors are also greatly indebted to Henri A. Gandolfo, sales representative—memorial counselor for Weiblen for 54 years, for furnishing much information about the cemeteries, the men who constructed the memorials, and the individuals for whom they were built, and William Groves, who furnished from his vast collection copies of unpublished drawings by W. R. Shaw. In addition, Mike Posey provided important photographs.

The editorial assistance of Mrs. Sally Evans and Mrs. Roulhac Toledano expedited the completion of this volume. Clerical and research assistants were Helen Schneidau, Maury Toledano, Ann Harris, Ann Evans, and Lou Hoffman.

STANTON M. FRAZAR
President, The Friends of the Cabildo, Inc.

INTRODUCTION

The cemeteries of New Orleans have always been objects of fascination to visitors to the city, and many early nineteenth-century travelers wrote extensively about their experiences and impressions of these old burial places and the burial practices. Among these was the architect Benjamin Henry Latrobe, whose comments are quoted in the text.

In the city's first cemetery, established before 1725 and located within the Vieux Carré, in the square bounded by Toulouse, Rampart, St. Peter, and Burgundy streets, burials were generally underground. Its site was recently excavated for the construction of a new hotel, and some remains were unearthed. Not even a tombstone remains, however, to mark the site of this historic burial ground where many of the city's founders were interred. Some remains and monuments may have been removed to the St. Louis Cemetery when this first burial ground was closed in 1788 and the land sold off as building lots in 1800.

Much of old St. Louis Cemetery I has disappeared over the years as streets have been cut through it on all sides. Nothing remains of the Girod street Cemetery, destroyed in 1957, except a few salvaged slabs now in the St. John Cemetery, to which the remains were removed, and a few bits of sculpture in the Louisiana State Museum. Other cemeteries have been the victims of neglect and of heartless vandals, and thus irreplaceable records of history and architecture have been destroyed.

There have been sporadic efforts in the past to do something to preserve the old cemeteries, and about 1923 a Society for the Preservation of Ancient Tombs was organized. The noted New Orleans writer Grace King was honorary president, and the historian and genealogist George C. H. Kernion was active president. This society with a reported membership of over 150, began a research project to determine the location and condition of the tombs of greatest historical significance and then undertook efforts to have them restored.

According to the New Orleans *States* of September 8, 1923, Mrs. Frank Wadill, vice-president of the society and chairman of the tomb committee "spent days in patient examination of the old St. Louis cemeteries," and church and cemetery records were studied. Mrs. J. P. Stockton then owned four volumes inherited from her great-grandfather, Ruffino Fernandez, in which he had taken notes of the location of plots in St. Louis Cemetery II which he carefully entered in these books. Here he recorded the purchase of burial plots and the erection of tombs, many of them between the years of 1823 and 1842, the first twenty years of the Claiborne Avenue Cemetery. The aims of the society were directed not only to New Orleans cemeteries but to old burial grounds in other parts of the state, and appealed through the press "to all patriotic men and women of New Orleans and Louisiana, who honor the memory of Louisiana's illustrious dead." As late as June 29, 1930, Grace King

INTRODUCTION

appealed in an article in the *Times-Picayune* for the restoration of the Protestant corner of the old St. Louis Cemetery, asking "Is there a more forlorn, desolate, neglected-looking spot in New Orleans than this old relic of history?" Some good was no doubt accomplished by these dedicated people, but the society evidently passed away with its leaders, and deterioration and neglect of the old tombs continued.

In the late 1930s the Works Progress Administration recorded the inscriptions on the tombstones in most of the old cemeteries. The results of this survey are many thousands of file cards housed in the library of the Louisiana State Museum. This is an invaluable record, for many of the old inscriptions have since disappeared.

A more recent and, in some ways, more successful effort was undertaken to save the old Lafayette Cemetery No. 1 on Washington Avenue and Prytania Street. As a result this historic cemetery was placed on the National Register of Historic Places kept by the National Park Service of the U.S. Department of the Interior.

Many of the newer cemeteries are now protected from neglect by perpetual care funds, but many of the older ones with tombs of unknown ownership or tombs of societies no longer existing are continuing to disintegrate. Efforts are being made to continue the work of salvaging the old Lafayette Cemetery, and some restoration has been attempted by the Archdiocese of New Orleans. Much more, however, is urgently needed, and this third volume on New Orleans architecture will undoubtedly focus attention and inspire positive action for the protection and preservation of what remains of this priceless historical and architectural heritage. Some forty cemeteries are discussed herein.

SAMUEL WILSON, JR.

NEW ORLEANS ARCHITECTURE

VOLUME III

The Cemeteries

Vaults of the Orleans Battalion of Artillery, with fence simulating old cannon and anchor chains.

New Orleans Cemeteries: A Brief History

LEONARD V. HUBER

When the French founded New Orleans in 1718, burials were made along the river bank. In 1721 Adrien DePauger, Royal Military Engineer, arrived to lay out the streets for the new town. The Vieux Carré, as we know it today, is essentially the town that he staked out. A cemetery was designated on the outskirts of the little settlement, and an early plan of New Orleans dated May 20, 1725 (fig. 1), shows it as extending along the upper side of St. Peter Street between the streets now known as Burgundy and Rampart. At the time the cemetery was laid out, the streets extended no farther back from the river than Dauphine Street. When the first efforts to fortify the city were made after the Indian massacre of the French at Natchez in 1729, a ditch, serving as a moat, was located along this street. This placed the cemetery outside the city limits, and it was reached by a winding road from the end of Orleans Street as shown on the plan of Gonichon drawn in 1731 (fig. 2). Inasmuch as New Orleans was then an entirely Catholic community, the first burial place was administered by the parish church of St. Louis.

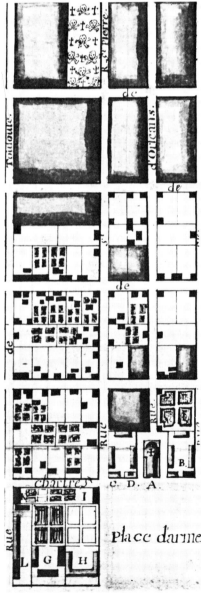

Fig. 1. Detail of plan of New Orleans dated 1725 showing St. Peter Street cemetery, indicated here by skull and cross-bones symbols. (Courtesy Samuel Wilson, Jr., Collection.)

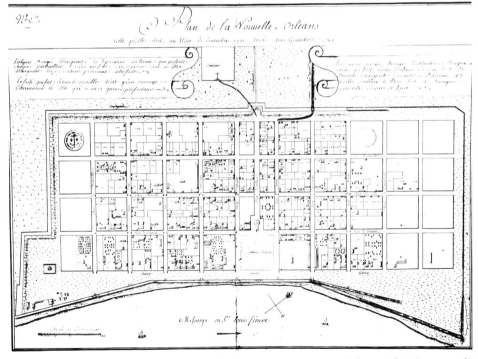

Fig. 2. Gonichon's plan of 1731 showing the first cemetery in New Orleans. This "graveyard" was designated as such in 1725 on an earlier plan. (Courtesy Samuel Wilson, Jr., Collection.)

3

Burial in the first cemetery was entirely below the ground, and because it was on a low and swampy site, the area was surrounded by ditches. The earth from the ditches was used to raise the level of the land, and the cemetery was enclosed by a wooden palisade. The little cemetery was thus described by DePauger in a letter which he wrote on February 9, 1724.

Not everybody was buried in the cemetery in the early days. Prominent inhabitants were entombed within the parish church throughout the colonial period, and interments took place occasionally in the small area of ground immediately adjacent to the church. When the engineer DePauger died in June, 1726, his remains were placed beneath the then uncompleted church which he had designed. Among the old records of the parish is an entry made in 1769 of "the burial of Mr. St. Martin which was granted freely within the church by virtue of the gifts which he had made to said church for repairing it." For the solemn service at his funeral, the church was draped in black and lighted by 272 candles.

On August 27, 1784, the Spanish Cabildo (governing body), "considering the danger to the public health . . . and especially knowing that the church and grounds are too small to permit further interments," ordered the wardens to refuse burials in the church other than those of distinguished inhabitants of the colony.

In 1742, under the direction of Father Charles, Capuchin Rector of St. Louis Church, the cemetery was surrounded with a five-foot brick wall. To build it, the wealthier contributed money to buy bricks and mortar, and the poorer classes contributed their labor. The wall was dedicated with great ceremony on All Saints' Day, 1743. A large wooden cross was erected in the center of the area.

For nearly seventy years the St. Peter Street Cemetery served the city. During that time, in 1762, Louisiana passed from the rule of France to Spain, and New Orleans grew from a village to a sizable little city. The year 1788 was one of calamity—the river overflowed, a great fire destroyed 856 houses and laid waste four-fifths of the city followed by a serious epidemic that brought death to many people. In that year the Cabildo, realizing that the cemetery was filled and being warned by local physicians that the proximity of the cemetery to the city could cause another outbreak of pestilence, ordered the cemetery closed to further interments. They ordered a new cemetery to be established farther from the center of population.

The new cemetery was to be selected in agreement with the Very Reverend Father Vicar General who would also see that it be "duly blessed in accordance with the rites of our Holy Church and fenced with pickets at the expense of the City Treasury; burial in the said cemetery may be started immediately, from which time burial in the actual [old] cemetery is absolutely prohibited." Thus came into existence St. Louis Cemetery I, which occupies the site between streets known today as Basin, Conti, Treme, and St. Louis. The site selected was at the edge of the city "in the rear of the Charity Hospital about 40 yards from its garden." It occupied a space three hundred feet square and until officially approved, was designated as temporary. On August 14, 1789, a royal decree was issued in which "His Majesty was pleased to approve the construction of the new cemetery." The burial grounds were then designated as permanent, and the authorities paid Antonio Guidry 523 pesos, 7 reales for "expenses and personal labor for fencing the new cemetery." The royal edict also decreed that the old cemetery "was to be eventually used as a site for the construction of houses."

It is interesting to note that, despite the founding of a new cemetery, burials in the St. Peter Street Cemetery continued for some years. In 1797, when Don Almonester y Roxas was building a new church of St. Louis (the cathedral) at his own expense, he thriftily made use of bricks from the wall of the old cemetery. The unfenced cemetery created an embarrassment for the Cabildo; they ordered the old cemetery fenced with pickets but declined to censure the philanthropic Don Almonester.

By 1800 the St. Peter Street Cemetery was divided into building lots and disposed of by the city council. Bishop Peñalver, however, intervened and submitted a claim as owner of the land in the old cemetery. In this claim a statement occurs mentioning that an earlier cemetery was located in the square bounded by Bienville, Chartres, Conti, and Royal streets until 1743. More than eighty years had passed since the city's founding, and the bishop depended on testimony of several old-time residents, but their statement is obviously in error, for contemporary maps and other records of the French colonial period clearly show that the Chartres Street square was used for residential purposes. The archbishop's claim to the St. Peter Street Cemetery was denied, but as late as 1802 he still tried to get possession of the land without success.

ST. LOUIS CEMETERY I (1789)

When one visits this venerable place today (fig. 3), he stands in the presence of the almost forgotten dead of a century and a half; the realization grows upon him that beneath the gray and often uncared-for ruins of once handsome tombs repose the remains of men and women who were at one time the most illustrious of New Orleans (fig. 4A).

The tombs in St. Louis Cemetery I are arranged with little regard for order. The shelled paths are tortuous; there are some grassy aisles and only a scattering of

Fig. 3. This wrought iron entrance gate of St. Louis I is a good example of the skill of New Orleans ironworkers of the nineteenth century.

Fig. 4B. The deteriorated condition of parts of St. Louis I is indicated in this scene.

Fig. 4A. Aerial view of St. Louis I showing its irregular aisles. At the upper left is the site of the Protestant cemetery.

Fig. 4C. A typical aisle in St. Louis I: a well-kept tomb at right; the brickwork showing through in patches of the society tomb at left; the lack of orderly planning ex-emplified by the tombs which block the aisle; and the young trees sprouting from Italian and Portuguese society tombs in the background.

shrubs and trees (fig. 4B). The plastered brick tombs of every conceivable shape lean this way and that. These tombs were made of brick, for there is no natural stone near New Orleans, and the least expensive permanent building material at hand was the soft red brick—burned in local brickyards. To preserve the brickwork it was necessary to use plaster and whitewash; some marble, imported at considerable expense, was employed, mainly for nameplates and tablets. Unfortunately, from exposure to the sun and rain of a century and a half, many inscriptions have become illegible, and some of the slabs have become warped or have perished completely.

The earliest recorded inscription in St. Louis Cemetery I was copied by a reporter from the *Daily Picayune* on All Saints' Day, 1903. It read: "*Ci git un mal heureuse qui fut victim de son imprudence. Vers une larme sur sa tombe, et un 'De Profundis' sil vout plait, pour son ame il n' avait que 27 ans, 1798.*" ("Here lies a poor unfortunate who was a victim of his own imprudence. Drop a tear on his tomb and say, if you please, the psalm 'out of the depths I have cried unto Thee, O, Lord,' for his soul. He was only 27 years old.") Could he have been the victim of a duel? In former days there were a number of inscriptions which ended, "*Mort sur le champ de 'honeur*" ("Died on the field of honor") for dueling victims, but these have apparently disappeared during the years.

Another early inscription tells of a mother's grief for a son who died far from home: "Here lies Prince Albert Monteculli, who died in 1822. His poor mother, Charlotte, Countess Laderche, Princess von Oettingen Wallenstein, praying for the repose of her son. Oh friends, it is a holy and salutary thought to pray for the dead that they may be loosed from their sins." The vault in which young Monteculli lies is so low to the ground that one must kneel to decipher the inscription.

Another vault contains the remains of Francis Benedict Van Pradelles, a Frenchman who came to America during the American Revolution. Van Pradelles fell in love with Cassandra Owings of a Baltimore county family, married her, and the couple returned to France. During the days of the French Revolution they fled to New Orleans, where they lived and raised a family of six children. Van Pradelles became a notary and the federal recorder of titles in Louisiana. In 1808 he contracted yellow fever and died, his funeral service in St. Louis Cemetery I being recorded by Père Antoine in the church records. Next year Cassandra Van Pradelles opened a boarding house at Conti and Chartres streets, but failing in health she determined to make a sea voyage to her old home in Maryland. Along the way she stopped at Beaufort, North Carolina, and the night before she was to sail north to Baltimore, she had a horrible nightmare in which she dreamed that the ship was attacked by pirates and that she was made to walk the plank. Frightened, she canceled her passage, but after an interval she took passage in another ship. The vessel never reached Baltimore. Years later in New Orleans a dying sailor told a visiting minister and a relative of the Pradelles family that he had taken part in the seizure of a vessel off the coast of North Carolina, and he remembered a woman passenger who had begged for her life because of her six fatherless children. The sailors forced her to walk the plank just as Cassandra had dreamed. Silver objects which had been in Cassandra's possession when she was lost were found in the sailor's possession after he died.

At the rear of the cemetery was a burial ground for non-Catholics, and in the rear of this burial ground was the graveyard for Negroes. Apparently some burials took place outside the confines of the walls of the Catholic cemetery.

St. Louis I, being on semiswampland, frequently flooded after heavy rains, and on at least one occasion, when the water of the Macarty Crevasse (1816) backed into the city, the cemetery had to be closed to funerals until the water receded and burials were made temporarily in a cemetery across the Mississippi. To remedy this situation, river sand was hauled into the cemetery from time to time.

The celebrated architect Benjamin H. B. Latrobe described St. Louis Cemetery I in his journal after a visit made on March 8, 1819:

> I walked today to the burial grounds on the Northwest side of town. There is an enclosure — for the Catholic Church — of about 300 feet square and immediately adjoining is the burial place of the Protestants, of about equal dimensions. The Catholic tombs are very different in character from those of our Eastern and Northern cities. They are of bricks, much larger than necessary to enclose a single coffin, and plastered over, so as to have a very solid and permanent appearance. . . . They are crowded close together, without any particular attention to aspect. . . .

> In one corner of the Catholic burying grounds are two sets of catacombs wall vaults, of three stories each. . . . Many of the catacombs were occupied, but not in regular succession, and the mouths of some were filled with marble slabs having inscriptions. But more were bricked up and plastered without any indication of the person's name who occupied it.

> The Protestant burying ground has tombs of the same construction, but a little varied in character, and they are all arranged parallel to the sides of the enclosure. . . . The monument to the wife, child and brother-in-law of Governor Claiborne is the most conspicuous and has a panel enriched with very good sculpture.

> There are two or three graves open and expecting their tenants; 8 or 9 inches below the surface they are filled with water and were not three feet deep. Thus, all persons here who are interred in the earth are buried in the water.

The Protestant Section

Part of the Protestant section of St. Louis I was in the way of an extension of Tremé Street, so in 1822 the city offered Christ Church a tract of land in the Faubourg St. Mary for a new cemetery. This was to be the Girod Street Cemetery; by 1838 most of the graves in the Protestant section were emptied and their remains removed to the new location. In 1840 what was left of the section on the west side of Treme Street was sold for building lots. Today all that is left of the Protestant section is a small desolate strip of land at the rear of the Catholic Cemetery, except for the well-cared-for tombs of the Thomas Layton family. This section also contains the graves of two young Americans who died in the defense of New Orleans against the British in 1814, and of one of their companions-in-arms who died of fever. There is also here a notable monument designed by Benjamin Latrobe in memory of Eliza Lewis, young first wife of Governor William C. C. Claiborne (1784–1804). Her child is buried here, and her brother, Micajah Green Lewis, who lost his life in a duel defending the honor of his brother-in-law (1805).

Some Pioneer Families in St. Louis I

St. Louis Cemetery I is the last resting place of a great many pioneer New Orleans families. Among the best known are: Etienne Boré (1741–1820), first mayor of New Orleans, on whose plantation Louisiana sugarcane was first successfully granulated commercially; his grandson, Charles Gayarré (1805–1895), the historian, who lies in the tomb with his grandfather, and whose pathetic little scroll monument on the roof of the low tomb was erected there by his admirer and fellow writer, Grace King;

Daniel Clark (1760–1813), wealthy Irish-born merchant, American consul in New Orleans during the last days of the Spanish regime and later territorial delegate to Congress; also Myra Clark Gaines (1805–1885) who, as his daughter, claimed immense tracts of land from the city of New Orleans in one of the longest (sixty-five years) and most complicated lawsuits of the nineteenth century; Paul Morphy (1837–1884), in his time the world's greatest chess player (fig 5); Blaise Cenas (1776–1812), the first United States postmaster of New Orleans: Stephen Zacharie, a banker; Bernard de Marigny (1785–1868), whose family was at one time fabulously wealthy and whose pecadillos finally brought him to poverty in old age; Colonel Michel Fortier (1750–1819), royal armorer and soldier who fought with the Spanish under Governor Galvez to help capture Manchac and Baton Rouge from the British, and who was later in life a member of the first City Council of New Orleans; Louis Moreau Lislet and Pierre Derbigny, jurists, who worked together to draw up the Civil Code of Louisiana. Derbigny was governor of Louisiana from 1828 until his accidental death on September 25, 1829, as a result of being thrown from his carriage by runaway horses; of Marie Laveau, one of New Orleans most notorious voodoo queens whose remains reputedly rest in a tomb much marked for good luck by chalked X's. Judge Victor Burthe's tomb, a handsome structure, is in need of repairs. Burthe was a wealthy landowner, political figure in state politics, and poet.

The pyramid-shaped brick tomb of the Varney family, now almost at the cemetery's entrance, was much closer to its center at the time John H. B. Latrobe sketched it in 1834, thus proving that a great many tombs were destroyed when Basin Street was opened and the walls of the present cemetery moved back (color plate 1). In other sections, the tombs of the Henry Dick and of Cesare Olivier and of the Pons family are noteworthy. Unfortunately the Byzantine chapel-tomb of the Jesuit fathers, which once stood in the rear of the cemetery to the left, was demolished in the 1920s (fig. 6).

Fig. 6. This quaint chapel-tomb of the Jesuit fathers in St. Louis I was built in the Byzantine style. Its architect probably was Father John Cambioso, who also designed the old Church of the Immaculate Conception. The wrought iron gates were particularly notable. The tomb fell into disrepair by 1920 and was demolished. (Courtesy Leonard V. Huber Collection.)

Fig. 5. This well-kept tomb in St. Louis I is the burial place of Paul Morphy (1837–1884), world champion chess player.

Society Tombs

Dominating the whole cemetery by its size is the tomb of the French Society which was erected in 1848. Another large society tomb is that of the Portuguese Benevolent Association which was built in 1850. The vaults of this tomb rise above each other in five tiers. A Spanish group, the Cervantes Mutual Benevolent Society's tomb, is surmounted by a tall rusticated obelisk. The vaults of the Orleans Battalion of Artillery are closed with iron plates, and the tomb is surrounded by a fence simulating old cannon and anchor chains, now falling into ruin (page 2).

The most striking society tomb in the cemetery is that of the New Orleans Italian Mutual Benevolent Society which was founded in 1848 (fig. 7). The tomb, a baroque marble circular affair, has twenty-four vaults and a receptacle in its basement closed by an iron door. It was designed by Pietro Gualdi, architect, and erected in 1857 at a cost of $40,000 under the presidency of Joseph A. Barelli who also built the unique memorial to his son in St. Louis Cemetery II. The Italian Society tomb, which is surmounted by a female figure which held a cross, features two niches, one of which contains a large statue representing "Italia" and the other that of a woman with two children representing "Charity" (fig. 8).

Oven Vaults and Tomb Burials

Of great interest are the wall vaults, the ovens, some of which today are in a state of picturesque dilapidation, the lower rows having sunk to such a degree that it is not possible to open them. When this new cemetery, St. Louis I, was planned in 1789 the Spanish custom of vault and society tomb burial influenced the builders (figs. 9, 10).

Fig. 7. This ornate marble tomb of the New Orleans Italian Mutual Benevolent Society was erected in 1857. By 1970, the tomb needed repair, as can be seen from the photograph. One of the female statutes is headless, the door to the receptacle has been torn from its hinges, the iron fence is broken, and vegetation sprouts from joints in the stonework.

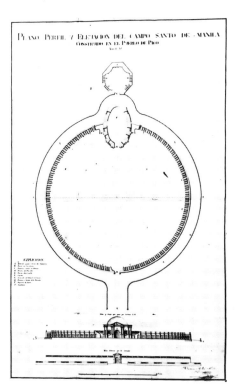

Fig. 9. Vault burial was introduced in New Orleans during the Spanish regime (1769–1803). This plan of the Campo Santo, or Cemetery of Manila, in the Philippines, from *Maps and Plans Filipinas, 135,* Archives of the Indies, Seville, Spain, shows above-ground vaults built into a circular wall and a chapel. The plan probably dates from the early eighteenth century. (Courtesy Leonard V. Huber Collection.)

Fig. 10. A multi-vault tomb for priests, similar to society tombs in New Orleans, located in the cemetery at Seville, Spain. Oven vaults, similar to those in old New Orleans cemeteries, can be seen in the background. (Photo by Leonard V. Huber.)

Fig. 8. This sculptured figure of Italia is one of three on the tomb of the New Orleans Italian Mutual Benevolent Society.

9

The Creole custom of using a single vault for a number of entombments is one that never fails to arouse the curiosity of visitors. As the occasion requires, the remains of the last occupant of the vault are gathered and pushed to the back of the vault, the decayed casket wood being removed and burned; the vault is then ready to receive another body.

In the private tombs, which generally consist of two vaults, one above the other, and a pit (caveau) or receptacle below, bodies are removed from the upper vaults and consigned to the receptacle to make room for further occupancy on the occasion of subsequent funerals. Thus a small, two-vault family tomb is used many times for the interment of several generations of its owners, a very practical and relatively inexpensive custom.

ST. LOUIS CEMETERY II (1823)

In 1820 the City Council, moved by the current belief that contagion of yellow fever, cholera, and other pestilential diseases were spread by "miasmas" emanating from cemeteries, determined to find a new site for a cemetery farther removed from the center of population. The site selected was along the Carondelet Canal, probably near present-day Galvez and Lafitte streets. The City Council had their surveyor estimate the cost of fencing the projected burial place, but an injunction by C. Pontalba, who owned a tract of land nearby, and a prolonged controversy with the wardens of the cathedral brought the plan to naught.

The council insisted on locating a new cemetery at least four hundred toises (twenty-four hundred feet) from the city limits and the nearest practical site on what is now Claiborne Avenue between Canal, St. Louis, and Robertson streets, was only about three hundred toises (eighteen hundred feet) from Rampart Street. The matter was finally settled when, after an enabling act by the state legislature, the city dedicated about 4/5th of Squares 38, 39, 40, and 41 as St. Louis Cemetery II, deeded it to the wardens of the cathedral, and fenced the site. The church consecrated it for burials in August, 1823.

Antoine Phillip LeRiche, a Paris-born architect-engineer, was appointed inspector of the cemeteries shortly afterwards. LeRiche carefully examined the soil of the cemetery and brought in a plan of the work that he proposed to do to start operations. In 1824 the wardens contracted with him to build thirty "tombs" (vaults) for whites and another thirty for Negroes at fifty dollars each; that same year LeRiche requested and the city let him use the Negroes of the chain gang to fill and grade the main aisles. Records in the archives of the cathedral indicate that considerable earth filling was added to the cemeteries from time to time and that numerous contracts for the building of wall vaults were made.

From contemporary city maps, the cemetery is shown as one continuous piece of property running from Canal to St. Louis Street. The division of the cemetery into separate squares (as it exists today) was done when Iberville, Bienville, Conti, and St. Louis streets were cut through. A meticulously drawn plan of the cemetery on Square 41 dated July 31, 1847, exists in the city archives (fig. 11). In 1937–1940 Joseph Carey, an engineer employed by the cathedral, surveyed and drew accurate plans of the four squares of the St. Louis cemeteries I and II.

Four-fifths of Square 38, the one facing Canal Street, though fenced, was only used

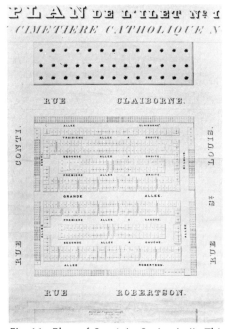

Fig. 11. Plan of Sq. 1 in St. Louis II. This square is bordered by Claiborne, Conti, Robertson, and St. Louis streets. (Courtesy Leonard V. Huber Collection.)

for a few scattered burials; it adjoined the property of Newton Richards, a builder of tombs and monuments who had bought it in 1840. In 1845 an individual with the improbable name of Increase Stoddard Wood bought out Richards and succeeded in getting the New Orleans City Council to sell him the rest of the square for $11,400 in March, 1846. To do this, the council had to annul the city's gift of the land, made twenty-three years previously to the wardens of St. Louis Cathedral, on the grounds that to extend the cemetery to Canal Street at that time would endanger the health of the rapidly growing city. The city agreed to indemnify and furnish the wardens with "the means of establishing a cemetery of greater extent in a location less dangerous to the public health." Experts appointed by the city, and wardens, were to select and approve the location of the new cemetery which "ought to be beyond Bayou St. John."

Increase Wood built a cotton compress on his land and eventually sold it to a brewing concern for which several large buildings were erected. These were demolished in the late 1960s, and an automobile agency erected a building on half of the site. When excavations for the foundations were made, remains of former burials were discovered.

Of the three squares which comprise the cemetery today, the burial places in the square between Iberville and Bienville streets are almost exclusively owned by Negroes. The square between Bienville and Conti streets contains the most elaborate tombs (fig. 12); the square between Conti and St. Louis streets is of lesser interest

Fig. 12. French Cemetery (St. Louis II), from sketch made about 1855. (Courtesy Leonard V. Huber Collection.)

Fig. 13. Bird's-eye view of Sq. 2, St. Louis II, from a photograph made by Charles F. Mugnier about 1890. (Courtesy Leonard V. Huber Collection.)

Fig. 14. Society of the Cazadores de Orleans tomb, St. Louis II, Sq. 2. When this photograph was taken in 1972 vegetation was beginning to cover the fifteen-vault tomb.

from an architectural point of view although there are several important tombs in it (fig. 13). All three squares are surrounded by wall vaults except the Robertson Street side of Square 2; and most of the Claiborne Avenue wall vaults are in ruinous condition.

St. Louis Cemetery II is well laid out with a straight center aisle and parallel side aisles. Like St. Louis I, this cemetery has a number of society tombs—multiple vaults built by mutual benefit groups for their members. Among the most important are

Fig. 15. Many Negroes were members of mutual benevolent societies. This dues card of Sam Mossey for 1926–1927 shows that he paid fifty cents per month, and one month (January, 1927) was assessed forty cents extra for the funeral of a fellow member. Mossey was a member of the Dieu Nous Protégé Society which owned a tomb in St. Louis I. (Courtesy Leonard V. Huber Collection.)

Fig. 16. An abandoned one-lot Negro society tomb, St. Louis II, Sq. 3. (Courtesy Leonard V. Huber Collection.)

Fig. 17A. Portrait of Margaret Gaffney Haughery (1813–1882), widely known as "Margaret" among the citizens of New Orleans at the time of her death. She was interred February 11, 1882, in the 24-vault tomb of the Sisters of Charity of St. Vincent de Paul in St. Louis II. The tomb was demolished in 1920 and the remains moved to lots 21, 22, and 23 in Sq. 3 of St. Louis III. A marble statue of Margaret was erected in 1884 in a park bounded by Camp, Prytania, and Clio streets. No stone marks her grave in St. Louis III. (Courtesy Leonard V. Huber Collection.)

Fig. 17B. The small tomb of Dominique You, privateer and expert cannoneer who fought in the Battle of New Orleans.

those of the Cazadores de Orleans (fig. 14), a group attached to the Louisiana Legion, built in 1836, at a cost of $15,000, and the Iberian Society, built in 1845 at a cost of $30,000. Both groups are of Spanish origin. There are many Negro society tombs in the square between Iberville and Bienville streets, some of them built four and five tiers high on a single lot (figs. 15, 16).

Notable Persons Who Lie in St. Louis Cemetery II

Within the confines of St. Louis Cemetery II (fig. 17A) lie the remains of many New Orleanians who lived in the first half of the nineteenth century. Among them are such notables as General Jean-Baptiste Plauché (1785–1860), a friend of Andrew Jackson, who commanded the Orleans Battalion at the Battle of New Orleans (Plauché tomb, main cross aisle, middle cemetery, page 85, fig. 40A; Francois Xavier Martin (1762–1846), jurist and author of the first history of Louisiana who is memorialized by a stubby obelisk (main cross aisle, middle cemetery, page 100, fig. 72); Pierre Soulé (1801–1870), orator, diplomat, U.S. senator, once ambassador to Spain, and Confederate provost marshal (page 80, fig. 22); Dominique You, pirate captain under Jean Lafitte who fought in the Battle of New Orleans, and who later became a useful citizen (fig. 17B). When he died in 1830 military honors were paid to his memory, banks and business houses were closed, and flags on ships and public buildings were placed at half mast (priest's aisle); Alexander Milne (1744–1838), a philanthropic Scot who at one time owned more than twenty miles of land along the borders of Lake Pontchartrain and for whom Milneburg was named. Milne, who died at the age of ninety-four, left a fortune to found homes for destitute boys and girls; his will is imperishably engraved on the surfaces of his ornate monument (priest's aisle, Square 2, middle cemetery page 101, fig. 76); Major Daniel Carmick (1772–1816), United States Marine Corps, who fought in the Battle of New Orleans and eventually died of wounds received in battle (Sq. 1, facing Robertson Street); James Freret (1838–1897), distinguished architect whose tomb is near Major Carmick's; Claude Tremé (1759–1828), owner of the large tract in which the cemetery is located and which was developed into the Faubourg Tremé (main aisle square between St. Louis and Conti streets); John Davis (1773–1839), gambler, promoter, owner of the Theatre d'Orleans; Louis Tabary, actor-manager who came to New Orleans in 1805 from Santo Domingo; Oscar J. Dunn, an octoroon plasterer and house painter who rose to be lieutenant governor of Louisiana when Henry Clay Warmoth became Reconstruction governor of Louisiana; Nicholas Girod (1751–1840), mayor of New Orleans, 1814–1815, whose residence still stands (the so-called Napoleon House, Chartres and St. Louis streets), finds his rest in a plain brick tomb; Charles Genois (1793–1866), mayor in 1838, in a much more elaborate granite one.

The Mortuary Chapel

Closely associated with the history of St. Louis cemeteries I and II was the mortuary chapel of Saint Anthony, now the church of Our Lady of Guadalupe, Rampart and Conti streets (fig. 18). The chapel was constructed in 1826–1827 by Gurlie and Guillot, architect-builders, to serve as a funeral church when the City Council forbade the holding of funeral services in St. Louis Cathedral since it was feared that the taking of dead bodies to the larger church was a means of spreading disease. A simple structure of brick, plastered, with an open arched loggia surmounted by a belfry and steeple, this little church was dedicated on December 27, 1827, by the beloved Pére Antoine and until 1860 was used solely as a mortuary chapel.

An interesting eyewitness account of a funeral service in the chapel and the subsequent burial services in St. Louis Cemetery II was written in 1835 by Joseph Holt Ingraham who wrote under the nom de plum, "A Yankee." In a book called *The Southwest,* he wrote:

Fig. 18. View of the Mortuary Chapel of St. Anthony (*circa* 1890), built in 1826 after funerals were forbidden in St. Louis Cathedral because of the fear of yellow fever contagion. It has been renamed Our Lady of Guadalupe and is still in service as the oldest church in New Orleans. (Courtesy Leonard V. Huber Collection.)

> I entered Rampart Street . . . and as I passed down the street to where I had observed, not far distant, a crowd gathered around the door of a large white stuccoed building, burdened by a clumsy hunch-backed kind of tower, surmounted by a huge wooden cross.
>
> On approaching nearer, I discovered many carriages extended in a long line up the street, and a hearse with tall black plumes, before the door of the building, which, I was informed, was the Catholic chapel. Passing through the crowd around the entrance, I gained the portico, where I had a full view of the interior, in which was neither pew nor seat, elevated upon a high frame or altar, over which was thrown a black velvet pall, was placed a coffin, covered also with black velvet. A dozen huge candles, nearly as long and as large as a ship's royal-mast, standing in candlesticks five feet high, burned around the corpse mingled with innumerable candles of the ordinary size, which were thickly sprinkled among them, like lesser stars, amid the twilight gloom of the chapel. The mourners formed a lane from the altar to the door, each holding a long, unlighted wax taper, tipped at the larger end with red, and ornamented with fanciful paper cuttings. Around the door, and along the sides of the chapel stood casual spectators, strangers and negro servants without number. As I entered, several priests and singing boys, in the black and white robes of their order, were chanting the service of the dead. The effect was solemn and impressive. In a few moments the ceremony was completed and four gentlemen, dressed in deep mourning, each with a long white scarf, extending from one shoulder across the breast, and nearly to the feet, advanced, and taking the coffin from its station, bore it through the line of mourners, who fell in, two and two behind them, to the hearse which immediately moved on to the graveyard with its burden, followed by the

carriages, as in succession they drove up to the chapel and received the mourners. . . .

Leaving the chapel, I followed the procession which I have described, for at least three quarters of a mile down a long street or road at right angles with Rampart Street, to the place of interment. The priests and boys, who in their black and white robes had performed the service for the dead, leaving the chapel by a private door in the rear of the building made their appearance in the street leading to the cemetery, as the funeral train passed down, each with a mitred cap upon his head, and there forming into a procession upon the sidewalk, they moved off in a course opposite to the one taken by the funeral train, and soon disappeared in the direction of the cathedral. Two priests, however, remained with the procession, and with it, after passing on the left hand the "Old Catholic Cemetery" St. Louis #1, which, being full to repletion, is closed and sealed for the "Great Day," arrived at the new burial place St. Louis Cemetery #2. Here the mourners alighted from their carriages and proceeded on foot to the tomb. The priests, bare-headed and solemn, were the last who entered, except myself and a few other strangers attracted by curiosity.

The cemetery is quite out of the city; there being no dwelling or enclosure of any kind beyond it. On approaching it, the front of the street presents the appearance of a lofty brick wall of very great length, with a spacious doorway in the centre. This gateway is about 10 feet deep; and one passing through it would imagine the wall of the same solid thickness. This, however, is only apparent. The wall which surrounds, or is to surround the four sides of the burial-ground (for it is yet uncompleted) is about twelve feet in height and ten in thickness.

Ingraham then described the wall vaults, which he estimated numbered about eighteen hundred. He continues:

When I entered the gateway, I was struck with surprise and admiration. Though destitute of trees, from the entrance to the opposite side through the centre of the graveyard, a broad avenue or street extends nearly a mile in length [sic]; and on either side of this are innumerable isolated tombs, of all shapes and sizes and description, built above ground. The idea of a Lilliputian city was at first suggested to my mind on looking down this extensive avenue. Many of the tombs were constructed alike and several were indeed miniature Grecian temples; many of them otherwise plain, were surmounted by a tower supporting a cross. All were perfectly white, arranged with the most perfect regularity and distant little more than a foot from each other. The whole cemetery was divided into squares, formed by these narrow streets intersecting the principal avenue. It was in reality a "City of the Dead."

There was a terrible epidemic in New Orleans in 1832 and still another in 1833. During the plague of 1833, in September alone nearly a thousand people died.* The sexton of St. Louis Cemetery II was hard pressed to find space for new graves. A new cemetery was urgently needed. The council, holding a special meeting, authorized the opening of a plot of land for burials which had been given to the city by Don Almonester during the Spanish regime situated on "Leprous Road," a section on the outskirts of town once abandoned to lepers.

A little over a year later the council passed an ordinance (March 5, 1835) which required that "the burying of all persons dying in the city of New Orleans or in the vicinity thereof shall take place in the cemetery established on land purchased from Mr. Evariste Blanc (in 1834), at the Bayou St. John." The ordinance exempted tomb and vault burials in existing above-ground structures but forbade further interments in the ground in all other cemeteries.

Blanc's land extended from present-day Broad Street along Orleans Street to Bayou St. John, a distance of more than a mile from the built-up section of New Orleans. Realizing that some means of transportation would have to be provided to

---

*Soon after, the City Council made it mandatory to bury any persons who died within twenty-four hours after death under penalty of a fine of $100. This was the beginning of a custom of relatively quick burials which largely exists in New Orleans today.

reach this distant burial ground, an enterprising capitalist by the name of John Arrowsmith (who also owned land in the vicinity) proposed to build a railroad for the transport of corpses and mourners from St. Claude Street out Orleans Street along the banks of the then open Girod Canal to the cemetery at Bayou St. John. The City Council on March 23, 1835, authorized the mayor to enter into a contract with Arrowsmith to build the road and specified that he was to provide separate cars for the transportation of the corpses of white people, of free colored persons, of slaves at fees which ranged from three dollars for whites to fifty cents for slaves; mourners were to be carried in other cars at twenty-five cents the round trip. However, no evidence of the actual existence of Arrowsmith's grisly railroad, nor the cemetery to which it was to run, has been discovered.

ST. LOUIS III (1854)

St. Louis Cemetery III (fig. 19) had its beginnings in 1848 when an act was passed by the legislature in March of that year under which the City Council privileged the Cathedral wardens to establish a new cemetery. The next year, on June 8, 1849, the wardens bought from Felix Labatut a tract of land on Esplanade "two arpents wide by 14 arpents deep for one and 16 for the other arpent" near Bayou St. John. The price was $15,000, and the wardens used money that the city had set aside for this purpose when they were dispossessed of Square 38 of St. Louis Cemetery II in 1846. The authorization by the city to establish the new cemetery was accepted by the wardens in December of 1850. It was not, however, until 1854 that the wardens advertised for bids for clearing the land and building fences and an entrance gate.

Fig. 19. This cemetery entrance is ornamented by a set of heavy iron gates, typical of New Orleans cast ironwork. The gates were fabricated by Francis Lurges, a well-known maker of ornamental iron. Gate overthrow now missing. (Courtesy Abbye A. Gorin.)

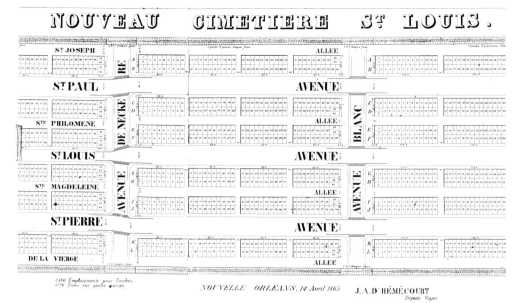

Fig. 20. Fragment of a plan of St. Louis III, drawn by P. A. D'Hemecourt, surveyor, April 14, 1865. The surveyor calculated there would be 2,580 plots for tombs and 5,176 "fours" or vaults. (Courtesy Leonard V. Huber Collection.)

Fig. 21. Aerial view of St. Louis III. Now virtually filled, this cemetery contains interesting tombs and monuments that have been erected in its closely built-up precincts.

Fig. 22. This tomb of the Hellenic Orthodox Community is in Byzantine style. Designed and erected by Victor Huber in 1928, it has been painted white, a deviation from its Byzantine character. (Courtesy Leonard V. Huber Collection.)

The plan for the first two "squares" of the new cemetery called for three main aisles, the center being named for Saint Louis and the other two for Saint Peter and Saint Paul; four smaller parallel aisles or alleés were named after Saint Mary, Saint Joseph, Saint Magdalene, Saint Philomene. After the cemetery was in use for some years, on April 14, 1865, a new plan was developed by P. A. d'Hemecourt, surveyor, which greatly extended the depth of the burial grounds (fig. 20). The main aisle was increased in width by ten feet at the expense of the two side alleés so that the cemetery presents a rather uncrowded appearance despite its multitude of closely built tombs.

The cross aisles for the new plan were named for bishops and archbishops of the diocese—Penalver, Dubourg, De Neckere, Blanc, Odin (and later Perché and Leray). D'Hemecourt's plan envisioned a small cruciform chapel at the entrance. This was never built, and the land was later sold as tomb sites. He calculated that there were 2,580 emplacements pour tombes (sites for tombs) and room to build 5,176 wall vaults (figs. 20, 21). As in the earlier St. Louis cemeteries, wall vaults were constructed. These give it a very picturesque appearance, as do the quaint tombs, many of which are now more than a century old.

Among the society tombs in the cemetery are the tombs of the Young Men's Benevolent Association (1866), United Slavonian Benevolent Society (1876), Hellenic Orthodox Community (1928) (fig. 22), and several vaults for priests and nuns.

Among the prominent personages who find their last rest in St. Louis Cemetery III are Father François Isidore Turgis (1805–1868), Confederate chaplain who spent his last years as pastor of St. Anthony's Church, the old Mortuary Chapel on Rampart and Conti streets, and whose modest monument was erected by his former comrades of the Army of Tennessee; of Valcour Aime (1798–1867), the fabulous Louisiana sugar planter who could once boast that he raised on his own land in St. James Parish everything to supply a gourmand's dinner, including wines and cigars; of Cyprien Dufour (1819–1871), lawyer and author of "Esquisses Locales"; of the Abbe Adrien Rouquette (1813–1887), poet and missionary priest who lived and worked for many years among the Indians in St. Tammany Parish who called him "Chahta-Ima" (remains removed from St. Louis II to the tomb of the priests); of Thomy Lafon (1811–1893), a highly respected mulatto philanthropist.

During the Civil War the body of Colonel Charles D. Dreux, the first Confederate officer from New Orleans to lose his life (July 5, 1861), was interred in St. Louis III after a tremendous funeral. Dreux's remains were removed to the tomb of the Army of Tennessee in Metairie Cemetery July 4, 1896.

One of the most interesting monuments in the cemetery is that erected by James Gallier, Jr, to the memory of his distinguished father and stepmother. This cenotaph bears the inscription:

> THIS MONUMENT IS ERECTED TO
> THE MEMORY OF
> JAMES GALLIER
> ARCHITECT OF NEW ORLEANS
> BORN AT RAVENSDALE, IRELAND JULY 24, 1795
> BY HIS SON AS A TRIBUTE TO HIS
> GENIUS, INTEGRITY AND VIRTUE
> AND OF
> CATHERINE MARIA ROBINSON
> BORN AT BARRE, MASSACHUSETTS
> WIFE OF JAMES GALLIER
> THEY WERE LOST IN THE STEAMER EVENING
> STAR WHICH FOUNDERED ON THE VOYAGE FROM
> NEW YORK TO NEW ORLEANS
> OCTOBER 3, 1866

All Saints' Day

November 1, All Saints' Day, is the New Orleans Memorial Day (color plate 4). For several weeks before, the cemeteries are sites of much activity. Tombs are often patched and freshly whitewashed. The tap-tap of the marble cutter's mallet is heard, for the names of those who recently took up residence must be carved. Vases of marble, of glass, and even bottles are brought. Then comes the great day. Thousands of chrysanthemums are brought to the cemeteries and reverently placed at the tombs. From morning to late afternoon the cemeteries are thronged, and by nightfall they are massed with flowers.

A diligent reporter for the *Picayune* visited the New Orleans cemeteries on All Saints' Day in 1879. This is what he wrote of the three St. Louis cemeteries:

The cemetery on Basin and St. Louis Streets #1 witnessed a large concourse of people. . . . Here the tomb of the Lusitanos Portuguese Benevoletnt Association is situated. It was draped in mourning and surmounted by various Portuguese flags. The Italian Benevolent Society's fine tomb was decorated with flags and draped in black. The Societe Française, Orleans Artillery, Catalan Society, Sieurs Bien Aimeé and other societies bedecked their tombs in becoming manner.

A detachment of Battery "B", Orleans Artillery, guarded the cemetery and gave the occasion a military aspect.

The Claiborne, Duralde and other family tombs were adorned with beautiful floral ornaments in the shape of crosses, wreaths, bouquets, etc.

The St. Louis Cemetery No. 2 was crowded with frequenters. Every tomb and every grave showed the presence of friends in whose hearts reverence for the dead is still fresh. The many society tombs, the Carriere tomb, especially, were decked with the fairest and most fragrant flowers.

The new St. Louis Cemetery, of No. 3, on Esplanade, near Bayou Bridge, was constantly filled with numbers of the city's wealthiest people. The many family tombs here were all decorated with costly vases and flowers. Some floral ornaments displayed here were truly magnificent and attracted much attention. Further down the broad avenue were the graves of many of the humbler portion of the Catholic population.

Writing in 1951, Elise Kirsch, reminisced of the All Saints' Days that she knew as a girl in the 1880s.* Miss Kirsch, who lived on Robertson Street near Esplanade, "in the nest of the Creole district" and whose grandfather, Alfred Barbier, is buried in the French Society tomb in St. Louis Cemetery I, wrote of the customs of the times:

> In the early eighties some tombs were decorated with tarlatan which was draped with artificial pansies and moss. Some of the tombs, especially the Society ones, had vases with flowers and also wreaths with seed pearls and glass beads which hung all through the day. As these were valuable, some of the members sat throughout the day to watch them.
> The bouquets were made of tiny, stiff chrysanthemums and the colored people always placed a cock's comb (a coarse red homegrown flower) in the center of them held by a stiff perforated paper. There were no large roses nor cultivated mums.
> At the gates and in different places in the cemeteries there were orphans seated at a table accompanied by a nun—there was a collection box where all people donated generously.

Customs have changed somewhat since these times. No longer are tombs draped in black and decorated with flags, and the nuns and orphans have vanished with the coming of the United Fund, but the custom of visiting the cemetery and bringing flowers on All Saints' Day is still a distinctive New Orleans observance.

GIROD STREET CEMETERY (1822–1957)

Christ Church was founded in 1805 by a number of prominent New Orleans Protestants. One of the first concerns of the infant congregation was for the burial of their dead. A committee called on the mayor and asked that the church be put in possession of that portion in the rear of the St. Louis Cemetery which had been set aside for the non-Catholic dead. The city was agreeable, and Christ Church came into possession of a cemetery before it had a permanent church in which its members could worship. Old vestry records show that lots in the place were sold for twenty-five dollars and that the sexton was given the privilege of charging three dollars to dig a grave and one dollar "for attending corpse to grave."

The city was growing by leaps and bounds, however, and in 1820, some fourteen years after it had been acquired, Christ Church was asked to give part of the land back so that a street could be cut through the cemetery. The vestrymen of the church then cast about for a larger and better site. Accordingly on August 10, 1822, the city council of New Orleans authorized Mayor Joseph Roffignac to sell to the congregation of Christ Church, represented by the Reverend James F. Hull, its rector, and the vestrymen of the church, a tract of land in the upper limit of the Faubourg St. Mary, having a frontage of 256 feet on St. Paul Street (now South Liberty Street) and running back to a depth of 594 feet and forming a "long regular [rectangular] square," between what is now Perrilliat and Cypress streets (about 3½ acres).

The resolution further described the land as "Two-thirds of the ground bought from Marie Moquin, wife of François Perrilliat, (whose tomb is in St. Louis Cemetery I), presently serving as a cemetery for the Protestants." The deed by which the church acquired the property provided that the tract was to be consecrated to the interment of all persons professing the Protestant or Catholic religion of any denomination or

Fig. 23. During the late nineteenth and early twentieth centuries it was fashionable to ornament the tops of tombs with sculptured Italian marble angels. Some were sculptured to order, but most were stock figures. In this view of St. Louis III there are so many angels one can almost hear the beat of their wings.

*"Down Town New Orleans in the Early Eighties"

sect. The habendum clause in the deed contained the following: "unto the members of the said congregation and their successors, to use and enjoy the tract of land presently sold as a Protestant Cemetery, until the Council of the City of New Orleans sees fit to change the location of this Cemetery by virtue of its proximity to the City, pursuant to which the said congregation can enjoy, use and dispose of the same as it sees fit in full ownership by virtue of these presents." The act of sale further stipulated: "This sale is made under further condition that the Wardens of the said Congregation, who so obligate themselves by these presents, will continually maintain the said tract of land in a good state of upkeep and will place thereon at their expense a sexton."

The price agreed upon was $3,140.67, and the purchasers were given the right to pay for the land over a ten-year period. Thus came into existence the cemetery which was known to the Creoles as the "Cimetiére des Hérétiques" or simply as "The Protestant Cemetery." Like all cemeteries in New Orleans, it was situated on the fringe of town. Girod Street was "The Swamp" to the rowdy flatboatmen of the day who caroused in the dens which lined it. At the end of the street was this cemetery. In early New Orleans, death was never very far away.

The cemetery was laid out with three aisles (a center and two side aisles) running from the front to the rear. These were bisected by twenty-two cross aisles although one of these was never cut through. Remains from the old cemetery in the rear of St. Louis I were removed to the new cemetery and entombed in a series of vaults near the left-hand side near the entrance.* Shade trees were planted, and the congregation erected hundreds of oven vaults which were offered for sale. As New Orleans grew more populous and its people wealthier, larger and finer tombs appeared. The first ones were generally built of the soft locally made brick so common in the older buildings of New Orleans. A few were built of the superior Philadelphia brick, and the use of white Italian marble became more and more common—first for tablets which closed the entrance of the tombs and later for the tombs themselves. Some of the more substantial tombs were made of Quincy granite brought to New Orleans by sea from Massachusetts (fig. 24).

The Girod Street Cemetery was a cemetery of above-ground tombs and vaults. Its walls contained 2,319 vaults; in addition to these, the vestry erected 526 vaults facing aisles within the enclosure; there were about 1,000 privately owned tombs of from one to three vaults each and more than 100 benevolent society tombs which contained from 12 to 70 vaults each.

Unfortunately, the cemetery was not an architecturally imposing place of last rest. True, it was well laid out with a wide central aisle and fairly regular side aisles, but somehow, despite several imposing tombs erected in it, Girod lacked the character of the newer Cypress Grove or the contemporary St. Louis cemeteries on Claiborne Avenue. It was noted for its society tombs, some of which rose eight tiers above ground. In the early 1850s, a visitor wrote of these tombs: "The largest and finest tombs in the Protestant Cemetery, (public or society tombs) are those owned and erected by slaves. The 'ovens' contain a large number of slaves; for any one who has money enough to pay for an oven can be deposited in this cemetery whether black or white, bond or free. The cost of burial in the ovens or in the vaults of the society tombs, is about twenty dollars. This is sometimes paid by the slave, and

Fig. 24. Monument erected over the grave (at left) of Colonel W. W. S. Bliss, veteran of the Mexican War, who died of yellow fever in the great epidemic of 1852. It was part of a row of tombs (center and right). The monument and Bliss's remains were moved to Fort Bliss, Texas, in 1957. (Courtesy Leonard V. Huber Collection.)

*A great many of these were still intact, and the remains in them were removed to Hope Mausoleum in 1957 when the cemetery was demolished.

frequently by the master. The slaves have, however, by means of the principle of association, erected fine monuments and tombs of their own. The following societies of slaves own their tombs: the First African Baptist Association, the Home Missionary Benevolent Society, Male and Female Lutheran Benevolent Society. This last society has a tomb containing upwards of seventy vaults—a very elegant, and costly edifice, entirely above ground."

The tomb of the "Sobriety Benevolent Ass'n." founded 1854, was surmounted by a small obelisk which had assumed a wholly new position on its base due to the vibration of passing trains. Some of the society tombs bore fanciful names, the invention of their Negro owners. Among them were Wide Awake Benevolent Society, Ladies of Labor Benevolent Association No. 2, United Sons of Honor Association, St. Mary Tabernacle No. 6, Morning Star Tabernacle No. 2, Pure In Heart Temple No. 1, Young and True Friends Benevolent Association.

The largest and finest of the "society" tombs in Girod Street Cemetery was built by the New Lusitanos Benevolent Association, a white group. This tomb, designed by J. N. B. de Pouilly in 1859, was really a mausoleum with a row of vaults on each side of a covered corridor. The portico was done in marble and granite with two substantial Doric columns ornamenting the facade. Iron gates (fig. 25, 26) closed the entrance, and the window at the rear of the corridor was protected by a cast iron grille.

Time and changing social and economic conditions gradually spelled the doom of the benevolent societies of New Orleans. More than fifty white groups were in existence in the 1870s; by the turn of the century, most of these had disappeared. The New Lusitanos Society continued to function for sixty-two years (until about 1920). Then its once proud tomb in Girod Street Cemetery was neglected and fell into decay. The plastered exterior gradually crumbled and fell off, exposing the brick wall; thieves stole the grille from the window at the rear of the tomb and vandals plundered the vaults. The cornerstone was pried loose for the few coins which it

Fig. 25. Proud members of the New Lusitanos Benevolent Association inspect their new society tomb in the Girod Street Cemetery on the day of its dedication in October, 1859. The tomb was decorated with black velvet panels trimmed with silver. Tomb designed by J. N. B. de Pouilly. (Courtesy Leonard V. Huber Collection.)

Fig. 26. The New Lusitanos tomb in the 1950s, shortly before it was demolished. (Courtesy Leonard V. Huber Collection.)

contained, and the memorial tablets on each side of the entrance fell and were broken. The heavy iron doors were cut from their hinges with an acetylene torch and stolen. Because it offered the shelter of a roof, the tomb became the favorite hangout for alcoholics who slept there for want of a better place to go. By 1956 the tomb was a gruesome wreck, but even as a ruin it had a certain dignity that nothing could destroy. To almost every visitor it was the most interesting structure in the cemetery.

The Girod Street Cemetery (fig. 27) was destroyed in 1957 after 135 years of existence. The mass removal of the bodies and the demolishing of its tombs and vaults prompted a great deal of criticism directed at Christ Church Cathedral, its owner. Many people, particularly those whose ancestors had been interred in this place, felt that the church should have continued to keep a sexton on the grounds to maintain the old cemetery. But there were other reasons why Girod Street Cemetery came to such a sorry end. One of them was the erroneous idea which was universally prevalent in the early nineteenth century concerning cemeteries — the idea that the *purchaser* and his heirs were to maintain their place of burial. A city ordinance, approved December 26, 1856, provided that the owners of tombs in New Orleans cemeteries could be fined $50 if they failed to keep their property in good repair when notified that repairs were needed. Like many another false idea, generally accepted as workable at the time, the passage of the years has shown the complete impracticability of such a maintenance arrangement. Families die, move away, or lose interest, and the once-proud memorial is neglected and falls into decay for lack of attention.

Christ Church, in common with other New Orleans churches of the time, used the revenue produced by the sale of land and vaults in its cemetery for current expenses; no provision was made for the eventual maintenance of the cemetery when all the ground was sold. This could have been eliminated by putting aside a percentage of the cemetery revenues each year to form a perpetual care fund, but such things were unknown in New Orleans in that day.

On January 4, 1957, the cemetery was officially "deconsecrated" by the Rt. Rev. Girault M. Jones, Episcopal Bishop of Louisiana, and between January 14 and March 8, 1957, the work of removing the bodies was accomplished. The white remains were reinterred in Hope Mausoleum, and those of the Negro dead were removed to Providence Memorial Park. Christ Church Cathedral provided, without charge, a special crypt in Hope Mausoleum for those families who desired the reinterment of their forebears. Besides the remains of the three ministers, Hull, Leacock, and Kleinhagen and of Richard Relf, Glendy Burke, and Jane Placide, the remains of members of fifty-five families were interred, each in its own individual, marked container, in this crypt. Two memorial tablets in Hope Mausoleum commemorate the event; a bronze tablet at the Memorial Park marks the spot where the mass reinterment of the Negroes was made.

Fig. 27. A jungle growth of vegetation choked the aisles and overran the tombs in the Girod Street Cemetery in its last days. (Courtesy Leonard V. Huber Collection.)

JEWISH CEMETERIES

The first Jewish cemetery in New Orleans was founded in 1828 by the Israelite Congregation Shanarai Chasset (Gates of Mercy). It was located in the suburb of Lafayette at Jackson Avenue and Saratoga Street, "fairly distant from the center of things in those days." In 1862 the congregation built a brick wall around the cemetery with an iron gate at its entrance. In this cemetery were buried the pioneer

Jews of German background, who had come to New Orleans after the Louisiana Purchase. The cemetery was demolished in 1957 and part of the site used to build a playground. All remains were removed to Hebrew Rest Cemetery (Gentilly) and reinterred, the graves being marked on a monument erected for that purpose.

The next Jewish cemetery to be constructed was started in 1846 shortly after Spanish-Portuguese Jews organized the Congregation Nefuzoth Yehudah. This was erected in the 4900 block of Canal Street and given the same name of the congregation—Dispersed of Judah. A stone in the main aisle was placed in memory of Judah Touro, benefactor of the congregation, who died in 1854. The largest monument in Dispersed of Judah is that of the Lazarus family which was erected as a memorial to Virginia, the eighteen-year-old daughter who died in 1897. The memorial to Lilla Benjamin Wolf (1869–1911) is in the shape of a marble chair. For many years it was Mrs. Wolf's custom to sit outside the family shop on South Rampart Street, and her survivors ordered the chair as her monument.

Temmeme Derech Cemetery in the 4800 block of Canal Street was founded in 1858. The founding congregation, a Polish group, disbanded in 1903, and a volunteer group ran the cemetery until 1939. In that year the Congregation Gates of Prayer absorbed the cemetery and renamed it Gates of Prayer (figs. 28, 29).

In 1867 there was a bad outbreak of yellow fever in New Orleans, and a number of immigrant Jewish persons died and were buried there. In some instances the names of the victims were not known, and in later years the cemetery authorities erected a large granite monument in their memory. In 1916 Temmeme Derech had a *metaher*

Fig. 28. Early marble headstone in the Canal Street Gates of Prayer Cemetery. The uplifted hands are symbolic of praise or prayer. (Photograph by Leonard V. Huber.)

Fig. 29. A view of the Gates of Prayer Cemetery. The monument in the shape of a lighthouse is to Harry Offner, a hardware dealer who served as president of the Lighthouse for the Blind, a charitable organization devoted to helping the blind by providing them a means of livelihood.

Fig. 30. *Metaher* at the entrance of the Gates of Prayer Cemetery on Joseph Street.

Fig. 31. Principal inscription on this head-stone, a monument to Louis Wolf (1856) in the Gates of Prayer, is in Hebrew.

built at the entrance of the cemetery in Egyptian style (used to conduct the committal ceremony at the time of burials). This building was demolished in the 1960s.

In the same square with Gates of Prayer are cemeteries known as Beth Israel and Chivra Thilim, the latter one being absorbed by Gates of Prayer on May 8, 1950. Another old Jewish cemetery is the one started in 1850 by the Congregation Sha'aray Tefilev (Gates of Prayer) of the city of Lafayette in uptown New Orleans. This, the Joseph Street Cemetery, was founded in what was then the edge of the uptown suburbs shortly after the Congregation Gates of Prayer came into existence. The cemetery was once surrounded with a brick wall which was replaced in 1897 by an iron fence (figs. 30, 31). The Hebrew Rest Cemetery in Gentilly was also established by the Congregation Shanarai Chasset which had built the first Hebrew cemetery on Jackson Avenue. In 1860–1861 they entered into contracts to build a *metaher* and enclosed two squares on Elysian Fields, Pelopidas and Frenchmen streets with brick walls at a cost of $7,850 (fig. 32). It is interesting to note that in 1881 the Portuguese Congregation, Nefuzoth Yehudah and the German Congregation Shanarai Chasset (Gates of Mercy) united to form the Touro Synagogue.

Fig. 32. Heavy cast iron gates of Hebrew Rest Cemetery.

In 1872 Congregation Temple Sinai purchased from Shanarai Chasset half interest in the Hebrew Rest Cemetery, and the two congregations formed a joint board, the Hebrew Rest Cemetery Association, to supervise the burial grounds. The cemetery was enlarged in 1894 by the purchase of land across Frenchmen Street, and 1900 brought the start of a general plan of beautification. Hebrew Rest Cemetery is the largest Jewish cemetery in New Orleans. All Hebrew cemeteries are neatly kept, and as is the custom in Jewish cemeteries, the graves face east.

In Metairie Cemetery there are two Jewish sections, and a number of Jews are buried in the nonsectarian cemeteries of the city. Other Hebrew cemeteries in the city are Ahavas Sholem, started in 1895, Anshe Sfard, Beth Israel, and the Jewish

Fig. 33. Memorial to Miriam and Abraham Haber in Hebrew Rest Cemetery is typical Victorian monumental design.

Fig. 34. Isaac Levy plot in Hebrew Rest is ornamented by a sculptured angel strewing flowers on the graves of Sam, aged 21, and Irma, aged 18. On the same plot is a broken column, its capital lying below it, a monument to Henry, aged 33.

Burial Rites cemeteries, all of which were started in 1936. The newest and probably smallest Hebrew cemetery was started in 1973 in a tiny triangular piece of land adjoining the Dispersed of Judah Cemetery by the Congregation Chivra Thillim.

LAFAYETTE CEMETERY NO. 1

Lafayette Cemetery No. 1, (Washington Avenue and Prytania Street) was established as the municipal cemetery of the city of Lafayette (fig. 35A). The square was purchased for $6,000 from Cornelius Hurst, and the cemetery was planned by Benjamin Buisson, city surveyor. The land originally had been part of the Livaudais plantation which had been subdivided into city squares in 1832. Lafayette Cemetery No. 1 was laid out with two center aisles (fig. 35B), but some sections built up haphazardly. For many years tall magnolia trees lined the principal aisles giving the place a restful, gardenlike appearance. The cemetery had been inclosed by a brick wall in 1858, and wall vaults were also built in certain sections.

In this cemetery are buried a great many persons of Irish and German origin who lived in the city of Lafayette. During the great yellow fever epidemics, the cemetery received many of the victims of the dread plague.

Some of the tombs in this old cemetery are well designed and well kept, but a far greater number are neglected, decaying, or even in ruins. The cemetery contains several historic tombs, among them that of Samuel Jarvis Peters, the father of the New Orleans public school system. General John B. Hood and his wife, who died within days of each other of yellow fever, and another Civil War figure, Governor Henry Watkins Allen, were originally interred in Lafayette Cemetery, but their remains have

Fig. 35A. Entrance gates to Lafayette No. 1. Two of the large magnolia trees and two of the newly planted replacements are in the background.

Fig. 35B. Aerial view of Lafayette No. 1. Large trees shade the Washington Avenue and Prytania Street sides. The two main avenues and some regularity of passageways are indicated, but the cemetery has many blind alleys.

since been removed. General Harry T. Hays also finds his rest in Lafayette Cemetery No. 1. The tomb of the Sewell family bore an inscription which mutely reflected the tragedy of the Civil War on the members of that family. It read:

"Have pity on me; have pity on me;
at least you my friends, for
the hand of the Lord has touched me" Job XIX :21

Died
On May 12, 1864 at Shreveport, La.,
and exile from his home
EDWARD W. SEWELL
aged 60 years.
A native of Cork, Ireland, and for 33 years
a resident of New Orleans.

On the 28th of the same month
in the same year
Was killed at the Battle of New Hope Church
Corporal WILLIAM WASHINGTON SEWELL
Of the 5th Co., Washington Artillery, C.S.A.
Only son of Teresa J. Murray and Edward W. Sewell
Aged 22 years 11 months
A Native of New Orleans
Leaving his widowed mother childless.

TERESA J. MURRAY
Widow of Edward W. Sewell
Native of Sheepwalk, Avoca, Ireland
Born 1817–Died 1882.

Unfortunately the slab containing this tragic story became loose and fell from the tomb and was broken.

When the city of Lafayette was annexed to the city of New Orleans in 1852, New Orleans inherited the Lafayette Cemetery with it. Because his compensation was meagre, the sexton had to resort to other means to gain a livelihood. As a consequence, most sextons were also marble dealers who erected tombs in the

Fig. 35C. One of the main aisles of Lafayette No. 1. The magnolia trees, replanted in 1970, can be seen next to the roadway. At the corner are the vaults of the Jefferson Fire Company No. 22, erected in 1852. This tomb, with its carved handpumper, is the victim of neglect.

cemeteries in their charge. This resulted in the neglect of proper overall maintenance and neglect by the families owning graves and tombs; it also added to the gradual dilapidation of the cemetery. By the 1950s a virtual forest of bushes and trees, some of them fifteen feet high, was growing on the roofs of vaults along Washington Avenue and tearing the masonry apart. In 1969 the municipality passed a bond issue to improve certain city cemeteries, among them Lafayette No. 1. To the great disappointment of the residents of the Garden District, in which the cemetery is situated, the city proposed to tear down the old vaults, put up a chain-link fence, and pave the entire width of the main aisles. Inspired by Mrs. John B. Manard, a committee was formed to stop these "improvements." Instead a study was made, the old vaults were rebuilt after the trees had been removed from their tops, and the cemetery's main aisles were replanted with magnolia trees (fig. 35C). As a consequence, today the old cemetery is much improved. A historical plaque was placed on the wall of the cemetery in April, 1970, which tells the cemetery's history and marks the restoration of the vaults.

LAFAYETTE CEMETERY NO. 2

Lafayette Cemetery No. 2 is located on Washington Avenue in a square bounded by Sixth, Saratoga, and Loyola streets. It was probably started in the 1850s, for in 1858 the city constructed 120 vaults in it. It was not until 1865, however, that the city authorities ordered a survey to be made and a plan designating avenues, alleyways and walks drawn. In June, 1865, such a plan was approved and adopted by the city. The plan showed 96 "corner lots," each 12 feet by 12 feet which were to be sold for $150 each, and 384 interior lots, each 12 feet by 5 feet 6 inches which were to bring $50 each. A section of the cemetery adjoining Sixth Street was set aside "for the occupancy of the colored population." In this section a number of society tombs were built (fig. 35D).

In 1868 the Butchers' Association built a large vault containing room for eighty bodies, and in 1872 the French Society of Jefferson built a vault for its members. These tombs have suffered from the ravages of time and weather, and the vaults of the various societies in the rear of the cemetery are in pitiful condition, many being overgrown with vines and abandoned.

Fig. 35D. This tomb of the Société Française D'Assistance Mutuelle in Lafayette No. 2 is in dire need of restoration. More than a century old, it is still an interesting example of the mortuary art of the time it was built. Note the two supplicating maidens.

Unfortunately, Lafayette Cemetery No. 2 is located in a neighborhood which has changed over the years from one of modest homes to that of a slum. Visitors are afraid to venture into the cemetery, and some families have moved out of the neighborhood. Except for its society vaults, the cemetery can lay very little claim to good or even interesting monumental architecture; it is just a run-down New Orleans graveyard. In 1973 old vaults along Washington Avenue, long neglected, were about to tumble down, and they were demolished.

CYPRESS GROVE (FIREMEN'S) CEMETERY

Irad Ferry, a member of a leading business firm in New Orleans and a fireman of Mississippi Fire Company No. 2 lost his life on January 1, 1837, in a fire on Camp Street. He was given an imposing funeral which was attended by his fellow volunteer firemen, the mayor, judges of the courts, and the governor of Louisiana. Interment was in Girod Street Cemetery. A monument to his memory was slated to be erected in this cemetery, but the founding in 1840 of the Cypress Grove Cemetery by the Firemen's Charitable and Benevolent Association caused a change of plans. In 1838 Stephen Henderson, a wealthy New Orleanian, willed the association, an organization of volunteer fire fighters, some property which they converted into a sum sufficient to buy a cemetery site on the banks of Bayou Metairie at the end of Canal Street. Cypress Grove, the new cemetery, was started in 1840, and the monument to Irad Ferry constructed at its entrance (fig. 36).

The Irad Ferry memorial, a broken Doric column symbolizing a life cut short, was designed by the architect de Pouilly after a monument in Père Lachaise in Paris that he used as a model which is in the Quaglia book of designs which he had brought with him when he came from France. At length, in early 1841, the Ferry monument and the improvements at the cemetery were complete, and a date was set for the dedication.

In 1841 the remains of firemen who had been buried elsewhere were reverently removed to this permanent city of the dead firemen.... Pursuant to notice given by President Bedford, the several fire companies and the Exempt Firemen's Association met in the Custom House yard, dressed in sombre black, and wearing crape on the arm; the company banners were draped in mourning, and two members of each company acted as pall bearers, wearing white scarfs with crape knots at the shoulder, and bearing urns, emblematic of the remains of their deceased comrades.... The actual remains were borne in five hearses, each with an escort; the first, escorted by members of the F. C. A. and Fire Companies 1, 2, 3, 4; the second by Louisiana Hose and Fire Companies 5, 6, 7; the third by Protection Hose; the fourth by Fire Companies 9, 12, 13; and the fifth by Liberty Hose and Fire Companies 14 and 15. In this order the procession moved through Canal, Camp, Poydras and St. Charles Streets, to the First Congregational Church. The Rev. Mr. Clapp delivered a eulogium.

. . . .

At the close of the services, the march was taken up again, the procession passing by St. Charles and Canal Streets to the railroad station, where the cars were in waiting to proceed to the cemetery, nearly a thousand persons being thus conveyed to the scene. Here President Bedford read the Church of England burial service, and the remains were committed to their final resting-place. The body of Irad Ferry was laid beneath the monument which had been erected by this time; that of George Clark was placed in a tomb erected to his memory by J. L. Clay; and the other remains were placed in a sepulchre provided by the Association. Their names were: William Mason, Augustus Brown, Henry Johnson, S. P. Bourdoux, Samuel Williams, Alfred Perryman, Benjamin C. Jolly, William Lofty, John F. Ross, William Smith and Peter McCullor.

Fig. 36. Irad Ferry monument, designed by J. N. B. de Pouilly, who was architect for many of the finer monuments and tombs in New Orleans cemeteries of his day. The tomb was adapted from a design in the book of illustrations of monuments he had brought with him from Paris. The broken column, however, was de Pouilly's own idea.

The cemetery was 2,700 feet in length and 244 feet wide; the purchase price and improvements cost $35,000.

The entrance pylons and lodges were designed in Egyptian style by Frederick Wilkinson (1812–1841) at a cost of $8,000. Wilkinson who was born in Pough-keepsie, New York, was a graduate of United States Military Academy at West Point. He came to New Orleans in 1831 where he practiced civil engineering (figs. 37, 38).

Many prominent Orleanians are buried in Cypress Grove which became the burial place for many Protestant families when the Girod Street Cemetery began to deteriorate. At one time there was a motto over the entrance to the cemetery which read: "Here to their bosom mother earth, take back in peace what thou has given, and, all that is of heavenly birth, God in peace recall to heaven." Each side of Cypress Grove was lined with brick wall vaults which have, through neglect, deteriorated to the point where they will have to be demolished. The tablets closing the mouths of the vaults have largely disappeared. Some vaults were the resting places of members of the volunteer fire department, and the vault tablets had little fire engines and quaint epitaphs carved on them (fig. 39).

There are several multivault tombs of volunteer fire companies in Cypress Grove Cemetery. Among them are the well-preserved vaults of the Perserverance Fire

Fig. 39. Vault slab of young William Kelly (1862). A figure of Kelly is carved standing beside the steam pumper. (Photograph by Leonard V. Huber.)

Fig. 37. Cypress Grove (better known to Orleanians through the years as Firemen's Cemetery) as it appeared to an artist about 1855. (Courtesy Leonard V. Huber Collection.)

Fig. 38. Aerial view of Cypress Grove. This cemetery contains many magnificent trees, some of which are shown here.

Fig. 41. Four tombs, all memorials to firemen, were erected at the entrance to Cypress Grove. This tomb, for Perseverance Fire Company No. 13, was built in 1840. The other three were the Philadelphia Fire Engine Company No. 14, the Eagle Fire Company No. 7, and the tomb of Irad Ferry.

Company No. 13 (fig. 41) which was designed by John Barnett, architect, and erected in 1840. This tomb, near the entrance of the cemetery is surmounted by a small dome held up by eight columns set in a circle. Also erected in the 1840s are the twin tombs of the Philadelphia Fire Engine Company No. 14 and the tomb of the Eagle Fire Company No. 7. In the latter tomb are interred the remains of the Reverend Theodore Clapp, who ministered to the sick and dying, and buried the dead in the great epidemics of the 1830s. The Reverend Clapp has left a vivid description of the terrible epidemics that he witnessed, in his book *Autobiographical Sketches and Recollections During a Thirty-five Years' Residence in New Orleans*. He was also a firm friend of the volunteer firemen. In the Eagle Fire Company tomb are also buried the remains of the Reverend Sylvester Larned, a pioneer Presbyterian minister who died in 1820.

Two of the most ornate tombs in the Cypress Grove Cemetery are those of the Robert Slark and W. H. Letchford families (page 107 fig. 86). Slark was a wealthy hardware dealer. These two tombs are unmarked as to builder, but from the character of the design, they were probably designed by Theodore Brune and erected by George Stroud since both men were prominent in the field of cemetery memorials at the time that Robert Slark died (1868). Newton Richards, pioneer tomb builder,

Fig. 42. The Quincy granite tomb of Newton Richards, a memorial craftsman, is now a century old and attests to the skill of its builder.

Fig. 43. Newton Richards (1805–1874), memorial craftsman.

finds his rest in a plain but substantial structure of granite from his native Northeast (fig. 42). Richards (1805–1874) came to New Orleans after having served an apprenticeship in the stone business in Boston. He moved first to New York and in 1831 came to New Orleans where he soon had a thriving business dealing in marble and granite for building fronts and in erecting tombs in the city's cemeteries. He also sold lime. Newton Richards' shop, 147 Customhouse Street (Iberville), was bought by him from the city after the council decided that the fourth square, which was originally part of St. Louis Cemetery II, was too close to the expanding neighborhood. Many examples of his craftsmanship exist to attest to his skill and good taste in design. Richards served as a director of the Mechanics' and Traders' Bank and as president of the Mechanics' Institute. He died on November 9, 1874, at the age of sixty-nine (fig. 43). Another tomb builder, a leader in his day, was George Stroud. He erected some of the most pretentious tombs in Metairie Cemetery and was active in the early days of Metairie. His tomb, on the main aisle of the cemetery, is marked simply Stroud's Tomb. A well-maintained tomb on this same aisle is that of Dr. Warren Stone, a New Orleans physician (died 1883) whose infirmary on Canal Street and Claiborne Avenue was a New Orleans landmark.

The remains of one of the best-known citizens of New Orleans of his day is that of James H. Caldwell, who was a builder of the first American Theatre, the first St. Charles Theatre, and the founder of the New Orleans Gas Light Company. One of New Orleans' mayors, foundryman Charles L. Leeds, is befittingly buried in a cast iron tomb (page 178, fig. 116A). Unfortunately this fine tomb is rusting away for lack of paint. Cypress Grove Cemetery is the tomb of Soon On Tong Association which was dedicated July 19, 1904 (fig. 44). This tomb was used for the temporary burial of Chinese. A small fireplace in the tomb was used during the ceremony to burn offerings. Food and drinks were also brought to these services. The remains were

Fig. 44. This view of the Soon On Tong Association receiving vault probably was made in 1904, shortly after construction. Local Chinese buried their dead here with ceremonies that included burning prayers (on paper) in a small fireplace at the rear of the corridor and bringing food and drink to the obsequies. The remains eventually were removed and sent to China, a custom that no longer prevails. (Courtesy Leonard V. Huber Collection.)

Fig. 45. The Maunsell White tomb, designed in the Greek Revival style by J. N. B. de Pouilly, is a memorial to a prominent citizen who is remembered as the creator of Maunsell White Peppersauce. The Slark tomb is in the background. (Courtesy Leonard V. Huber Collection.)

eventually shipped back to China for burial in the homeland. The Chinese of today bury in the ground in Greenwood Cemetery.

Maunsell White, merchant, veteran of the Battle of New Orleans, who invented the Maunsell White Peppersauce, and who was described by Lafacadio Hearn as "immortalized among epicures" for his concoction, lies in a fine marble tomb which was designed by de Pouilly (fig. 45).

William G. Vincent (1828–1916), a veteran of the Mexican and the Civil wars, is entombed in a granite tomb on which is inscribed a summary of his eventful career. Vincent was president of the antilottery league which, after a long and bitter fight, put the Louisiana State Lottery out of business.

In the last few years Cypress Grove has suffered from neglect of some of its best tombs and loss of much of the fine cast iron fence work. The old vaults along each side of the cemetery have been practically denuded of their tablets, and the mark of the vandal is everywhere.

The combination of sexton and marble dealer is in evidence in most of the older cemeteries of New Orleans. This is true of Cypress Grove-Greenwood cemeteries. A firm, the Greenwood Marble Works composed of F. Bradley and E. D. Eaton, advertised in the 1871 city directory. In the 1890s Samuel T. Gately became superintendent and operated a marble yard at the entrance of Cypress Grove, and at his death his wife took over the business. She was aided by John F. Lally who until his death in the 1960s was associated with the two cemeteries. After Mrs. Gately's death Leonard E. Gately assumed management, and he has associated with him his two sons, Leonard III and Tracy Gately.

CYPRESS GROVE CEMETERY NO. 2

Cypress Grove No. 2 existed on the right rear side of Greenwood Cemetery. It was here that the indigent dead were buried until Canal Boulevard was cut through in 1911, and the roadway covered most of the area. A section remained in use until 1920.

ST. VINCENT DE PAUL CEMETERIES I, II, III

These walled cemeteries, also called the Louisa Street cemeteries, are in lower New Orleans (fig. 46). Nothing definitive can be ascertained about their origin although the city directory of 1857 lists the date of the charter as 1844, and writers in the past make reference to its founding by simply saying, "The cemetery was founded by a priest." It was acquired in 1857 by Señor Jose Llula, "Pepe Llula," the famous Spanish duelist, who operated it along with other business enterprises. When Llula died in 1888 the cemetery was inherited by his daughter, the wife of Manuel Suarez. On her death shortly thereafter, the property went to her seven children. Each of the four girls and three boys received shares in the cemetery property worth $20,000. Poor management by the heirs caused borrowings to be made from Albert L. Stewart, and in 1910 Stewart bought out the heirs and assumed other debts. The Stewart family has continued its ownership of the cemeteries to the present. In the past three quarters of a century they have built hundreds of vaults and tombs in the three cemeteries, including a two-storied community mausoleum in the third section (fig. 47).

The large family tombs of the Zaeheringer, Nothacker, Frantz, and Schoen families are notable. There are hundreds of smaller tombs of pedestrian design; the cemeteries are literally jammed with them.

In a vault in St. Vincent de Paul are the remains of Mother Catherine Seals, a widely followed Negro spiritual leader who died in 1930, and a large marble tomb of the Tinka-Gypsies holds the remains of their queen, Marie, who died in 1916 (fig. 48).

ST. PATRICK CEMETERIES I, II, III

There was a large influx of Irish immigrants to New Orleans in the 1830s. Like the German immigrants who came to this city, they were strangers in a strange land, and it was only natural that each group clung to others of the same native background. The Irish, universally Catholic, had no place to worship except with their Creole fellow Catholics, and it was not long before the Celts founded their own place of worship, St. Patrick's on Camp Street. Their next move was to find land and start a

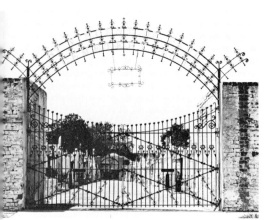
Fig. 46. The Piety Street gate of St. Vincent de Paul I.

Fig. 47. Brick wall surrounding St. Vincent de Paul III.

Fig. 48. Rows of tombs characterize the St. Vincent de Paul cemeteries.

cemetery of their own, and in 1841 the vestry of St. Patrick's bought a site near Metairie Ridge from a free man of color named Gabriel Jason and received permission from the city council to start a cemetery. Since the site was divided by Canal Street and by Metairie Road (now City Park Avenue), it was natural that each section of the new cemetery should be consecutively numbered: Numbers 1, 2, and 3.

The cemetery was just a dozen years old when the most frightful epidemic of yellow fever took place, and many of the unacclimated Irish were its victims. In the single month of August, 1853, eleven hundred persons were buried in the St. Patrick cemeteries. The burial of this enormous mass of bodies in so short a time must have taxed the cemetery's facilities to the utmost and probably accounts for the irregularity of the plan of St. Patrick No. 1 where most were buried. The dead simply came too fast to the cemetery and had to be buried in hastily dug graves which were at times mere ditches or trenches (fig. 49).

St. Patrick No. 2 fared better, the plots being laid out with regularity. It has a great many more above-ground tombs in it in contrast to the almost universal earthen burial in St. Patrick No. 1. St. Patrick No. 3 still has lots available. St. Patrick No. 2 is noted for headstones which bear interesting religious carvings (fig. 50). Many of these have been destroyed by hurricanes, but a number were photographed by the author in 1957–1958 and are illustrated in this book (fig. 51). In St. Patrick Cemetery No. 3 is the tomb of the Christian Brothers and the copings of the Sisters of Mercy and the Catholic Maritine Club. It also contains a small community mausoleum erected in the late 1960s.

On All Saints' Day, 1891, a mound surmounted by a calvary was dedicated in St. Patrick No. 1. The statuary group designed by Charles A. Orleans consisted of a wooden cross twenty feet high with life-sized statues of the crucified Christ, Mary Mother of Jesus, His beloved disciple John, and Mary Magdalene. The statues were cast in Paris. The Ancient Order of Hibernians served as a guard of honor.* St. Patrick

*In 1973 the calvary was removed to make way for the construction of a community mausoleum.

Fig. 49. The Graham monument stands out among hundreds of humbler monuments in St. Patrick No. 3.

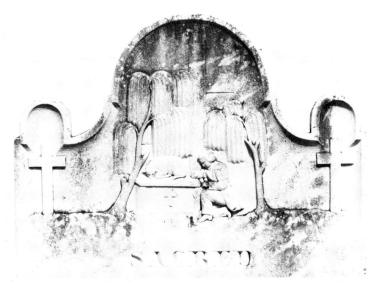

Fig. 50. The Lyons family headstone is an interesting example of the primitive carvings found on many monuments in St. Patrick No. 2.

Fig. 51. View of St. Patrick No. 2 shortly after Hurricane Betsy. Many of the headstones are made of marble only two inches thick and were blown from their bases and broken. (Photograph by Leonard V. Huber.)

33

No. 2 has a Pieta, erected by the church's pastor, Father Raymond Carra. Father Carra also had a large altar featuring a crucifix erected in memory of Domenick Carra in St. Patrick No. 3, and the same cemetery is graced by a statue of the good saint himself. At the entrances of the three cemeteries are sculptured stations of the cross. Plots in St. Patrick No. 2 were originally laid out to preserve a huge oak tree near the center aisle of the cemetery. This tree has long ago disappeared, but the semicircle of tombs which bordered it remains. When City Park Avenue was widened in 1909 a thirty-seven-foot strip of land from the front of St. Patrick No. 3 was acquired by the city from the church.

A simple marble headstone in St. Patrick Cemetery No. 1 marks the grave of the pioneer jazz musician Emile "Stalebread" Lacoume. "Stalebread" organized a skiffle band around the turn of the century when he was still a youngster, and even though he became blind, he played in jazz bands in the 1920s and 1930s. He died in 1946 at the age of sixty-one. One of the most interesting characters who finds his rest in the St. Patrick Cemetery is William Blair Lancaster (1826–1896), a native of St. Augustine, Florida, a lawyer who studied in Paris. In that city he came under the influence of Frederick Ozanam, a churchman who founded the world renowned Society of St. Vincent de Paul, an organization of men pledged to help those who were down on their luck, the unfortunate, and down-and-outers. Lancaster became a Catholic convert, and when he returned to the United States in New Orleans, he and the priest at St. Patrick's Church formed the first branch of the society in the South. In 1955, under the guidance of Monsignor Henry C. Bezou, then pastor of St. Patrick's Church, Ozanam Inn, for homeless men, was established on Camp Street. Monsignor Bezou had a plot set aside in St. Patrick No. 1 for the burial of indigents who died at the inn, so in the same cemetery lie the founder of the local St. Vincent de Paul Society and those who benefited by his charitable act.

In the early 1900s there was a small marble shop in St. Patrick Cemetery No. 1 run by Frank J. Pierre. This was located on Canal Street in a corner of the cemetery. Pierre was also sexton. He was succeeded by Jules F. Peytral, Jr., who was also in the marble and granite business. Peytral's successor was Jason Otis, who served for thirty years, 1943–1973. In 1966 the St. Patrick cemeteries, which had long suffered neglect, were taken over by the Archdiocese of New Orleans. These, as well as St. Louis cemeteries I, II, and III, the St. Roch cemeteries, St. Joseph cemeteries, and St. Vincent Soniat Street Cemetery were placed under a single management, and efforts have been made to improve and rehabilitate them.

ODD FELLOWS REST

The Independent Order of Odd Fellows, a secret benevolent society, had its New Orleans beginnings in 1831. It was not until 1840, however, that the membership began to increase and in 1847 that the Grand Lodge of the order purchased a triangular piece of land for a cemetery adjoining St. Patrick Cemetery No. 2 at the intersection of Canal Street and Metairie Road (now City Park Avenue). The site was bought for $700 from Henry Mitchell and later enlarged by donations of land from the Firemen's Charitable Association, Henry Bier, and George Allan. The plot was on relatively high land, and when the backwaters of the crevasse of 1849 inundated that section of New Orleans, the Odd Fellows site remained above the overflow (fig. 52).

The new cemetery was dedicated with great pomp and ceremony on February 29,

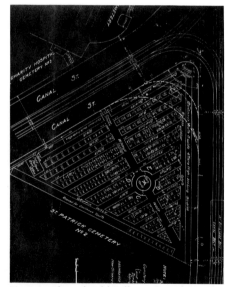

Fig. 52. Plan of Odd Fellows Rest drawn by city engineers. The broken lines at the left center indicate a proposed cutoff at the intersection of Canal Boulevard and City Park Avenue. A later plan called for the removal of the entire cemetery, but neither plan was implemented.

1849. A grand procession was led by two circus bandwagons, one from Stone and McCollum's Circus, drawn by "sixteen splendid horses," and a second from the circus troupe of S. P. Stickney which was drawn by four horses. Then followed a "funeral car" (fig. 53). This vehicle bore a sarcophagus of "quite imposing appearance . . . fitted up in a very appropriate manner, covered with emblems of mourning and was drawn by six fine grays driven by Mr. Stickney, who is one of the brethren." The "funeral car" carried the remains of sixteen deceased members of the organization that had been gathered from other cemeteries. These remains were the first interments in the new cemetery.

THE FUNERAL CAR, DESIGNED AND EXECUTED BY MR. DUBUQUE.

Fig. 53. This funeral car was used by the Odd Fellows in 1852 in memorial ceremonies commemorating the deaths of John C. Calhoun, Henry Clay, and Daniel Webster. Illustration is from a booklet describing the ceremonies. (Courtesy Leonard V. Huber Collection.)

The procession, after leaving the Place d'Armes, traversed some of New Orleans's principal streets including Chartres, Esplanade, Royal, Canal (upper and lower to Rampart), Camp, and St. Joseph to the head of the New Basin Canal. Here the Odd Fellows entered carriages and boarded thirty-five chartered omnibuses for the trip along the New Basin Shell Road to the site of the cemetery three miles away. At this point the procession stretched out for a mile. The officers of the Grand Lodge made the trip by water aboard a passenger barge.

Eventually the walks were laid out in the cemetery and named for Louisiana past grand masters of the Order. By 1852 two hundred vaults had been erected and the tomb of the Teutonia Lodge No. 10 finished. Two sides of the cemetery were enclosed with wall vaults and by the 1930s nearly all land in the small cemetery had been sold and built upon (fig. 54).

There are a number of interesting memorials in Odd Fellows Rest. One of these is that of the Howard Association, an organization of young men in New Orleans whose mission was to render emergency aid to victims of the yellow fever epidemics. A sculptured bas-relief of the English philanthropist and social reformer, John Howard (1726–1790), for whom the group was named, ornaments the front of the tomb. Alas, there is no one to take care of the Howard tomb, and in 1973 it was

Fig. 54. This 1965 photograph of the vaults in Odd Fellows Rest shows a heavy growth of roof-top weeds. This was later removed, but weeds are beginning to reappear. (Photograph by Leonard V. Huber.)

Fig. 55A. The Howard Association of New Orleans originally was composed of thirty young men, mostly clerks, who banded together in 1837 to aid the sick in times of epidemics. The association was named after John Howard (1726–1790), an English philanthropist and prison reformer who had campaigned successfully for reforms in jails and lazarettos in his own country and throughout Europe. The Howard Association performed magnificently during the yellow fever epidemics that periodically scourged New Orleans. The association no longer exists, however, and the tomb, with its bas relief of John Howard, is neglected and weed-grown.

Fig. 55B. The name in the pavement in front of this tomb designates it as the vault of Southwestern Lodge No. 40. The structure probably was built as the tomb of I.O.O.F. Teutonia Lodge No. 10, however, because the carving in the center panel bears the German words *Freundschaft Liebe und Warheit* (Friendship Love and Truth).

weedgrown (fig. 55A). The society tomb of Southwestern Lodge No. 40, Independent Order of Odd Fellows, with its intricately carved ornamentation and which bears the German words *Freundschaft und Warheit* meaning Friendship and Truth, is probably the original Teutonia Lodge No. 10 tomb which was constructed about 1851 (fig. 55B). The cast iron gates of the Odd Fellows Rest, with their interesting symbols of the fraternity such as the widow and her children, the beehive, the all-seeing eye of Deity, the world, the cornucopia, the Bible, the initials I. O. of O. F., and the five-pointed stars are being slowly destroyed by vandals. (figs. 56, 57, 58).

In the 1960s the traffic situation at the intersection of Canal Street, City Park Avenue, and Canal Boulevard had become so serious that the city of New Orleans offered this Grand Lodge of Odd Fellows a proposal to move the cemetery. After months of negotiations the city authorities and Grand Lodge failed to reach an agreement and the cemetery still remains where it has been since its founding in 1849. Today Odd Fellows Rest is in great need of proper maintenance, and the high hopes and fine words of its founders have been forgotten long ago.

Fig. 57. Mother and children pattern on gates of Odd Fellows Rest. (Photograph by Leonard V. Huber.)

. 56. These cast iron gates of Odd Fellows Rest
ce were painted in vivid colors. When this
otogaph was taken in 1962 only a small bit of
e panel was missing. By 1973, however, one
ire upper panel was gone. (Photograph by
onard V. Huber.)

Fig. 58. Odd Fellows symbols panel in cemetery gate. (Photograph by Leonard V. Huber.)

GREENWOOD CEMETERY

So successful was Cypress Grove Cemetery that the Firemen's Charitable and Benevolent Association bought more land, and the Greenwood Cemetery was founded (1852). Greenwood is smaller in acreage than Metairie Cemetery, yet because of the smaller size of its lots (6 feet by 9 feet) far more families have their places of burial in Greenwood. There are about 20,500 lots in Greenwood, and the cemetery accounts for about a thousand interments a year. The cemetery was planned to utilize the maximum amount of land for grave lots, so aside from five memorials at its entrance set in a lawn space, no attempt was made to beautify it by architectural or landscape features.

The five featured memorials at the entrance to Greenwood are: the Confederate monument, the Firemen's monument, the Elks tomb, and the tombs of Michael McKay and John Fitzpatrick. The Confederate Monument in Greenwood Cemetery was erected through the efforts of the Ladies Benevolent Association of Louisiana (fig. 59). It marks the mass grave of six hundred Confederate soldiers whose remains the association had gathered. A contemporary at the time of its dedication wrote in the *New Orleans Republican:*

> The following is a brief description of the monument: A mausoleum of masonry about fifteen feet square and six feet in height. The sloping sides are turfed. On top is a granite

Fig. 59. Busts of four military leaders of the Confederacy adorn the Confederate monument at one entrance to Greenwood. Shown here below the statue of the Confederate soldier are the marble likenesses of Generals Stonewall Jackson, Robert E. Lee, Leonidas Polk, and Albert Sidney Johnston.

Fig. 60. New York sculptor Alexander Doyle had a virtual monopoly on statues erected in New Orleans in the post – Civil War era. This one of a sturdy volunteer fireman is the central ornament of the Firemen's Monument (1887). (Courtesy Leonard V. Huber Collection.)

gallery about eight feet square in the center of which stands a marble pedestal nine feet high. Surmounting the pedestal is a statue representing a Confederate soldier, fully armed. The statue is of Carrara marble and is seven feet in height. . . .

On the south face of the base of the pedestal is the inscription: "Erected in memory of the heroic virtues of the Confederate soldiers, by the Ladies' Benevolent Association." Just above the inscription, on the south side of the monument, is placed a life size bust of General R. E. Lee, on the western side a similar bust of Stonewall Jackson, on the side toward the north one of Albert Sidney Johnston and on the east side of [Leonidas] Polk.

The monument was designed by the architect Benjamin M. Harrod and was erected by the memorial contractor, George Stroud. It cost $11,385. The statuary was carved in Italy.

The Confederate monument was dedicated April 10, 1874, the first of the Civil War memorials to be erected in New Orleans. New Orleans was still under carpetbag misrule and the city's people far from prosperous, yet the zeal of the women of the Ladies Benevolent Association was such that they raised nearly $30,000 in eight years; they expended $18,500 of this aiding destitute widows and orphans of Confederate soldiers and used the balance to pay for the removal of the remains of several hundred Confederate soldiers and for the erection of the monument. At the dedication, the Reverend B. M. Palmer gave the opening prayer. H. N. Ogden was orator of the day, and Dr. William T. Leacock gave the benediction.

Each year on Confederate Memorial Day, June 3, the United Daughters of the Confederacy mark the day by decorating the Confederate monument with flowers.

The second of the impressive memorials at the entrance of Greenwood Cemetery is the Firemen's monument (fig. 60). Its design, neo-Gothic, was probably inspired by the Sir Walter Scott monument in Edinburgh. The Firemen's monument is situated at the center of a fifty-eight-foot square mound which rises five feet. Its base is eighteen feet square, and the monument is forty-six feet in height. The shrinelike body of the monument consists of a cluster of Gothic arches surmounted by a steeple. The figure of a volunteer fireman is placed under the arches and the names of twenty-three volunteer fire companies are engraved on the monument's base. The monument was designed and erected by Charles A. Orleans at a cost of $14,000. The material used was Hallowell, Maine, granite. The Italian marble statue is six feet high and was designed by Alexander Doyle of New York and carved by the artist Nicoli. The monument was erected by the Firemen's Charitable Association to celebrate the fiftieth anniversary of its founding and to memorialize the brave volunteer firemen who had lost their lives in fighting fires during the past half-century. The orator at the dedication was Lawrence O'Donnell.

Each year on March 4 the officers of the Firemen's Charitable and Benevolent Association gather at the monument and commemorate Volunteer Firemen's Day by the presentation of a wreath in memory of departed members. March 4 was a holiday featuring parades by the volunteer fire companies in the days before a paid fire department was organized in 1891.

Other multivault tombs in Greenwood are those of the Swiss Society and the New Orleans Typographical Union, which was founded in 1855, the first labor union in this region (fig. 61). The beautifully designed double tomb of A. T. and W. O. Thompson on Magnolia Avenue also faces Canal Street. This white marble tomb in Gothic style had suffered damage from a hurricane and the passage of years but was recently restored to something of its original beauty (page 106, fig. 85).

An interesting tomb at the corner of Magnolia and Myrtle avenues of Greenwood is the Woodruff-McLeod memorial (fig. 62). Daniel Woodruff and William McLeod lost their lives on March 16, 1854, when a wall fell on them at a fire on Magazine Street. Both were members of Mississippi Fire Company No. 2. A year later the cornerstone of their tomb was laid with Masonic ceremonies, but when the tomb was completed, McLeod's widow objected to having her husband's body removed from the Girod Street Cemetery, where it was interred when he died, so the tomb contains only the remains of Woodruff. The expense of erecting the tomb was borne by the Common Council of the City of New Orleans. Today the tomb is in need of repairs.

Opposite the Firemen's monument is the tomb of Lodge No. 30 of the Benevolent Protective Order of Elks. The tomb is in the shape of a grassy mound (tumulus) surmounted by the bronze figure of an elk, the symbol of the fraternity. Under the

Fig. 61. This society tomb of the New Orleans Typographical Union was built about 1912 by Victor Huber. The date at the top of the tomb, 1855, refers to the date of the founding of the union, the first labor union to be established in the city. (Photograph by Leonard V. Huber.)

Fig. 62. In the days before firemen were paid for their work, volunteer firemen were highly regarded by their fellow citizens. When they lost their lives in the line of duty, as did Woodruff and McLeod, members of Mississippi Fire Company No. 2, they became heroes overnight. To show their regard for the bravery of these two men, the city council had this tomb erected in their memory.

Fig. 63. This tumular tomb of Lodge No. 30, Benevolent and Protective Order of Elks, is near the entrance to Greenwood.

mound is a marble chamber which contains eighteen vaults (fig. 63). The granite entrance to the tomb is done in Doric style with two fluted columns supporting an entablature. The second symbol of the Elks, a clock, the hands of which point to the hour of eleven, is worked into the pediment. Bronze doors close the entrance. The tomb was erected in 1912 by Weiblen, who warned the engineer in charge that the structure was on unstable ground and that it should have a pile foundation. His words went unheeded, and as a result the tomb is tilting due to an improper foundation. The first entombment took place in Decmber, 1912.

Adjoining the Elks tomb are two tombs of presidents of the Firemen's Charitable and Benevolent Association. The first is that of Michael J. McKay who was president for sixteen years. This was erected by the Samuel T. Gately Marble and Granite Works in 1938. The tomb of John Fitzpatrick is the last of the tombs facing Canal Street. John Fitzpatrick (1844–1919) was mayor of New Orleans 1892–1896 and president of the Firemen's Association for twenty-seven years. The tomb was designed by Edwin L. Zander, the engineer employed by the association and erected by Victor Huber in 1926. The tomb, like many of the old-time buildings of New Orleans, was erected on a matte of heavy pecky cypress planks by order of the engineer. The Firemen's monument, as well as some of the other tombs in the group, lean. All were built on the banks of the old Metairie Bayou, and the subsoil has subsided causing the structure above it to tilt.

Another multivault tomb which faces Canal Street is that of the Police Mutual Benevolent Association. It was constructed of white marble in 1917 and contains twelve vaults. The tomb features a policeman's cap and badge carved on its pediment (page 123, fig. 115).

Nearby is the monument to Abial Daily Crossman (1803–1859), mayor of New Orleans, 1846–1854. This memorial consists of a graceful fluted column bearing a symbolic urn on its capital. The Crossman plot is encompassed by an iron fence (fig. 64A).

The Robert Roberts family memorial off Myrtle Avenue features an Egyptian obelisk. Roberts (1822–1881) was a manufacturer of millwork. From his factory came supplies of Victorian brackets and other wood ornamentations of hundreds of

Fig. 64A. Monument to Mayor A. D. Crossman, who held the city's highest office during the tragic yellow fever epidemic of 1853. (Courtesy Leonard V. Huber Collection.)

houses built in uptown New Orleans in the mid-nineteenth century. A catalogue of his designs is in the Tulane University Library.

Parts of Greenwood have felt the heavy hand of time. Both tombs and receiving vaults have suffered from neglect as survivors died and because the association did nothing to check the decay of some of their most interesting architectural sepulchers. The saddest of all, and one that should have never happened, is the neglect of the iron tomb on Myrtle Avenue that contains the mortal remains of Isaac Newton Marks, its president and dedicated leader from 1855 to 1891 when the paid fire department took over from the volunteers. Marks was born in 1817 in Charleston and came to New Orleans in young manhood. He soon became a successful business-man which gave him the means to serve as alderman and to head or serve on the boards of other firms. Starting as a volunteer fireman in 1843 when he joined Perserverence Company No. 13, he became president of the company and later president of the Firemen's Charitable Association. He was a wise and energetic leader, and in 1855 on the twenty-first anniversary of the association he was presented with a silver service of unique design that cost $1,000.* When the Firemen's monument was dedicated in 1887 the speaker of the day hailed Marks in his address, saying:

> In conclusion, Mr. President, to speak what I know is the sentiment of the whole fire department: that among our honored chiefs living or dead, to none are we more indebted for the great success and high standing of the fire department than yourself. For half a century you have assisted to guide our Association, and now, with integrity unquestioned you stand . . . as a peer among the good and great men of the city, while with us firemen you are a pillar of our existence and have a place in our hearts forever . . . on our roll of honor your name is inscribed; in our memories your name will live, yea, in our hearts we declare you the noblest Roman of them all.

Fine words, but Isaac Marks has been forgotten by the descendants of those who listened to the words of the orator that day. But it is not too late to make amends; the iron tomb of Isaac Marks can be rehabilitated and put under perpetual care by the association so that this important leader's memory will be kept alive and his tomb preserved.

On Cedar Avenue is the tomb of Samuel Locke. The tomb, a granite structure, was erected by Newton Richards more than a hundred years ago. A large tree fell on the tomb and knocked it askew. It also broke one of the granite posts surrounding it, but the tomb itself is still structurally sound. Next to it is a large marble column erected to memorialize John Oliver Locke, a member of Fenner's Battery who died during the Civil War on January 12, 1864, at the age of twenty-five. An epitaph on the side of the tomb reads:

Rest, gentle youth, thou hast found peace at last
When war no more its gloomy cloud may cast
O'er anxious hearts, nor snatch from earthly view
The forms we love, without a last adieu.
The void thou leavest in our sorrowing breasts
As brother, son and friend ever attests
Our loss, thy gain, we trust in brighter spheres,
But fond remembrances shall in coming years
Dwell on thy kindly virtues and recall
Each tone and look and gesture
All the frank expression of a guileless mind
Of modesty and worth alike combined!

*This service is in the possession of the Insurance Company of North America.

Fig. 64B. Many carved memorials on vault slabs and tombstones grace Greenwood. Among them is the above, engraved with the word *Hope*, with a sculptured anchor, the symbol of hope, and ornate and skillfully executed lettering:

Erected
By his wife
In Memory of
JOHN HOUSTON
who died
of Cholera
July 20, 1849:
Aged 33 years
11 months, 8 days
(Photograph by Leonard V. Huber.)

Fig. 64C. This fantastic tomb is decorated with no less than ten crosses and boasts two metal shrines. It is an excellent example of cemetery folk art. (Photo by Leonard V. Huber.)

By a miracle the falling tree did no damage to the monument of young Locke.

An imposing granite tomb on Hawthorn Avenue bears the family name of Marcy. This tomb is ornamented by small columns and Romanesque capitals and contains three openings. Among the tombs in Greenwood is that of Warren Easton, the educator for whom the high school on Canal Street is named; that of Dan C. Byerly, "gallant soldier and journalist who fell in one of the heated political conflicts which grew out of the bitterness of the days of reconstruction." In the pavement of the tomb of Captain Eugene Gaspard (1839–1889) there is carved a marble ship, and there are here and there stones which bear epitaphs of hope, faith, or submission to God's will (fig. 64B).

Through the century that has passed, Greenwood Cemetery has built up with thousands of tombs and copings (ground plots) (fig 64C). Near the entrance the tombs are mostly of brick or Georgia marble but as one goes deeper into the cemetery the marble gives way to granite, limestone, and concrete. Unfortunately in some sections, great numbers of the tombs are poorly designed and crowded too closely. Only of late years has the Firemen's Association begun the sale of its lots with mandatory perpetual care included, something that should have been done half a century ago.

ST. JOSEPH CEMETERIES NO. 1 and NO. 2

The St. Joseph Cemetery No. 1 on Washington Avenue was dedicated in 1854 by the St. Joseph German Orphan Asylum Association. Thomas Keosh was president and George Hirsch secretary. There was a dual purpose in the founding of this cemetery—first, to provide a place of burial for the German immigrants and their descendants who lived in the suburb of Lafayette and, second, to provide a source of revenue for the nuns of the Sisters of Notre Dame who managed the St. Joseph German Orphan Asylum. The first superintendent of St. Joseph Cemetery was Mathias Huber whose term of office was from 1855 to 1870.

The cemetery filled with such rapidity that an addition became necessary, and on July 2, 1873, permission was given by the city council to extend the cemetery to the block behind the first section. This too filled, and in time the cemeteries became somewhat dilapidated. When the streets surrounding it were paved and the bills for the paving were presented, the sisters found that they had a liability on their hands instead of the income-producing property that had for years been a source of revenue. They asked to be relieved of their property, and Archbishop Joseph F. Rummel accepted it for the diocese. It was then that Stanley J. Guerin, an interested Catholic layman, came to the rescue of the cemeteries. He instituted reforms, and under his hand the neglect which had set in was stayed and the cemeteries made presentable once more.

A feature of St. Joseph Cemetery No. 1 is the chapel which is the original church of the former St. Mary Assumption Parish (fig. 65). The frame building which was constructed in 1844 seated eighty. It was moved in 1862 when the St. Mary's Assumption Church in the present St. Alphonsus Parish was constructed. In this cemetery one sees the family names of old-time uptown residents such as the Wegmanns, the Babsts, the Fabachers.

In the second St. Joseph Cemetery is a miniature Gothic chapel complete with

Fig. 65. The original chapel of the St. Mary's Assumption Congregation was moved to St. Joseph No. 1 in 1862. Built in 1844, it is one of the oldest buildings in uptown New Orleans.

Fig. 66. This former tomb of the Redemptorist fathers provides a variation in the otherwise dull and repetitious monumental design which characterizes the St. Joseph cemeteries.

copper flêche. This was once the tombs of Redemptorist priests but is now owned by the Smith family (fig. 66).

The St. Joseph cemeteries contain hundreds of copings (earthen burial plots). These are sometimes as high as three feet from the sidewalk, built that way so that a grave need not be dug deeply below grade. In them, families bury and rebury; this is also the custom with tomb burials; on one tomb there were the inscriptions of two dozen of its occupants. When wall vaults that once bordered the cemetery on Washington Avenue were removed, monument dealers unfortunately were allowed to erect a row of poorly designed spall tombs* which spoil the entrance. Since 1966 when the Archdiocesan Cemetery group was formed, the cemeteries have been well managed and well maintained. In 1972 a bronze historical plaque was placed at the entrance of St. Joseph Cemetery No. 1 by the Archdiocesan cemeteries group.

CARROLLTON CEMETERY
(Sometimes called the Green Street Cemetery)

The burgeoning suburb of Carrollton was incorporated as a city in 1845 and historian William H. Williams, writing in 1876, described the cemetery (fig. 67):

> A cemetery was established as an appendage to the town government, and owned by the corporation. It is situated in the rear of the town, formed by the sedimentary deposit from the waters of the Macarty crevasse. The height of the land renders it suitable for burying in the ground — the most pleasant and beautiful as well as the most permanent mode of preserving our dead [sic].
>
> The grounds are now becoming handsomely improved with tombs, trees, shrubbery

---

*Tombs made of small pieces of granite or marble, the refuse of marble yards.

Fig. 68. In 1855 Valentine Munck combined the duties of undertaker and sexton for the Carrollton Cemetery. His advertisement above tells the entire story: a hearse, a coffin, tombstones in the background, and Munck leaning on a shovel, one of the tools of his trade. (Courtesy Leonard V. Huber Collection.)

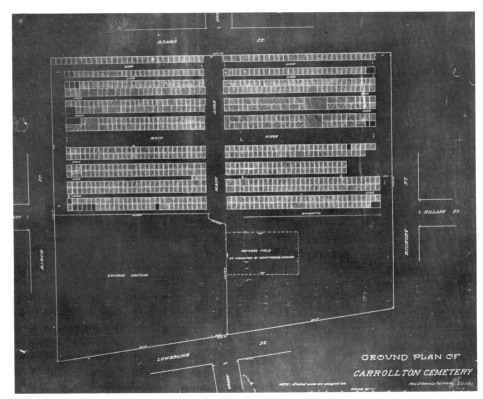

Fig. 67. This plan of the Carrollton Cemetery drawn in 1917 shows an orderly section for whites, a "colored section" not laid out in aisles, and a "potters field as indicated by scattered graves."

and flowers. The dead of forty years lie reposing here; many, it is true, now wholly neglected and forgotten; while on the other hand, the honored and well remembered names here scattered around on marble, are so many and so familiar to us all, that we feel, in the walks in our cemetery, as if we were moving in the midst of our friends.

A cemetery journal in the Kuntz collection records that the first lot sold in this cemetery was numbered 405, purchased on November 8, 1849, by Neil Cochran for $15 which was the price for many years thereafter. Carrollton was annexed to the city of New Orleans in 1874, and the management of the cemetery passed into the hands of the city government.

Under municipal management, Carrollton has had far from satisfactory maintenance (fig. 69). Many of the early tombs in the cemetery, like the twenty-four-vault society tomb of Die Deutsche Freundschaftsbund (German League of Friendship), which bears the date 1850, are badly in need of repairs. In 1969 the city issued bonds for cemetery improvement, and today the Carrollton Cemetery's main aisles are paved, and there is improved drainage, but as Williams noted in 1876, "the dead . . . are now wholly neglected and forgotten."

There are no tombs of great architectural value in Carrollton cemetery. On the main aisle is the tomb of Frederick Fischer who came to Carrollton in 1839 and nearby the twin tomb of the Kirchoff and Lochte families, and throughout the cemetery are tombs of pioneer families such as the Heatons, Herrles, Thielers, Gogreves Deibels, and O'Dwyers.

Fig. 69. This wooden headboard of Walter Davis, who was "berried" on February 9, 1936, was typical of the simple, impermanent monuments erected in the Negro section of Carrollton. (Courtesy Leonard V. Huber Collection.)

ST. MARY CEMETERY (CARROLLTON)

This desolate spot, located near the Carrollton cemetery (Spruce, Adams, Cohn, and Lowerline streets), was so weedgrown in September, 1973, when the author visited the place that he feared to enter it. The cemetery originally was the property of the Catholic Church but the city authorities took it over in a swap of land with the church in 1921.

ALGIERS CEMETERIES: ST. BARTHOLOMEW, ST. MARY, AND DUVERJÉ PRIVATE CHAPEL AND BURIAL GROUND

St. Bartholomew Cemetery (Square no. 213) on Newton, Diana, and Nunez streets was deeded to the Catholic Church by the Duverjé family on December 19, 1848, on condition that it always remain a cemetery. The cemetery was started the next year, and by the 1860s it had become so crowded that a newer cemetery was needed. The new cemetery occupies Square no. 188, Newton, Diana, Nunez, and DeArmas streets. Ten lots were acquired from 1861 to 1866 and an eleventh in 1923. This is St. Mary Cemetery. Both cemeteries partake of the same characteristics as those on the other side of the river in New Orleans—copings and tombs and society tombs (fig. 70).

The family of Barthelemy Duverjé had its own cemetery in Algiers. Started as a burial place for his slaves by Duverjé, a wealthy landowner, the cemetery was enclosed first with a wood fence and later by a brick wall and a chapel. The little cemetery occupied nearly a city block. Duverjé's descendants built a house for the keeper of the cemetery, and the place was always well maintained. The family tomb of the owner was built of granite from Quincy, Massachusetts, in Egyptain style. The little cemetery was the scene each year of a family reunion on All Saints' Day. First, Mass was held in the chapel, and those who gathered would repair to the cemetery

Fig. 70. This brick tomb of James Mitchell in St. Mary's Cemetery, Algiers, is typical of family tombs of the 1880s and 1890s when it probably was erected. (Courtesy Richard Remy Dixon Collection.)

Fig. 71. St. Bartholomew Cemetery features a large crucifix (left center). This photograph, made either on All Saints' Day or the day after, shows that nearly all the graves and tombs are decorated with flowers. (Courtesy Richard Remy Dixon Collection.)

and spread a picnic lunch. A tragic incident occurred in the 1840s when a prominent member of the family, a wealthy merchant, despondent from financial losses, repaired to the cemetery, wedged a sword between two tombs and ran himself through.

Duverjé left five daughters who married into the families of Villeré, Olivier, Robelot, LaVigne, and Coycault (and later after the death of Coycault, Wharton) and eventually this generation, too, used the cemetery when death came. By 1915 J. G. Olivier, a grandson of Barthelemy Duverjé, realized that the cemetery was in the way of a growing community and that it might fall into unsympathetic hands, resolved to demolish it after getting permission to move the nearly four hundred bodies interred in it. Duverjé's Egyptian-style tomb was moved to Metairie Cemetery in 1916, the old chapel demolished and the cemetery eventually made into a playground. A rough granite marker, inscribed Barthelemy Duverjé Place, keeps alive the name of this pioneer citizen of Algiers.

ST. VINCENT CEMETERY (SONIAT STREET)

St. Vincent Cemetery (Soniat Street) is composed of two squares, the first of which was chartered in 1859 by the Congregation de la Mission. The first features a pair of rather high vault structures at the end of its main aisle. At the top of the vaults is a platform which may be reached by an outdoor staircase. On the platform there is a marble crucifix, but, both arms of the Christus are missing. From this vantage point may be seen the two copings of the religious with their granite markers identifying the graves of the sisters who were members of the Sisters of Charity of St. Vincent de Paul. To the left of the viewer is the second section of this cemetery, which, except for a single tomb and a small public mausoleum, is composed entirely of ground burials (copings). The right side of this cemetery is patronized by Negroes and the left side by whites.

Although the cemetery is neatly kept there is not a single tomb or headstone in it that could be termed outstanding. One exception, possibly, is the sealed granite coping and memorial to Father Lester Kavanaugh under whose auspices the fine church of Our Lady of Lourdes on Napoleon Avenue was constructed. In tombs on the main aisle are the remains of Emilien Perrin, a leader in the real estate business and of George J. Glover (1838–1932) a general contractor who erected many large buildings in New Orleans. St. Vincent's was under the management of the priests of St. Stephen's Church (Napoleon Avenue) until 1966 when it was taken over by the Diocesan Cemetery group.

VALENCE STREET CEMETERY

The Valence Street Cemetery, once known as the City Cemetery of the City of Jefferson, (Valence and Saratoga streets) was, like a number of other uptown cemeteries, laid out to take care of the population of the city's expanding suburbs. When the city of New Orleans annexed these suburbs it also inherited the cemeteries. Besides Valence Street Cemetery, examples are Lafayette No. 1 and No. 2 on Washington Avenue and Carrollton Cemetery, Green Street. The date of its founding is uncertain, but a report of the city comptroller in 1869 designated the cemetery as a property 300 by 300 feet valued at $7,500. The city erected a fence around the cemetery in 1892, paved the sidewalks in 1895, and in 1898 caused filling to be made "in order to eliminate a health menace occasioned by the existing poor drainage."

The Valence Street Cemetery is not a prepossessing place. Like most city cemeteries, it is not well maintained either by the city or most of the families who have places of burial in it. There are a number of decaying society tombs like the vaults of the St. Anthony of Padua Italian Mutual Benefit Society; the St. Joseph's Sepulchre of the Male and Female Benevolent Association (1872) (fig. 72) and the Ladies and Gentlemen Perserverence Benevolent Association (1893). John David Fink (died 1856), the German philanthropist for whom the former Fink Asylum was named is buried in this cemetery in a tomb to which his remains were removed from the Girod Street Cemetery when that cemetery was demolished.

The Valence Street Cemetery is used by both whites and Negroes.

ST. JOHN CEMETERY — HOPE MAUSOLEUM

St. John Cemetery in the 4800 block of Canal Street was founded in 1867 by the St. John Evangelical Lutheran Congregation. It was the second Protestant cemetery to be established in New Orleans, the first having been established by Christ Church (Episcopal) in 1822. The cemetery was originally known as the First German Evangelical Lutheran St. John Cemetery (fig. 73). The cemetery as originally laid out contained about 750 lots, size 6 by 9 feet, and there was space against the perimeter for receiving vaults. The cemetery was operated by the church for sixty-two years, until 1929.

During the ownership of the church some nineteen hundred interments were made at St. John and about 400 lots sold at prices that varied from $40 to $75 per lot. There was a space approximately 100 by 320 feet at the rear of the cemetery which had not been used for burials since it was occupied by the sexton's house and vegetable garden, and there was another partly unoccupied parcel measuring 133 by 54 feet facing Canal Street at North Bernadotte. In the 1920s Canal Street was repaved and North Anthony Street paved. The city charged the paving to the owners, St. John Congregation, and since the bill was a large one and the revenues from the cemetery were hardly enough to pay the sexton's salary, the congregation decided to sell the cemetery. The sale was made to Victor Huber, a memorial craftsman who was also a member of the congregation and who had supervised its operations and set up a small perpetual care fund for the church. Huber made a cash settlement with the congregation and agreed to assume the street-paving bills and retain the name St. John Cemetery although it was understood that the cemetery would be made nonsectarian. (When the church had owned it secret societies were not allowed to hold ceremonies in it, and Catholic priests were forbidden by their bishops to officiate at services in it.)

St. John Cemetery Association was then formed and incorporated under state law and Victor Huber and his sons, Leonard, Albert, and Elmer began the erection of vaults and tombs. The elder Huber had seen community mausoleums on a trip to the West Coast, and he conceived the idea that a similar mausoleum, as a logical development of New Orleans above-ground burials, would prove successful in the Crescent City. Accordingly, plans were made and construction on the first wing of Hope Mausoleum on the vacant ground in the rear of the cemetery started in 1931.

Fig. 72. The decaying structure of the St. Joseph's Sepulcher of the Male and Female Benevolent Association in the Valence Street Cemetery. Note the nine small vaults at the top of this society tomb. They were intended for the entombment of babies since there was a high rate of death among infants.

Fig. 73. Rahders tomb, erected in 1876, in St. John Cemetery. It is said that when the well-to-do family lost a child, they sold one of their houses and used the money to build this tomb. In the background is a wall of Hope Mausoleum.

Fig. 74. The German word atop the hand-clasp on the Richard Koch headstone in St. John means Farewell. (Courtesy Leonard V. Huber Collection.)

Fig. 75. Although Hope Mausoleum occupies almost half the ground in St. John Cemetery, there are numerous private memorials as well. Among them is this sarcophagus Walter Ward had built for his mother Sarah in the 1930s. It was designed by Albert Huber and erected by Victor Huber and Sons. The design was influenced by that of the tomb of Napoleon Bonaparte in the Invalides in Paris which Ward wanted copied. (Courtesy Leonard V. Huber Collection.)

Fig. 76. The Red River Pilots Association erected this tomb (probably in 1870) for burial of its members. The emblem of the profession, a steamboat steering wheel, ornaments the pediment of the tomb in Masonic Cemetery. (Courtesy Leonard V. Huber Collection.)

NEW ORLEANS ARCHITECTURE

Hope Mausoleum through the years has expanded as the need for more space has grown, and in 1973 the building contained more than 8,000 crypts and included a crematory, the first to be constructed in Louisiana. Interments in St. John and in Hope Mausoleum now exceed 13,500. Hope Mausoleum is a noteworthy example of the prudent use of land for burials; the relation of land use in the mausoleum over conventional earthen interment is about 20 to 1. St. John has always been well kept, and today a substantial perpetual care fund generated from sales of crypts in Hope Mausoleum is a guaranty for its future maintenance.

The cemetery contains several interesting carved headstones (fig. 74), relics of its earlier days, but Hope Mausoleum, which was designed by Albert R. Huber, is its principal feature. For many years Otto Burandt was sexton of St. John, and after his death Thomas Williams held the position. The sexton lived on the grounds of the cemetery in a house which stood on the corner of Iberville and North Anthony Street. This house was demolished in 1941, and the house at 4821 Iberville Street was purchased and remodeled into a home for the superintendent. The present superintendent is John D. Lahare who in 1962 succeeded his father, William J. Lahare, Jr., who had held the office for more than thirty-two years.

Members of the present generation of Hubers who own St. John Cemetery are the great- and great-great-grandsons of Friedrich Robbert, one of the cemetery's founders and the fourth and fifth generations to be continuously connected with its operation (fig. 75).

MASONIC CEMETERY

The Masonic Cemetery, one of a number to come into existence shortly after the Civil War, was founded in 1865 by the Grand Lodge of the State of Louisiana, Free and Accepted Masons. Petition to establish a cemetery for Masons was made in March, 1865, while the city was still under military occupation. The resolution granting permission was signed by Captain Stephen Hoyt, U.S.A., who was acting mayor. The Masonic Order took no chances however, and had a new resolution passed giving them permission to build their cemetery on January 18, 1868. The cemetery is in two sections and is located on land facing Bienville Street between St. Louis Street and City Park Avenue. The wide main aisle is paved with brick, and the cemetery except for a receiving vault on North Anthony Street is surrounded by an iron picket fence.

Masonic Cemetery contains a number of interesting lodge tombs, the oldest probably being that of the Perfect Union Lodge, founded in 1793. This odd structure consists of vaults on either side of a corridor and a set of steps on its exterior by which one may gain the roof. Other lodge vaults are those of the George Washington Lodge No. 65, the Alpha Home Lodge No. 72, Louisiana Relief Lodge No. 1, and that of Étoile Polaire No. 1, a lodge founded in 1794. On the main aisle is the society tomb of the Red River Pilots Association (1869), a group long extinct (fig. 76).

The burial places owned by most Masonic lodges are for ground interments (copings); among them is the interesting coping of the Osiris Lodge No. 300 which is graced by two polished columns which were salvaged in the 1920s when the old Masonic Temple on St. Charles Avenue was demolished. Other lodge copings are the Union Lodge No. 172, Orleans Lodge No. 397, Ionic Lodge No. 374, Friends of

Harmony No. 58, Trowel Lodge No. 386, Mount Moriah No. 59, Quitman Lodge No. 76, and the two copings of Linn Wood No. 167.

A large columnar monument was erected to the memory of Samuel M. Todd who was grand master of Louisiana Masonic lodges in 1859, 1868, 1870, 1871 and 1872, besides holding office as grand commander of the Knights Templar of Louisiana in 1866 and 1867. There is a coping of cast iron on the plot of William G. Bedford who died in 1876. A number of granite tombs for individuals and families includes those of Dr. J. G. Harz (1848–1936), a long-time resident of Canal Street; L. P. de la Houssaye (died 1913) who was grand master of the state in 1904–1905; R. G. Holzer (1844–1906), a Swiss who founded a metal concern which is still in business; of John I. Plume and the Morgan-Pajewski family.

The land in Masonic has nearly all been sold, and there is the problem of maintenance since obligatory perpetual care was begun only lately. The present superintendent is Nolan L. Bergey. J. D. Ryan and Shelton P. Hubbard succeeded Benjamin Weaver who was superintendent for nearly a quarter of a century.

ST. ROCH CEMETERIES I, II

St. Roch Cemetery (fig. 77) was started by Father Peter Leonard Thevis, a young German-born priest who was pastor of the Holy Trinity Catholic Church in lower New Orleans. In 1868, a year after he had come to Holy Trinity, there was an epidemic of yellow fever, one of numerous epidemics that periodically plagued New Orleans. Father Thevis remembered that in Europe, at times of pestilence, people prayed to ask for the intervention of St. Roch, one of the Church's "Fourteen Holy Helpers," to alleviate their misery. He himself prayed and urged his congregation to pray to invoke the help of St. Roch, and he made a vow that he would build with his own hands a chapel to the saint if members of his church were spared. The story is told that none died and Father Thevis built the chapel. Father Thevis also planned a *campo santo* or cemetery in which he would build his shrine. The cemetery was started in 1874. It was modeled after the famous Campo Santo dei Tedeschi near St. Peter's in Rome. Like the older New Orleans cemeteries it was surrounded with wall vaults. At intervals small chapellike niches were constructed, and in them were placed figures of the stations of the cross.

The chapel, which one writer said reminds him of a kitchen clock, was designed to resemble the diminuitive chancel of a Gothic church (fig. 78). It was completed and dedicated on August 16, 1876. The altar in the chapel is of carved and painted wood; in its reredos is a small statue of St. Roch, the pilgrim, with his staff, gourd, and faithful dog, who by tradition brought him food when he lay ill and deserted. When Father Thevis died, his remains were placed under the floor in front of the altar.

Since its erection St. Roch's chapel has been a favorite shrine of the faithful. Thousands have come to pray or burn a candle for wishes asked or granted (fig. 79). Roger Baudier, Catholic historian, wrote of St. Roch's: "There pervades over the Camp Santo and its fascinating Gothic chapel an Old World atmosphere and charm, an other-world air, and a soul-satisfying sense of peace and spirituality. Here one sees before one's own eyes mighty faith, living hope, inspiring piety and Christian beliefs put into living practice." Another section of the cemetery was added in 1895 when St. Michael's chapel-tomb was built. This structure, with its flying arches, fell

Fig. 77. The entrance lodges and gates of St. Roch Cemetery. Father Thevis' Chapel is in the background.

Fig. 78. St. Roch's Chapel. The crucifix in front of the chapel was built over a well which was known as "the wishing well." The marble figure of an infant is an *ex voto* presented by a grateful mother whose child had been cured of an illness. (Courtesy Leonard V. Huber Collection.)

Fig. 79. The altar of the St. Roch shrine, 1937. At right are the "thanks blocks," and to the left are the representations of various parts of the human body placed there as *ex votoes* by grateful persons who felt their prayers to the saint had been answered. These objects have since been moved to a room at the side of the shrine. (Courtesy Leonard V. Huber Collection.)

Fig. 80. St. Michael's chapel-tomb, St. Roch Cemetery No. 2.

into a ruinous condition by the 1920s, but it was eventually restored and is today in good repair (fig. 80).

The first square of St. Roch's has long been filled with family tombs and ground plots. In the near future the land which remains in the section to the rear of the original cemetery will also be fully occupied.

METAIRIE CEMETERY

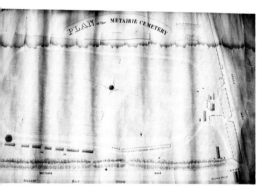

Fig. 81. Photograph of a rare plan by P. A. d'Hemecourt, deputy city surveyor, dated August 19, 1872, showing the Metairie Race Course just before the Metairie Cemetery was planned. The grandstand (lower center) and the stables (lower left) were situated along Metairie Road, and the course itself (now Metairie Avenue in the cemetery) is shown with auxiliary buildings. (Courtesy Leonard V. Huber Collection.)

With its ample acreage, its beautiful palms and other trees, shrubs, and lagoon, Metairie Cemetery is a fine setting for the more than seven thousand tombs and plots which dot its 150 acres. Metairie is unique among the cemeteries of the United States; it is the only one that was converted from a racetrack. The site, relatively high ground on the banks of Bayou Tchoupitoulas (Bayou Metairie) was laid out in 1838 as the Metairie Race Course (fig. 81). The Metairie track soon became a leading racing center, known throughout the South. In 1854 the famous match races between Lexington, a horse from Kentucky and Lecompte, a Louisiana horse (representing Mississippi) were held there. Although Lecompte was bested in this grueling series, the horse had won the hearts of Louisianians, and a town near Alexandria where his stud farm was located, was named in his honor.

The Civil War (1861–1865) brought great changes to life in Louisiana, and although an attempt was made in 1866 to restore racing at the Metairie track the racing association had financial difficulties, and there were disagreements among the members of the board of directors which resulted in the closing of the track. At this time New Orleans was ripe for the development of a new cemetery—one patterned after the great rural cemeteries of the eastern part of the Union with their spacious, landscaped grounds. All of the New Orleans cemeteries of this time (except Greenwood) were surrounded by wall vaults or were small in size, and the promoters of the new cemetery envisioned a burial ground that had an uncrowded, parklike appearance as a background for the more elegant types of tombs and monuments which had, in the quarter century before this, been developing in New Orleans.

The new cemetery owners, called the Metairie Cemetery Association, were granted a charter in May, 1872, and the land acquired by an act of sale passed in July of that year. The capital stock was $120,000, but apparently little cash was put up.

The president of the old racing association, Duncan Kenner, became a member of the board of the Cemetery Association. Other members were William S. Pike, first president of the association, Gus A. Breaux, Charles T. Howard, John A. Morris, and W. C. Lipscomb. Charles T. Howard and John A. Morris were principal owners of the Louisiana State Lottery and William S. Pike, a banker, was Howard's son-in-law. Breaux was a lawyer and Lipscomb, a cotton broker.

The cemetery was designed by Benjamin F. Harrod, an architect who utilized the 1 1/16-mile track of the race course (now Metairie Avenue), as the principal avenue (fig. 82). A receiving vault was one of the first structures erected in the cemetery and this still exists. The cemetery was beautified by trees and shrubs, and it soon became well patronized by most of the leading families of the city. The first interment took place in 1873 when the body of Dr. James Ritchie was interred in a small tomb on Central Avenue. The original entrance to the cemetery (fig. 83) was followed in 1883 by the erection of a stone lodge flanked by two stone arches, but this too was demolished in 1953–1954 because of the erection of the overpass at City Park Avenue and Pontchartrain Boulevard (fig. 84). The cemetery was laid out with broad avenues and small paths which were wide enough for the passage of vehicles. A feature of the cemetery which added greatly to its beauty was its lakes—Horseshoe Lake (fig. 85) and Lake Prospect. Horseshoe Lake was part of Bayou Metairie which had been enlarged by digging. This lake was to the left of the cemetery and has been filled in to make room for widening Metairie Road. Lake Prospect still exists. Both lakes were ornamented with picturesque little stone bridges (fig. 86). In 1885 a suit was brought against the Canal Bank for all land occupied by a major portion of Lakeview, West End, and the Metairie Cemetery. This involved an alleged royal grant but the case, which was eventually sent through at least four courts, ended in that the cemetery had its title confirmed. Another case in which the city of New Orleans tried to levy a toll on the bridge crossing the New Basin Canal for all traffic, including funerals, resulted in a compromise.

Fig. 85. Lakefront view of tombs near the Metairie Cemetery entrance. (Courtesy Leonard V. Huber Collection.)

Fig. 82. Aerial view of Metairie Cemetery. The layout of roads was greatly influenced by the original track of the Metairie Race Course.

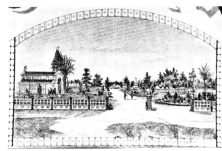

Fig. 83. View of the Metairie Cemetery entrance, about 1875. (Courtesy Leonard V. Huber Collection.)

Fig. 84. Metairie Cemetery lodge building, with twin-arched driveways, was built in 1883 and served until 1953 when it was demolished to make way for the Metairie Road overpass. (Courtesy Leonard V. Huber Collection.)

Fig. 86. This marble bridge once spanned Horseshoe Lake in Metairie Cemetery. The lake has been filled and the bridge demolished to make room for the widening of Metairie Road. (Courtesy Leonard V. Huber Collection.)

Two legendary stories are attached to the Metairie Cemetery. One of them is that Charles T. Howard, one of the founders of the cemetery, was blackballed when he tried to become a member of the exclusive Metairie Jockey Club which owned the racetrack. Charles Howard had made his fortune in the Louisiana State Lottery Company and was regarded by his contemporaries as a "rough diamond." When he was not admitted to the club, so the story goes, he swore that he would make a cemetery out of the racetrack. Charles Howard died in 1885, and in his ornate mausoleum on Central Avenue in Metairie Cemetery sits the mysterious marble figure of an old man with his finger to his lips.

The other legend is probably based on fact. In 1914 Josie Arlington (color plate 8), a notorious madame of the New Orleans red-light district, commissioned Weiblen to build a mausoleum for her. The tomb was built of a polished reddish granite, and it is said that a red light from the toll barrier along the New Basin Shell Road reflected in the shiny sides of the tomb, the cemetery at that time not having been built up. Someone discovered this red glow in the Arlington tomb, whose owner by that time had died and was buried in it, and the tale became an overnight sensation. Officials of the cemetery, it is said, planted out the pathway of the light, and the tomb became as sedate as any of the others, but the tradition still exists, and ever so often strangers inquire about it.*

In 1908, largely through the efforts of the association, the Louisiana legislature passed Act No. 190, the important law which permits cemetery corporations to take cemetery tombs and plots in trust for their perpetual maintenance. About 1910 an adjacent area was acquired, and the Metairie Annex was developed after most of the land in the original cemetery was sold.

The long-time secretary of Metairie Cemetery was Samuel H. Bell, who held this office from 1878 until his death in 1925. Under his direction the operation of the cemetery was a most successful one. Bell was succeeded in 1925 by Numa V. Bertel who held the office until 1951. One of the first superintendents of Metairie Cemetery was William Benson, and William J. Lahare was the superintendent from the early 1900s until his death in 1937. Benson had laid out the cemetery with the assistance of superintendent Paul Scholz in 1893. Harold Magin held the office until 1951.

Metairie Cemetery is the last resting place of many of the best-known families of New Orleans. Through the years no less than seven governors of Louisiana, including William C. C. Claiborne, the first American governor of Louisiana, are buried there. Six mayors of New Orleans, the best known of whom are Martin Behrman and de Lesseps S. Morrison find their rest in Metairie. Forty-nine kings of Carnival are buried there, and since many of the queens have married and changed their names, only a dozen or so are identifiable.

If one starts at the new gatehouse of the cemetery and proceeds to the right on Metairie Avenue, he will first see twin tombs erected by Victor Huber for William B. Bloomfield, a successful rice broker and Presbyterian layman, memorials to the Bloomfield and Affleck families. These are of the style current around 1910. Across the road is a sarcophagus memorial designed by Jean F. A. Lorber for his own memorial. Among the sarcophagus tombs is the Missouri red granite monument-tomb of James Hearn and his wife. When Hearn died his tomb was in process of being built, and the Episcopal bishop who officiated held the commital service at the cemetery dressed in his robes of office, and this, with the unfinished monument in

*Josie Arlington's remains were eventually removed by relatives to an ordinary vault and the tomb sold to J. A. Morales.

the background, made an impression on one viewer which has remained with him all his life.

Nearby are the well-proportioned twin tombs of the brothers Witherspoon, J. T. and Thomas, cotton brokers, which were designed by architect Rathbone DeBuys and built by Weiblen. Here also is the tomb of Harry Fitzpatrick who was a champion athlete in his younger days and who was a well-known auctioneer. The impressive tomb of George W. Clay, a cotton broker, was designed by Charles Lawhon and erected by Weiblen. Another attractive tomb designed by Charles Lawhon is that of Oliver O. Provosty, one time chief justice of the state of Louisiana.

The Poer-Cohen-Allee tomb was designed by Albert R. Huber and erected by Victor Huber (fig. 87). The design with its enormously thick stones was inspired by the tombs in the Valley of the Queens in Egypt. This tomb has granite walls two feet thick, and the roof stones, which weigh thirty tons, were cut at the quarry since the rough stone from which they were made was too heavy to transport. The tomb of Frank J. Matthew, painting contractor, was designed by Emile Weill, architect, and constructed by Weiblen.

Fig. 87. Reminiscent of tombs in the Valley of the Queens is this tomb built in the 1920s for William L. Poer by Victor Huber. It has walls two feet thick and enormously heavy roof stones. (Courtesy Leonard V. Huber Collection.)

One of the most impressive groups of tombs and mausoleums in Metairie Cemetery is that of the Vaccaro and D'Antoni families. Nearby is the grave of the Reverend Albert R. Edbrooke, an Episcopalian priest. The monument is in the shape of a rock-faced cross. On the same avenue is the grave of New Orleans architect, Moise Goldstein, a memorial tablet of fine proportions and beautiful ornamentations which he designed himself. An unusual tomb is that of the Kimmel family. This tomb was erected by Weiblen and features a bronze figure of a woman strewing flowers on the grave.

The impressive mausoleum of the Eastwick family is the last resting place of Marie Celeste Stauffer, widow of George Spencer Eastwick, who left a good part of her estate to the Eye, Ear, Nose and Throat Hospital. This money was used by the hospital authorities to build a modern annex to the hospital. Other mausoleums nearby are George A. Diasselles', a contractor, built by Weiblen and the Montelepre mausoleum designed by Albert R. Huber and erected by Victor Huber. At one time the pink marble from Tennessee was used to construct several tombs in Metairie Cemetery. One such tomb is that of Thomas Simms. This and marble from Georgia and Alabama have withstood the climate of New Orleans much better than marbles from Italy and Vermont.

Situated on Metairie Avenue, which was at one time the race course of the Metairie Jockey Club, is the tomb of John A. Morris, eastern capitalist and a sponsor of the Louisiana lottery. His tomb, which is on a large plot, was built by Charles Orleans. Other tombs nearby are those of the physician Dr. Samuel Choppin and the lawyers John and Charles Chaffe. The Emory Clapp sarcophagus surmounts a grassy mound (page 83, fig. 35). Governor John M. Parker is buried in the Airey coping. Stanley O. Thomas, who is further memorialized by Stanley Thomas Hall at Loyola University, is buried in a polished granite tomb which was erected by Charles Orleans. One tomb holds the remains of two New Orleans steamboatmen, Captain Thomas Pickles and Captain A. M. Halliday. The family operated ferries which bore the names of both Captain Pickles and Captain Halliday.

In certain sections of Metairie Cemetery a great number of tombs were erected by Pierre Casse. Among them are the tombs of the Brewster, McGinty, McCloskey, and James J. Reiss families, and there are others which bear the stamp of Casse's craftsmanship. There are a number of double tombs—two families in a single

Fig. 88. Alexander Doyle, a New York sculptor, designed numerous figures of Confederate leaders during the 1880s. Doyle is shown here with a full-sized study of the equestrian statue of General Albert Sidney Johnston. After it was completed in 1887, the statue was sent to New Orleans and placed atop the Army of Northern Virginia tomb. (From *Frank Leslie's Illustrated Newspaper*, July 17, 1886.) (Courtesy Leonard V. Huber Collection.)

Fig. 89. Dedication of the Albert Sidney Johnston monument in Metairie Cemetery in 1887 aroused great public interest. It also was the inspiration for "Heroes' March," composed by William d'Equede and "written expressly for the unveiling of the statue of General Albert Sidney Johnston and dedicated to the Louisiana Division of the Army of Tennessee." (Courtesy Leonard V. Huber Collection.)

structure. One of these is the tomb of J. C. Scofield and Edwin Shanks. This tomb is surrounded by an iron fence with a graceful harp design. The Keppler and Stumpf tombs were erected by George Stroud who did a number of tombs in this vicinity.

The Zahn tomb was built from granite salvaged in 1894 from the fire of the second St. Charles Hotel. The Gothic Georgia marble tomb of Joseph Lenes was designed by Charles Lawhon and built by Weiblen. Lenes Hall on Baronne Street adjoining the Jesuit Church of the Immaculate Conception is another memorial to this family. Henry Greenwall, pioneer theatrical manager, is memorialized in a tomb not too far away from that of his contemporary in the theatrical business, David Bidwell. Similarly, the tombs of two hotel men, Grunewald (Grunewald-Roosevelt-Fairmont Hotel) and Monteleone (Monteleone Hotel) are erected in this same neighborhood. The triumvirate of haute cuisine, Jules and Roy Alciatore (Antoine's), Leon Galatoire (Galatoire's), and Arnaud Cazenave (Arnaud's) all rest in Metairie. An architecturally interesting tomb off Metairie Avenue is that of the Lefebvre family. This structure of red brick contains a number of vaults and is the only one of its type in the cemetery (page 77, fig. 16).

The first tomb to be erected in Metairie Cemetery was that of Dr. James Ritchie, a small single vault structure on the main aisle. Dr. Ritchie's tomb bears the inscription, "More Bent to Raise the Wretched than to Rise." Nearby are those of Frank T. Howard and William Pike, cofounders of the Cemetery Association. Pike was the third Rex, king of Carnival of 1873. An impressive tomb near the former entrance of the cemetery is that of Captain Salvadore Pizzati which was erected by Charles A. Orleans. The story goes that Captain Pizzati ordered that his favorite rocking chair be placed in the lower receptacle of his tomb.

One of the larger memorials in Metairie Cemetery is that of the mausoleum of the Benevolent Association of the Army of Tennessee erected at the former main entrance of the cemetery. It consists of a vaulted Gothic chapel in which are forty-eight vaults; the tomb is covered by a large grassy mound (tumulus) and is surmounted by an equestrian statue of General Albert Sidney Johnston (fig. 88). At the right of the entrance to the tomb is a marble statue of a Confederate sergeant calling the roll. This statue, like the equestrian statue above it, is the work of Alexander Doyle, a New York sculptor. The sergeant's face was modeled after a photograph of a New Orleans Confederate soldier, William Brunet, a sergeant of the Louisiana Guard Battery who lost his life at the Battle of New Hope Church, Georgia, in 1864. The statue was the gift of Charles T. Howard, and it was dedicated before a large group of people on May 20, 1886. Next year, on April 6, 1887, the bronze equestrian statue of General Albert Sidney Johnston was dedicated and the *Daily Picayune* ran a special illustrated edition to commemorate the affair (fig. 89).

The most celebrated personage to find his rest in the Army of Tennessee Tomb is General P. G. T. Beauregard who sleeps eternally with the remains of the men who were soldiers in his and other Confederate armies. General Beauregard died in 1893. Nearby is the beautiful Lacosst sarcophagus memorial erected from a design by the architects Burton and Bendernagel (fig. 90). It was erected by Weiblen of Alabama marble, and the carving is regarded as the finest example of this craft in Metairie. Eugene Lacosst (1854–1915) was a successful stock speculator and an amateur musician whose specialty was whistling. Lacosst left substantial legacies to Charity Hospital and Delgado Museum.

The largest memorial in Metairie Cemetery is that erected by Daniel Moriarty in memory of his wife who died in 1887 (fig. 91). Her remains were moved to Metairie

Fig. 90. Memorial to Eugene Lacosst, stock speculator and amateur musician, is one of the most costly and ornate in Matairie Cemetery. The design resembles that of the monument to William Cullen Bryant in New York, but the Lacosst sarcophagus is much richer. Burton & Bendernagle were architects, and the work was erected by Weiblen.

Fig. 91. The largest and most imposing monument in Metairie Cemetery is the shaft Daniel Moriarty had erected in memory of his wife. The scale of this memorial is immense. A man can stand under the arms of the Latin cross that surmounts it. (Courtesy Leonard V. Huber Collection.)

Fig. 92. The four granite maidens around the base of the shaft of the Moriarty monument have been referred to by local wags as Faith, Hope and Charity—and Mrs. Moriarty. The fourth figure, however, represents Memories. (Courtesy Leonard V. Huber Collection.)

Cemetery about 1905, and the huge granite spire topped with a cross of the same material was erected. The spire and its bases were so heavy that a railroad spur track had to be built to the site to transport them from the quarry. In 1914 Victor Huber erected the sidewalk of Mount Airy granite around the circular plot. The stones, each of which weighed eleven tons, caused the drays carrying them to the cemetery to cut deep ruts into the gravel with which Canal Street was then paved.

At one time, probably between 1903–1923, there was a style of building huge granite tombs with polished sides, fronts, and roofs. These tombs were usually constructed of Quincy, Massachusetts, granite, but some are of Barre, Vermont, granite and at least one of Elberton granite and a few of red Missouri granite. Among these are tombs of J. S. Rainey, Dr. B. M. Palmer, Hardie, Allgeyer, J. Blackman, Segari, and Ellis families. The Shakspeare tomb of Mayor Joseph Shakspeare, early foundry owner, and that of Alexander Hutchinson are of polished red granite. Also of red granite are the coping and headstone of Albert Weiblen, the tomb builder whose organization was responsible for probably more than half the work in Metairie Cemetery.

An attractive plot is the imposing mausoleum of Lawrence Fabacher of the family of pioneer brewers. Close to each other are the tombs of two tycoons, Julius Kruttschnitt, who rose to be president of Southern Pacific Lines, and Thomas Woodward whose name is still borne by Woodward, Wight and Company, Ltd., a leading machinery, mill, and hardware supply firm. Further along the aisle is the ground burial plot of William Ratcliff Irby who was head of a large tobacco firm. He became interested in the preservation movement in the Vieux Carre in later life and bought the lower Pontalba Building and willed it to the Louisiana State Museum. He also bought the Banque de la Louisiane building, now Brennan's Restaurant, the former home of Paul Morphy, the chess wizard, and presented it to Tulane

55

Fig. 93. Weeping dog on the Masich family plot.

Fig. 94. Monument to the Louisiana Division of the Army of Northern Virginia, topped by the granite figure of General Stonewall Jackson. (Courtesy Leonard V. Huber Collection.)

University. Mayor T. Semmes Walmsley is buried in the coping of his wife's relatives, the Havard family. The Maginnis family tomb was the work of Charles A. Orleans. The small granite tomb of the family of F. Masich is ornamented by a life-sized marble figure of a weeping dog (fig. 93). The story goes that the dog would not come away from his master's grave; eventually he perished waiting for him to return, and the family had his image carved in stone where he keeps perpetual watch. In the center of the cemetery there is a circle, and around it are three 1890s style ornate tombs of the families of Peter O'Brien, Samuel Gilmore, and Joseph Hernandez. Samuel Gilmore was city attorney and the father of Martha Gilmore Robinson, one of the city's most energetic civic workers.

One of the largest granite tombs near the center of the original cemetery is that of Colonel Cuthbert Slocomb, Civil War veteran, volunteer fireman, and a pioneer in a hardware business that survived until the 1930s. This was built by Stroud. The J. L. Harris tomb is memorable for the fact that some of its stones are so heavy that when they were being carted to the cemetery they broke the bridge across the New Basin Canal. The monument to the Reverend Thomas Markham, which was designed and built by Weiblen, consisted of a base and an eight-ton obelisk surmounting it. This was picked up by the wind during Hurricane Betsy in 1965 and dropped to the earth and broken.

Another military monument is that of the Washington Artillery Battalion. It is a cenotaph since no one is buried below it. The structure was erected on land donated by the Metairie Cemetery Association, and it was dedicated in 1881.

A memorable Confederate memorial is the Stonewall Jackson monument, better known as the tomb of the Association of the Army of Northern Virginia (fig. 94), which occupies a large circular site at the rear of the cemetery. Its column towers some thirty-eight feet over the grass-covered tumulus containing fifty-seven vaults in which are interred the remains of Confederate veterans. The front side of the die of the monument is inscribed "From Manassas to Appomattox" and the reverse side "Army of Northern Virginia, Louisiana Division." A third side is inscribed "Intaminatis Fulget Honoribus," and a fourth has reliefs of the flags of the Fifteenth Louisiana and the Zouaves. The figure at the top of the column is of the indomitable General Thomas J. Jackson, "Stonewall" to his men and to history.

The exercises to dedicate the monument were held on May 10, 1881; seats were provided for five thousand persons, and a huge crowd attended the unveiling. A band played solemn music, a poem written for the occasion was read, and General Fitzhugh Lee, nephew of Robert E. Lee, made the principal address. When former Confederate President Jefferson Davis died on December 6, 1889, he was given a state funeral and his body placed in the tomb of the Army of Northern Virginia. The casket containing his remains was removed from the tomb on June 1, 1893, and shipped to Richmond for permanent burial. The crypt in the Metairie tomb was sealed and never again used for burial (figs. 95, 96).

Civil War figures whose graves are in Metairie Cemetery are those of General Richard "Dick" Taylor, son of President Zachary Taylor, and one of the best strategists and bravest fighters of the Confederacy; Colonel George Moorman, CSA; General John Bell Hood, CSA, whose remains were moved to Metairie from Lafayette Cemetery No. 1; General Fred N. Ogden, who led the White League in the battle of September 14, 1874, to crush the Metropolitan Police, and in the final takeover of the state government when Francis T. Nicholls was elected governor in 1876; and John A. Stevenson who built the cigar-shaped Confederate ironclad "turtle" Ma-

nassas used in the defense of New Orleans in 1862. A long epitaph tells of his civic and patriotic services.

Pearl Wight, cofounder of Woodward, Wight & Company, Ltd., like his partner Woodward, finds his rest in Metairie Cemetery in a handsome mausoleum designed by Charles L. Lawhon and erected by Weiblen. Nearby is a ground plot of the Barthel-Waterman family which is dominated by a reproduction of Thorwaldsen's *Christus* in bronze. The red granite tomb of Henry Wenger, at one time the owner of a celebrated beer garden in New Orleans, is near the tomb of Joseph A. Walker. In this neighborhood is also the tomb of Judge George H. Braughn, a founder of the Rex organization and for years its secretary and manager.

Walking through Metairie Cemetery one sees the names of persons successful in the businesses or the professions of New Orleans, such as the grave of Dr. J. T. Nix, a well-known physician, and that of Hugh McCloskey, who lies in a private mausoleum. McCloskey was president of D. H. Holmes, famed New Orleans department store, and of the New Orleans Railway and Light Company. In the Denegre plot is buried the man who introduced football to New Orleans, Thomas L. Bayne, and who, with his brother Hugh, had played football at Yale. The first game was played on New Year's Day, 1890, between two squads of Tulane University. Another coping which is surmounted by a beautifully carved column marks the grave of Ensign Hugh A. Aiken (page 93, fig. 56A). A monument to the memory of David C. Hennessy, superintendent of police, who was assassinated on October 15, 1890, by members of Sicilian Mafia in New Orleans, was erected in Metairie Cemetery (page 93, fig. 58).

A monument of Moresque design, constructed of a dark Belgian limestone, was erected for General Beauregard's son-in-law, Charles Larendon. At one time a miniature nude female figure in a boat hung suspended from a chain under the dome but this has disappeared.

Two handsome mausoleums (Avenue E) just a short distance apart, were built for two lumber tycoons whose timber holdings in southwest Louisiana adjoined each other. Frank B. Williams rests in an Egyptian-inspired mausoleum designed by the architects Favrot and Livaudais (page 103, fig. 80). This tomb also holds the ashes of the early movie actress Marguerite Clark and the remains of her sportsman husband, Harry Williams, a pioneer in the development of aviation in Louisiana. Also in this memorial are the ashes of General L. Kemper William and his wife who founded the Historic New Orleans Collection, a museum of New Orleans antiquities. The Downman tomb was designed by Charles L. Lawhon, and both were erected by Weiblen.

Metairie Cemetery also contains the grave of Edward G. Schlieder, a wealthy brewer who left a fortune to establish the Schlieder Foundation. The cemetery boasts of the beautifully done Celtic cross on the Rogers-Palfrey-Brewster plot (fig. 98). This cross was designed by Elizabeth Rogers Palfrey and Charles L. Lawhon. The tomb of Eliza Poitevent Nicholson, the editor of the *Picayune,* who died at the age of forty-seven in 1896, and that of her husband, George Nicholson, is marked by a monument featuring a bronze newspaper. Robert Ewing, a power in politics in the early 1900s and owner and publisher of the *Daily States,* also finds his last rest in Metairie, as does William Carter Stubbs (died July 7, 1924), author, scientist, educator, who was internationally known for his work in the sugar industry and who was an expert in the efforts to develop pest-resistant sugarcane.

Three tombs in the vicinity of the pyramidal tomb of the Brunswick family are

Fig. 95. When Jefferson Davis, former President of the Confederacy, died in New Orleans on December 6, 1889, the funeral obsequies lasted until December 11. Davis' casket is shown here in the council chamber of City Hall. (Courtesy Leonard V. Huber Collection.)

Fig. 96. The remains of former Confederate President Jefferson Davis were entombed with great ceremony in the vaults of the tomb of the Army of Northern Virginia. This photograph shows veterans and the guard of honor awaiting the arrival of the funeral cortege. The monument was festooned with mourning garlands for the occasion. (Courtesy Leonard V. Huber Collection.)

Fig. 97. A row of Italian mutual benevolent society tombs in Metairie Cemetery. But for Italian immigrants, the societies that built them are gradually disappearing. Membership in a mutual benevolent society with the right of burial in the society's tomb was highly prized.

Fig. 98. Rogers-Brewster-Stillwell Celtic cross in Metairie Cemetery, inspired by the large crosses of this type erected many years ago in Ireland. The designers have skillfully included numerous Christian symbols (the Reverend Mr. Brewster, one of those commemorated, was an Episcopalian priest). Symbols include the dove (Holy Ghost), the True Vine, the Eucharistic cup, and the interlaced XP. A magnificent example of the stoneworker's art.

those of F. W. Tilton, Alexander and Josephine Hutchinson, and Richard A. Millikin. All three families are memorialized otherwise for their philanthropies—Tilton and Hutchinson at Tulane University and Millikin at Charity Hospital. George Soulé, pioneer business school educator, whose college is still in existence, lies in a tomb with an attractive glass window. The tomb bears the inscription "At the tomb knowledge ends and hope begins." Near the Soulé tomb are the twin tombs of A. M. and J. B. Solari, whose fancy grocery store on Royal and Iberville streets was known throughout the world.

In that part of the cemetery facing Metairie Road are buried a number of personages of more than ordinary interest. In the little Greek temple tomb of Dr. C. Edmund Kells rests this pioneer in X-ray work in dentistry who, because the effects of X-rays on human tissues were not known when he started his experiments with this device, suffered the loss of most of his fingers.

The massive domed Quincy granite mausoleum of John Dibert was erected in the early 1900s by Weiblen from a design by Jean Duffy, an interior decorator (color plate 7). The tomb memoralizes John Dibert, a wealthy foundry owner and his wife, a philanthropist, whose name is enshrined for her gifts to Charity Hospital. Another man of medicine is interred on the same avenue with the Kells and Dibert memorials. He is Dr. Arthur W. de Roaldes who was one of the founders of the Eye, Ear, Nose and Throat Hospital. The de Roaldes tomb bears an engraved coat of arms of the family, and each spring pink lilies bloom on the plots alongside the tomb. Further along the same avenue is the graceful circular columned pergola of the Benjamin Saxon Story family (page 90, fig. 49). The design of this memorial was suggested by the Temple of Vesta at Tivoli in Italy. At the center of the pergola there is a shaft on which are engraved scenes from the plantation in St. Bernard Parish which had been owned by the family.

The Langles cenotaph and its puzzling inscription at the base, "Angele Marie Langles 105 La. 39," is a curious memorial (figs. 99, 100). Angele Langles and her mother Pauline Costa Langles were well-to-do residents of New Orleans. Planning a trip to France, they both made wills before sailing on the French steamer *La Bourgoyne*. Two days out of New York on July 4, 1898, the steamer sank, with the loss of more than five hundred lives, the Langles among them. Since the wills of both women involved different sets of heirs, the courts were called upon to decide which of them had died first. A lengthy legal dispute arose, and the case eventually went to the Louisiana Supreme Court. The court's decision was that the daughter, being younger, was presumed to have survived the mother. Since the daughter's will had called for the erection of a tomb for herself, the court, against the wishes of the heirs, ordered that the sum of $3,000 from her estate be used for the purpose of erecting a cenotaph in her memory. The executor of her estate caused her name and legal reference to the case to be engraved on this monument to suggest that all who pass might learn the circumstances under which the memorial was erected and read the opinion of the Supreme Court of Louisiana commanding its construction (fig. 101).

The canopied sarcophagus tomb of Isaac Delgado is near the Langles memorial. Delgado, a wealthy sugar factor left fortunes to found the Delgado Museum (now New Orleans Museum of Art), the Delgado Central Trade School (now Delgado Junior College), and to Charity Hospital (page 83, fig. 36).

An interesting marble tomb is that of A. G. Williams, a candy-maker who developed a confection called Heavenly Hash. Before he died he ordered that his tomb be constructed to resemble a Greek Orthodox chapel. The tomb was designed by the architect Samuel Stone and erected by Victor Huber.

The Barthelmi Duverjé tomb is the oldest in Metairie. Of Egyptian design, it was constructed of Quincy granite, probably about 1835 or 1840. An inscription on the base reads "Erige en Algiers 1806," but this is incorrect since the stone of which it is made was not quarried for commercial use until the 1830s. The tomb was originally in the cemetery of the Duverjé family in Algiers, Louisiana, and was taken down and re-built in Metairie Cemetery in 1916 when the Duverjé heirs gave the site of their Algiers cemetery for a playground.

A tomb of California granite was designed in the 1920s for the Legendre family by Albert R. Huber and erected by Victor Huber. This tomb is noted for its graceful lines and fine moldings (fig. 102). In the same section of the cemetery is the tomb of Augustus Bernau, an attorney. His tomb is of Byzantine design since he was of Greek origin and the tomb is surmounted by a cupola in which hangs a little bell. On the side of the tomb is inscribed parts of Bernau's speech made when the cornerstone of the lodge building at the original entrance of the cemetery was laid in 1883.

In the annex of Metairie Cemetery are some very striking memorials. The mausoleum of William Helis, Greek oil magnate, was designed by Ralph Phillippi who used as a model the temple of Nike on the Acropolis of Athens (page 88, fig. 46). The Helis mausoleum was erected by Weiblen. By his own request Helis' casket lies on Greek soil brought from his native land and placed in his tomb.

A very striking monument is that erected by Edith Allen Clark on the Clark plot. This consists of a cast bronze panel, a Pieta, the work of the sculptor de Weldon who created the famous Iwo Jima War Memorial in Washington, D.C. Another sculptured memorial is the Capretto monument with its beautiful life-sized granite figures of the Madonna and Child, sculptured by Albert Rieker. Mayor de Lesseps S. Morrison, mentioned earlier, is buried in the newer part of the cemetery. The grave of the well-known painter, Andres Molinary, is marked by a simple boulder of red Missouri granite. A unique memorial marks the grave of Captain Le Verrier Cooley, one of the last of the great Mississippi steamboatmen. It is the bell of his best-loved boat, the *America* (fig. 103).

Dorothy Dell (Goff), a local beauty queen and motion picture actress, who lost her life in an automobile accident, is buried in the Goff tomb. In the Gulotta tomb rests the scrappy little fighter, Pete Herman (Gulotta), who was twice world's bantamweight champion. Herman became blind as a result of his fighting career, and for years ran a night club in the Vieux Carré. He died April 14, 1973, aged 77.

Also in the Metairie Cemetery are the mausoleums of Albert Briede, funeral director, Aloysius Fabacher, head of a drayage business, and of a real estate operator named Seidel. All these tombs were designed and erected by the Acme Marble and Granite Company.

Unfortunately the graceful entrance to the Metairie Cemetery had to be destroyed when the City Park overpass was built. The new entrance with its fountain was designed by Richard Koch, architect, in 1961, and another lodge or cemetery office was constructed. Metairie Cemetery was sold in 1951 by the Morris estate, which owned most of the stock of the association, to the late John Weiblen who, with his wife Norma, directed its affairs and made many improvements. John Weiblen died in 1956, and his wife became president and managed its affairs until 1969, when she sold her interest to the Stewart Enterprises.

Fig. 99. The Langles monument, with its intriguing inscription. (Photograph by Leonard V. Huber.)

Fig. 100. The Langles monument. (Photograph by Leonard V. Huber.)

Fig. 101. In the same section as the Langles monument, commemorating a mother and daughter lost in the sinking of the steamer *La Bourgoyne* in 1898, are the tombs of the Aldige family. Three members of the latter were also on the voyage, and they, too, perished. The sculptured angels, the prow of a ship, and an anchor were created to memorialize the incident. (Courtesy Leonard V. Huber Collection.)

Fig. 102. This handsome tomb of Joseph Amilcar Legendre faces Metairie Road. (Courtesy Leonard V. Huber Collection.)

Fig. 103. This appropriate monument to a steamboatman is the bell of his favorite steamer, the *America*. Beneath it lies the body of one of the last of the great Mississippi River captains, LeVerrier Cooley. (Courtesy Leonard V. Huber Collection.)

Fig. 104. Most of the headboards in Holt Cemetery are just that—wooden boards painted white and inscribed with name and dates. The fancier ones are topped with a jig-sawed cross, but all of them weather, decay, and soon perish like the bodies of those they mark. (Courtesy Leonard V. Huber Collection.)

HOLT CEMETERY

Locust Grove cemeteries No. 1 and No. 2 were in Squares 360 and 363 on Freret Street between 6th and 7th streets. These were cemeteries for the indigent dead, and they were mostly used for Negroes. Land for Locust Grove No. 1 was bought by the City Council in 1859 for $3,000, and the No. 2 cemetery was opened in 1876. However, by 1879 the Committee of the Council on the Locust Grove Cemetery decided to close both and open another one in the southeast corner of lower City Park Avenue. (In those days City Park extended from Bayou St. John along Metairie Road, now City Park Avenue, for quite a distance past St. Louis Street.) The committee recommended that the new cemetery be started because it was on a high-ground site on Metairie Ridge and also because it was removed from habitations, and third, the site was "superior to the old cemeteries in that the bodies of the indigent dead were not brought through the heart of the city but could be carried through the extreme upper and lower portions of the city by means of the shell roads." Locust Grove cemeteries were closed, and in 1905 the ground was used to build the Thomy Lafon School and a playground.

Holt Cemetery originally ran 400 feet on City Park Avenue and was 600 feet deep (fig. 104). The ordinance of 1879 appropriated $500 for fencing the plot, and the cemetery was named for Dr. Joseph Holt, city board of health official. There was an addition to Holt Cemetery in 1909, and the cemetery was increased by a plot on St. Louis Street, 300 by 450 feet, on what was then called Monroe Street, and an appropriation of $1,120 was made to fence it. This is one city cemetery where ground for burial may be obtained for the cost of digging the grave. The ownership of the grave remains with the family of the deceased as long as they keep the plot clean. Unfortunately, for many years there has been no attempt by most families to maintain the graves, and the cemetery has a long history of being a weed patch each summer (fig. 105).

MOUNT OLIVET CEMETERY

Mount Olivet Cemetery was founded some time after World War I by J. Henry Blache, a real estate developer. It is located off Gentilly Road at Norman Mayer Boulevard. The cemetery is not well planned; there is a lack of cross aisles, and the erection of a large community mausoleum near the entrance adds to the difficulty of ingress for automobiles. Mount Olivet consists largely of ground plots (copings) although there are a number of above-ground tombs. None of these, with the possible exception of the Lawless mausoleum, are of architectural interest. When visited in September, 1973, the cemetery roads were in poor shape, although the plots in the cemetery were fairly well kept.

CHARITY HOSPITAL CEMETERY

This cemetery fronts Canal Street and runs to Banks Street. It is located between Cypress Grove and St. Patrick cemeteries, and is now almost lost to view since its frontage on Canal Street is hidden behind an oil station and a large flower shop. In this graveyard are buried thousands of the indigent dead who died in Charity Hospital.

During four days in September, 1847, Charity Hospital Cemetery received the corpses of eighty-seven persons, and the cause of death in sixty-eight of them was listed as yellow fever. When the new Charity Hospital was constructed in 1937, earth from the foundations was carted to the hospital cemetery and the whole level of the land was raised several feet.

THE MEN WHO MADE THE MONUMENTS

The pioneer marble dealers who erected monumental work in the early cemeteries of New Orleans have been treated in another chapter. This section deals with the men who were engaged in the monument business after Newton Richards, whose career came to an end in 1874. Among his contemporaries were George Stroud and Pierre Casse who did much work in the early days of the Metairie Cemetery. That cemetery was just six years old when there arrived in New Orleans a thirty-six-year-old Canadian by the name of Charles A. Orleans (fig. 106). Orleans had previously had a checkered career in the building trades in Chicago, New York, and, for a while, in Paris. He was reputed to have made and lost two fortunes, and it is quite probable that he came to New Orleans after a siege of bad luck in Chicago. At any rate he liked the city, and being a pleasant and affable man, he made friends quickly.

With a new and modern cemetery as a challenge, Orleans turned to the business of building tombs and cemetery memorials. He employed Theodore Brune, an architect who was quite good at design, and made a connection with a granite manufacturer in Hallowell, Maine. Soon he was building one fine mausoleum after another in Metairie Cemetery and elsewhere. In an advertisement published in 1894 (fig. 107), he listed his office at 224 Carondelet Street and stated that he had erected three-fourths of all the principal granite vaults and monuments in New Orleans in the sixteen years previous, and this was no idle boast. Orleans was the unchallenged leader of monument firms in New Orleans until about 1891 when he lost the competition to design and build the monument erected in memory of David C. Hennessy, superintendent of police, who had been shot in an ambush by activists from the New Orleans Sicilian colony. Orleans continued in business almost until his death which occurred on April 2, 1923. His remains were interred in the Kennedy-Orleans tomb, tomb 4, office square, range No. 4, St. Louis Cemetery III. No inscription marks his resting place.

As Charles Orleans' star began to sink in the 1890s, that of Albert Weiblen (fig. 108) began to rise. Weiblen had come to New Orleans from Germany in 1887, and starting from scratch he built his firm into one of the largest in the South during a career which lasted more than eighty years. Weiblen's first big break came when he was the successful bidder for the erection of the Hennessy monument. Weiblen's office and display were located at 825 Baronne Street, and in 1906 he moved his works to a sizable plant at 501–25 City Park Avenue at St. Louis Street. He employed good designers, notable among whom were Charles L. Lawhon and Ralph G. Phillippi, and his firm was largely responsible for the high quality in design and workmanship of most of the memorial work in Metairie Cemetery. Besides his monument work, Weiblen leased a quarry at Stone Mountain, Georgia, and furnished granite work for such large contracts as a bridge in Philadelphia and the

Fig. 105. Holt Cemetery is blessed with a magnificent live oak tree, but most of the graves beneath it are unkempt, desolate, and apparently forgotten.

Fig. 106. Charles A. Orleans (1839–1923), monument designer and contractor.

Fig. 107. An 1894 advertisement of Charles A. Orleans, "designer and contractor of monumental, statuary and building works." (Courtesy Leonard V. Huber Collection.)

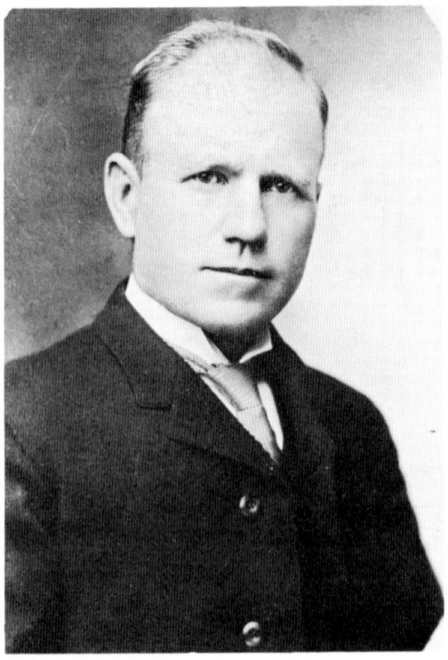

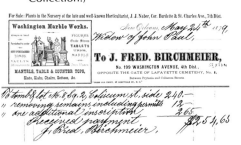

Fig. 108. Albert Weiblen (1868–1967). (Courtesy Leonard V. Huber Collection.)

For Sale: Plants in the Nursery of the late and well-known Horticulturist, J. J. Naber, Cor. Burdette & St. Charles Ave., 7th Dist.

Washington Marble Works.

Always on hand —or— Furnished to order —to— suit purchasers TOMBS VAULTS Monuments

FIGURES Grabe Stones TABLETS URNS, MARBLE —and— Iron Vases

MANTELS, TABLE & COUNTER TOPS, Slate, Slabs, Chairs, Settees, &c.

New Orleans, May 24th 1879,

Widow of John Paul,

To J. FRED. BIRCHMEIER, SEXTON

No. 199 WASHINGTON AVENUE, 4th Dist.,

OPPOSITE THE GATE OF LAFAYETTE CEMETERY, No. 1,

Between Prytania and Coliseum Streets

"PRESS JOB PRINT, 48 BIENVILLE ST., N. O."

To tomb & lot No. 8 Sq. 2, Coliseum st. side	240.—
" removing remains including permits	12—
" one additional inscription	2 65
Received payment	$254,65
J. Fred. Birchmeier,	

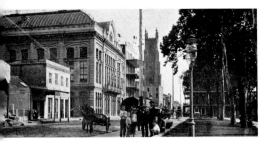

Fig. 109. Quaint bill dated May 24, 1879, and presented to a customer for the erection of a tomb by J. Fred Birchmeier, marble dealer and sexton of Lafayette No. 1. (Courtesy Leonard V. Huber Collection.)

Fig. 110. One of the few photographs extant of a nineteenth-century marble works. An 1887 view of Camp Street near Lafayette, with the shop of Kurscheedt and Bienvenue partially visible at the left. At the corner is the marble and granite works of James Hagan. St. Patrick's Hall is at the center. (Courtesy Leonard V. Huber Collection.)

Cuban Capitol in Havana. Weiblen lived to be ninety-nine and died in 1957 a few months short of his one-hundredth year. His sons, Fred and George, operated the quarry in Georgia, and George eventually finished the sculpture on the famed Stone Mountain Confederate figures before his death in 1971.

In 1951 the Weiblens purchased the controlling interest in Metairie Cemetery, and on John Weiblen's death in 1956 Mrs. Norma Merritt Weiblen took over the management of both the memorial firm and the Metairie Cemetery. In 1969 the firm and cemetery were sold to the Stewart Enterprises and the name Weiblen, after a period of more than eighty years, disappeared from the roster of monument firms in New Orleans.

Two of Weiblen's employees who had much influence on the work that went into Metairie Cemetery were Henri A. Gandolfo, sales–counsellor who spent fifty-eight years with the firm, and Ralph A. Phillippi, a designer of great ability whose career extended over forty years.

There were a number of smaller dealers in New Orleans who did monument work. Among them were the Birchmeiers, father and son (fig. 109), who had a plant on Washington Avenue and Gottlieb Huber (no relation to Victor Huber) who operated a small plant near the St. Joseph Cemetery; Samuel T. Gately and his sons and grandsons who with John F. Lally have been in business at Greenwood and Cypress Grove cemeteries since 1891; the Peytrals, Jules father and son and Rachel, wife of Jules Peytral, Sr. Jules, Jr., was superintendent of the St. Patrick cemeteries in the 1920s, and his uncle Felix was superintendent of the Dispersed of Judah Cemetery at about the same time. Andrew Kolwe had a small shop on City Park Avenue in the 1920s–1930s.

At one time or another J. A. Kramer, John Quinn, J. J. Healey, C. J. Badger, Charles Puneky, and Armand Rodehorst had offices or shops at or near the Greenwood–Cypress Grove–Odd Fellows Rest–St. Patricks group of cemeteries.

Schutten and Fallon had a large shop on Scott and St. Louis Streets, and Louis Reynolds also had a sizable shop at City Park Avenue and St. Louis Street. James Trebuquet, George J. Deynoodt and his son Joseph; the Karchers, John and his son Walter, had shops near St. Louis Cemetery III on Esplanade. J. V. A. Backes and his son Eugene had a shop on Washington Avenue as did the brothers C. and G. Sill. N. F. Gunther combined the duties of sexton at St. Roch's with the business of monument worker. The Schaefers, father Charles and son Henry, were dealer-sextons of the Hebrew Rest cemeteries in Gentilly for a combined fifty-eight years, and the owners of the cemetery erected a fountain in their memory in 1948. Charles Mabel and William A. D. Weaver were wholesale granite dealers to the trade in the 1920s and 30s.

Among the mechanics whose skill was responsible for engraving were René Boneé, Louis and Charles Puneky, Vincent Cerrito, Justin Brossette, and Raymond Lincoln. Among the marble cutters were Emile Decker, Ferdinand Bahrdt, Alex Casse who was also a good marble setter, the Donellan brothers, Mike and Edward Gatto and Albert Delord. The setters who come to mind are George Dench, Albert and Paul Cazalot, Charles Dittman, and Ben Williams, a Negro, the last two of whom set much of Weiblen's work in Metairie Cemetery.

COLOR ALBUM

Plate 1. St. Louis I in 1834, sketched by John H. B. Latrobe. (Courtesy Historic New Orleans Collection.)

Plate 2. View of St. Louis I.

Plate 3. Supposed tomb of Voodoo Queen Marie Laveau, St. Louis I. The plastered brick monument is marked with Xs for good luck.

Plate 4. Wall vaults in St. Louis II, Sq. 3, on All Saints' Day, 1972.

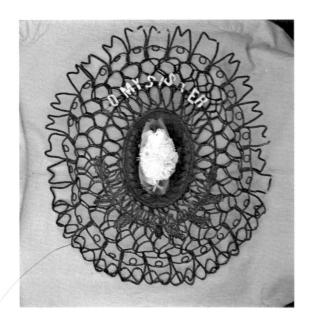

Plate 5. Immortelle. Bead-on-wire wreath with porcelain roses in center. Elegant memorial typical of those used for more than a century in New Orleans cemeteries. (Courtesy Historic New Orleans Collection.)

Plate 6. St. Roch Cemetery chapel and Campo Santo (21 inches by 32½ inches). Oil on canvas, signed by R. W. Grafton. (Courtesy W. E. Groves Collection.)

Plate 7. Dibert family tomb (John Dibert, d. 1912), Metairie Cemetery. An impressive classical temple tomb built by Weiblen of polished Quincy, Massachusetts, granite, with bronze ornamentations and large bronze urns.

Plate 8. J. A. Morales family tomb, Metairie Cemetery. This monument, formerly known as the
Josie Arlington tomb, was designed and built by Albert Weiblen in the early twentieth century.
Bronze sculpture is signed by F. Bagdon, 1911.

Plate 9. Peniston-Duplantier tomb, St. Louis II, Sq. 2., designed by J. N. B. de Pouilly in 1842 and built by Monsseaux. The design was inspired by the prostyle Greek Doric temple. The width at the front center is 7 feet, 6 inches.

Influences on 19th-Century Funerary Architecture

PEGGY McDOWELL

A microcosm of nineteenth-century architectural styles fills the paths and avenues of the New Orleans cemeteries. Most of the tomb designs are based on classical, Gothic, Egyptian, and Near Eastern revival trends popular in nineteenth-century Europe and America. The revival styles found a special place in funerary design. The cemetery uniquely allows many different styles to exist harmoniously side by side.

The practical aspect of above-ground burial was only a small factor that contributed toward a tradition of elegant and often costly funerary architecture. Most New Orleanians, because of their European ancestry, were sympathetic toward the tradition of above-ground tombs. Pride and fashion motivated many New Orleanians to abandon the modest and practical early tomb designs in favor of styles that reflected international trends and tastes, namely the romantic revival styles. In France and Spain, as in other European countries, above-ground funerary structures were not unusual. In the early nineteenth century, Paris evinced an exceptional interest in elegant funerary design. New Orleanians, aware of the trends and styles in Paris, were surely influenced by contemporary Parisian cemeteries, especially the cemetery of Pere Lachaise which was established in 1804.

The majesty and elegance of Pere Lachaise exerted a great influence on funerary traditions and illustrates the innovative interest of the nineteenth-century European in sophisticated and prestigious sepulchral chambers set apart from cathedral or churchyard atmosphere. This interest was evident in cities other than Paris. Pere Lachaise helped serve as an inspiration for the establishment of an impressive metropolitan cemetery in London — Kensal Green.

Stimulated by romantic attitudes, many nineteenth-century cemeteries in the tradition of Pere Lachaise, Kensal Green, and St. Louis I and II share a common architectural vocabulary which contributed toward an international style. The forms and types employed by many nineteenth-century designers of tombs had precedents in ancient, medieval, and renaissance commemorative monuments. Sarcophagi, columns, temples, and pyramids were easily adapted to nineteenth-century funerary designs. Unfortunately, frequent repetition resulted in monotonous tautology. Variations in surface ornamentation, scale, and, occasionally, freely interpreted and combined styles allowed for diversity and for that element of the unpredictable that excites the eye.

Inspiration came from many sources. The influence of Giovanni Battista Piranesi, an eighteenth-century Italian artist known for his engravings and etchings of ancient ruins, cannot be underestimated. His imagery not only records in dramatic variations of greys and blacks the ancient Roman ruins, but also interprets fanciful com-

Fig. 1. An eighteenth-century print by Giovanni Battista Piranesi, from a private collection.

Fig. 2. Illustration from an early nineteenth-century publication—*Le Père Lachaise ou recueil de dessins aux traits et dans leur juste proportions des principaux monumens de ce cimetière*. This volume was at one time owned by J. N. B. de Pouilly. It is now in the collection of Leonard V. Huber.

binations of styles and types based on antiquity. The illustrated Piranesi print (fig. 1) exemplifies his interest in imaginative commemorative shrines and memorial structures. Combined in one print are Greek, Roman, and Egyptian types. Piranesi especially helped spread the popularity of Egyptianism. Often the same imaginative conglomeration of styles occurs in nineteenth-century funerary design. An illustration (fig. 2) from an early nineteenth-century publication on Pere Lachaise, now in the collection of Leonard V. Huber, clearly indicates the illustrator's awareness of Piranesi. A similar aggregation of tomb types and styles is evident in the print by Alfred R. Waud of St. Louis I (see jacket).

In nineteenth-century France, scholars often promoted the study of period and area styles. Architecture students in Paris were exposed to a variety of designs and structures from many areas of the world in reference volumes such as J. N. B. Durand's *Recueil et parallèle des èdifices de tout genre, anciens et modernes* (1800). Durand's illustrations from ancient Greece and Rome, as well as exotic India, Egypt, and the Orient, gave further impetus to eclectic romanticizing under an academic guise. This interest found its way into funerary design. Enough variations in the romantic architecture vocabulary existed to please the divergent tastes and finances of the majority of clients. Fortunately, local interest in revival styles coincided with a greater availability of marble and granite made possible by increased shipping into the port of New Orleans from the New England states and from Italy. With these materials local designers had the means to range from simplicity to grandeur and to create monuments comparable to those in the contemporary cemeteries of Europe. It was no longer necessary to import ready-made tombs and tombstones. Beginning in the 1830s, local professional architects turned their attention to designing tombs. Funerary architecture was elevated from the craftsman level. The architect who did most to inaugurate a sophisticated approach to tomb design was Jacque Nicolas Bussiere de Pouilly. He was the first significant architect of cemetery art in New Orleans, and his work provides the focal point of the following analysis of designs in the romantic tradition. Constructed tombs designed by de Pouilly and documented from original sketches include:

Fouche family tomb, St. Louis II, Sq. 1. Italian marble. P. H. Monsseaux, builder, 1836.
McCall-Jones family tomb, St. Louis I. Marble. Monsseaux, builder, 1857.
Dupeire family tomb, St. Louis II, Sq. 2. Marble. Monsseaux, builder, sketch dated 1845.
Dusuau family tomb, St. Louis II, Sq. 2. Sandstone. Monsseaux, builder, sketch dated 1846.
Ursin Bouligny, Jr., family tomb, St. Louis II, Sq. 2. Monsseaux, builder.
J. M. Caballero family tomb, St. Louis II, Sq. 2. Marble.
Malard family tomb, St. Louis I. Plastered brick.
Peniston (and Duplantier) family tomb, St. Louis II, Sq. 2. Marble.
J.-B. Plauché family tomb, St. Louis II, Sq. 2. Marble. Monsseaux, builder, sketch dated 1845.
Lacoste family tomb, St. Louis II, Sq. 2. Granite. Newton Richards, builder, 1849.
Miltenberger family tomb, St. Louis II, Sq. 2. Granite. Newton Richards, builder, 1850.
Maunsel White family tomb. Cypress Grove. Marble. Monsseaux, builder, 1869.
Grailhe family tomb, St. Louis II, Sq. 2. Marble. Monsseaux, builder, 1850.
Kohn family tomb, Cypress Grove. Granite.
A. D. Crossman monument, Greenwood Cemetery. Granite. 1859.
Irad Ferry monument, Cypress Grove. Marble. Dedicated 1841.
Orleans Artillery Battalion tomb, St. Louis I. Plastered brick.
Iberia Society Tomb, St. Louis II, Sq. 2. Monsseaux, builder. (Original sketch proposed for "Cazadores Volantes, 1843–45," built in St. Louis II, Sq. 1.
Société Francaise, St. Louis I. Plastered brick.
Lusitanos Society Tomb, Girod Street Cemetery. Plastered brick with marble columns and details. Now destroyed.

TYPES AND STYLES

Early Brick Tombs

St. Louis I contains the earliest extant brick tombs that offer insight into the styles that proved most feasible in the premier stages of New Orleans tomb design. Although their modest, functional designs cannot boast of a schooled architect, the tombs are not without variety and charm, and reveal the skilled hands of the craftsman who probably served as designer as well as builder. Benjamin H. Latrobe described and sketched the tombs he observed in St. Louis I in 1819: "The Catholic tombs are very different in character from those of our Eastern and Northern cities. They are of bricks, much larger than necessary to enclose a single coffin, and plaistered [*sic*] over. . . . They are of these and many other shapes of similar character covering each an area of 7 or 8 feet long and four or five feet wide and being 5 to 7 feet high." Another visitor gave a slightly different description of the St. Louis cemetery printed in an 1833 newspaper account:

The tombs were all above the ground, those who can afford it will never be buried underground. The tombs are chiefly or all of brick, some plastered over, some not, they are from 2½ to 3 feet high and there is a little hole or front door into which the body is put. Some of the tombs in this, the Catholic burying ground, are elegant and well walled over. . . . A few flower pots were on the summit of some. Others had little railings for a guard, and many had inscriptions.
This graveyard is on a dead level and on a rainy day inundated with water.

The brick tombs that impressed Latrobe were higher than those described in the 1833 account, where the coffin chambers are on low foundations of one or two courses. The Latrobe sketches (fig. 3), which illustrate impressive podiums that elevate the crypt above ground level, reveal the probable reason for the different impression. In St. Louis I it is difficult to analyze many of these structures because

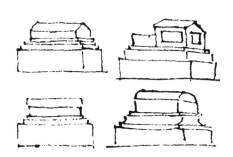

Fig. 3. Sketches of various tombs in St. Louis I by B. H. B. Latrobe in his 1819 diary. See *Impressions Respecting New Orleans*, edited by Samuel Wilson, Jr., 1951.

they have sunk below the present ground level, and the addition of several feet of soil for fill in the early nineteenth century further hid many foundations. The podium became increasingly popular in the nineteenth century, since it was practical as well as compositionally pleasing. It was desirable to raise the burial chamber well above the wet and marshy land that was "on a rainy day inundated with water."

Brick tombs were usually constructed with two or more horizontal or vertical chambers for multiple burials. The soft brick was usually plastered and then whitewashed. Two basic types of tombs were popular in the first half of the nineteenth century (fig. 4). The first, a simple structure with a flat top of one or more stepped platforms, was probably a local version of the ancient Greek table tomb, as illustrated by the Jean Lanusse (d. 1812) tomb in St. Louis I (fig. 5), and by the Nicolas Girod (d. 1840) tomb in St. Louis II (fig. 6). Theoretically, the structure evolved from the early simple building of a casket-sized rectangular enclosure, which was later easily modified in scale to contain a single or several burial chambers as in the Étienne Boré tomb in St. Louis I (fig. 7). Those tombs with double parallel chambers

Fig. 4. St. Louis I. Examples of brick tombs typical of the early nineteenth century. The right tomb, family of H. Castarede (d. 1838), has a slightly elevated pediment atop the façade. The main structure is covered by a low-pitched roof. The left tomb is a stepped-top monument. The white tomb in the background illustrates the use of the truncated pediment. All three are plastered and whitewashed.

Fig. 5. Jean Lanusse (d. 1812), St. Louis I. An example of a brick stepped tomb with inscription slab placed on the top. This form probably originated from the early technique of placing the casket on a low foundation of brick and building the monument over it. Several similar tombs, dating before 1815, are in St. Louis I. Most of the plaques on these early monuments are inscribed in a delicate script that is still visible even though badly weathered.

often functioned as family tombs, for example, the Brown (d. 1849), LaBranche-Fernandez tomb in St. Louis I (fig. 8). Another modification was the addition of a triangular pediment to the façade, a motif occasionally elevated to create a false facade as seen in the Michel Fortier (d. 1819) tomb in St. Louis I (fig. 10). Further variations can be seen in the Pierre Brousseau (d. 1846) tomb (fig. 11) in St. Louis I, and in the Dominique You (d. 1830) tomb (page 12, fig. 17B) in St. Louis II, which exemplify the stepped-top type with a truncated pediment that often held a vase or cross.

The stepped-top tomb was exceptionally popular in St. Louis I and II, and

Fig. 7. Etienne Boré tomb, St. Louis I. This stepped-top monument, built in the second decade of the nineteenth century, illustrates the use of two vertical chambers for multiple burials. Etienne Boré was the first mayor of New Orleans under Governor Claiborne and was the first man to granulate sugar commercially. His grandson, the historian Charles Gayarré, is also buried in the tomb. The small scroll marker on top was added later as a tribute by fellow historian Grace King.

Fig. 6. Nicolas Girod (d. 1840), St. Louis II, Sq. 2. Girod was mayor of New Orleans in 1814 and 1815. His tomb is a typical stepped-top brick design with a narrow front opening that made it possible to reopen the tomb for further burials. Today these structures are too small to contain a modern casket. The slate plaque is signed by Viau.

Fig. 8. William Brown-Labranche-Fernandez tomb, St. Louis I. An example of the expanded brick stepped-top tomb with double horizontal chambers. The Brown (d. 1849) plaque is signed by Monsseaux.

Fig. 9. Prosper Foy and Florville Foy (d. 1903), St. Louis III. A later version of the stepped-top tomb in granite. Florville Foy was one of the leading tomb builders in nineteenth-century New Orleans.

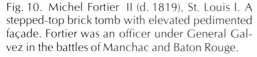

Fig. 10. Michel Fortier II (d. 1819), St. Louis I. A stepped-top brick tomb with elevated pedimented façade. Fortier was an officer under General Galvez in the battles of Manchac and Baton Rouge.

Fig. 11. Pierre Brousseau (d. 1846), St. Louis I. A stepped-top brick tomb with truncated pediment. The flattened top of the façade often held a vase or cross.

continued in popularity into the late nineteenth century. Numerous monuments of this type in marble and granite as well as brick can be found in all the major cemeteries; the tomb of builders Prosper Foy and Florville Foy in St. Louis III is a typical granite version of the early brick form (fig. 9).

A second basic brick design employs a pitched roof instead of the flat or graduated stepped-top. The triangular pediment is defined by the end gables, or a larger pediment was added to the facade (figs. 4, 12). Scale can be successfully varied in the pitched roof tomb; it is especially expanded upward for family or benevolent society tombs. The tombs of the so-called Voodoo Queen, Marie Laveau (color plate 3), the chess genius, Paul Morphy (d. 1884), and of Bernard de Marigny (d. 1868) are various examples of the pitched roof design. Tall narrow tombs with vertical single chambers are numerous in St. Louis I and II (page 12, fig. 16).

Obviously there are additions to the two basic styles of the flat and pitched roof designs. Tombs topped with barrel vaults were occasionally constructed, as well as some capped by semicircular lunettes above the facade (fig. 13).

The use of the barrel vault in the construction of crypts in early family and wall tombs was visually similar to the structure of bakers' ovens, hence the analogy *oven vaults* or *oven tombs* (fig. 14; color plate 4). The technique required much skill and demonstrates the competence of the local brickmasons. By the mid-nineteenth century, lintel slabs had replaced the barrelled inner chambers in the wall vaults (fig. 15). The builders of these wall vaults usually had to satisfy specific requirements set up by building committees. A contract between the town of Carrollton and Alexander McKee to build thirty-six vaults for $500 in the Carrollton Cemetery, entered June 27, 1855, included the following specifications: "These thirty-six vaults will be built in two separate piles or blocks each containing eighteen vaults, six in the length and three in the height. . . . Each block of vaults will be eighteen feet long, nine feet wide and of such height as shall be hereinafter required, and will be proportioned and built in accordance with the plan prefixed to these specifications."

Brick tombs were constructed throughout the nineteenth century because of the adaptable and economical nature of the material. Fine examples of quality brick

Fig. 12. Large tomb, earliest date, Marie Eugenie Girod, d. 1887. Small tomb, infants of F. Menard, St. Louis I. Two examples of brick pitched-roof tombs with elevated pedimented façades. There are occasional examples of small children's vaults and tombs in the early cemeteries.

Fig. 14. View into wall vault, St. Louis II, Sq. 2. An example of barrel vaulting in brick.

Fig. 15. A nineteenth-century view of Lafayette No. 1. The wall vaults were constructed with marble lintel slabs. Immortelles are visible on several vaults. (Courtesy Historic New Orleans Collection.)

Fig. 13. View of Lafayette Cemetery No. 1. Many of these monuments are topped by barrel vaults and semicircular lunettes.

Fig. 16. Lefebvre family tomb, Metairie Cemetery. Built in late nineteenth century.

Fig. 17. Left, John Hughes, right, Mark Thomas, Cypress Grove. Both built 1855.

construction and ornamentation can be seen in the Hermann and Freret family tombs in St. Louis II, in the Lefebvre tomb of the 1880s in Metairie Cemetery, where the brick was probably specially molded for the design (fig. 16) and, in Cypress Grove, the tombs of the John Hughes, Mark Thomas, and François Vallette families (fig. 17). Of interest also are the Malard and the large French Society tombs in St. Louis I, both by de Pouilly (figs. 18A, B, 19A, B).

Fig. 18A. Sketch by J. N. B. de Pouilly for Malard family tomb. (Courtesy Historic New Orleans Collection.)

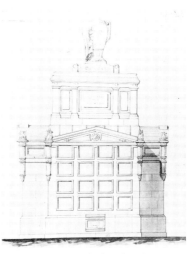

Fig. 19B. Original sketch of Société Française Tombe. Note the cruciform plan that was not followed through in the final version. It is also doubtful that the large draped vase was elevated above the monument. (Courtesy Historic New Orleans Collection.)

Fig. 19A. Société Française de Bienfaisance et d'Assistance. This plastered brick tomb with bronze ornaments is the largest in St. Louis I. Designed by J. N. B. de Pouilly. The monument is in need of repair and is overgrown with trees and bushes.

Fig. 18B. The Malard tomb, probably built in the 1840s, as it appears today. St. Louis I.

THE CLASSICAL REVIVAL STYLE

In New Orleans cemeteries the classical revival predominated. Greek and Roman design elements can be discerned in the earliest pedimented brick tombs in St. Louis I, which illustrate a modest attempt to imitate the classical. To dwell in death in an ideal, i.e. classical, environment had favorable connotations to purchasers of tombs.

The neoclassical style was admired by the academically oriented French. Excavations at Pompeii and Herculaneum, begun in the eighteenth century, offered new insights into Roman antiquity. The French Revolution and the Napoleonic campaigns intensified an interest in Roman art and fashions. Winckelmann's history of ancient art extolling the Golden Age of Greece reflected and inspired an ideological interpretation of the ancient Greeks. During and after the Renaissance, the art of the classical Greeks was idealistically associated with a utopian phase of human perfection that, according to the classicists, should be emulated.

The Sarcophagus and Related Forms

The classical sarcophagus, originating from Greek and Roman prototypes, was a traditional funerary structure. The word *sarcophagus* literally translated from Greek means "to consume flesh," and in ancient Greek times the term described a type of coffin cut from a limestone with caustic properties. The body quickly disintegrated within this stone receptacle. By association sarcophagus came to mean any stone coffin. The body, placed within a cavity hollowed out from the stone, was covered with a heavy stone lid; the covering lids described friezes of figures, a reclining figure, or, more frequently, architectural decorations such as the pedimented roof with acroteria. The illustrated examples (fig. 20) are from Durand's *Recueil et parallèle des èdifices*.

By employing functional and decorative modifications, modern designers made good use of the ancient sarcophagus type. The body, lying within a wood or metal coffin, was placed in front or side opening. (In New Orleans, the narrow front opening covered with an inscription plaque was preferred.) The top of the sarcophagus form retained the architectonic lid effect, and its dimensions could be successfully altered to enclose a single coffin or several coffins. The sarcophagus could be placed within a larger mausoleum or built to stand in the open air. In New Orleans it is more usual to find this type standing along the avenues of the numerous *campo santos*. (The early brick tomb with pitched roof and triangular pediment was probably a simplified version of the sarcophagus form.)

De Pouilly was exposed to the sarcophagus design during his formal studies in Paris. He was aware of the illustrations in Durand's *Recueil et parallèle des èdifices* and the similar tombs in Parisian cemeteries. The de Pouilly design for the Fouche family tomb (1836) was exceptionally popular and typical of one treatment of the sarcophagus motif (fig. 21A, B). The ornamentation is restrained and limited to inverted torches, a traditional symbol of death, on the four corners, a small cross in the center front of the pediment, and small anthemion motifs on the acroteria. The design allows for the addition of a marble urn on the center top of the tomb, and one duplicate of this design, in St. Louis I, includes the urn. Another copy is located in St. Louis II, Square 1.

The pedimented sarcophagus, either elevated by a podium or resting on a low

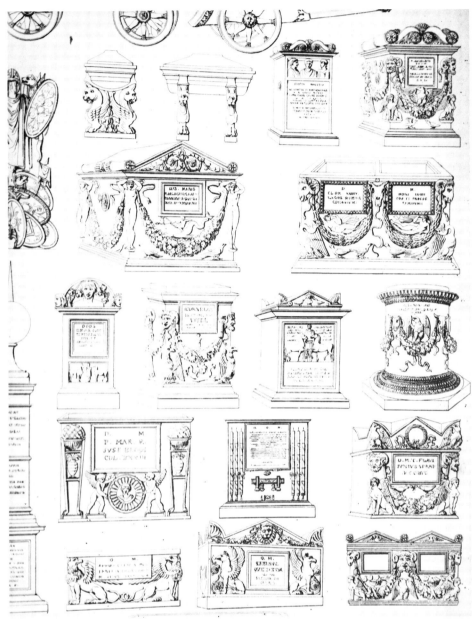

Fig. 20. Detail, Roman sarcophagi, plate 77, *Recueil et parallèle des èdifices de tout genre, anciens et modernes* by J. N. L. Durand, 1800.

Fig. 21A. Fouché family tomb, St. Louis II, Sq. 1. Designed by J. N. B. de Pouilly.

Fig. 21B. Sketch for Fouché tomb from de Pouilly's notebook. Notation on sketch indicates tomb of Italian marble, P. H. Monsseaux, builder, and date, 1836. (Courtesy Historic New Orleans Collection.)

foundation, is one of the most popular tomb types in local nineteenth-century cemeteries. Impressive in its simplicity is a low marble or granite sarcophagus with little or no ornamentation. This austere version of the sarcophagus, illustrated by the Pierre Soulé (d. 1880) tomb, with a heavy vase now fallen from the top, the Labarre tomb, in St. Louis II, Square 2 and the Saulet tomb in St. Louis I, was often repeated with minor variations in the mid-nineteenth century (fig. 22). It was a favorite type of the builder P. H. Monsseaux, who executed most of de Pouilly's designs, and it may have been a stock model in his and other tomb builders' workshops. Florville Foy constructed many tombs in St. Louis I and II using the sarcophagus form; some of these, like the Dufossat and the Mioton family tombs, because of their similarity, were probably stock designs. The tomb of Amable Charbonnet (d. 1832), imported from Paris and bearing the signature of Duvey-Marbrier, Rue St. Andre, Popincourt

Fig. 22. Pierre Soulé (d. 1870), St. Louis II, Sq. 2. Soulé was born at Castillon, France, and became a U.S. senator, ambassador to Spain, and Confederate provost marshal.

Fig. 23. Amable Charbonnet (d. 1832), St. Louis II, Sq. 1. The name of the Paris maker of this tomb is deeply inscribed on the lower right front, Duvey-Marbrier, Rue St. Andre, Popincourt No. 2.

Fig. 24. VanBenthauysen family tomb, Lafayette No. 1. Signed James Hagan builder.

Fig. 25. Barelli tomb, St. Louis II, Sq. 2. Built 1856.

Fig. 26. McCall-Jones tomb, St. Louis I, design attributed to J. N. B. de Pouilly or the younger Joseph Isidore de Pouilly. Signed Monsseaux, 1857.

No. 2 (fig. 23), illustrates decorative carvings and ornamentation typical of many tombs of the sarcophagus type built in nineteenth-century Paris. The limited amount of high and low relief sculptures on nineteenth-century New Orleans tombs, compared to Parisian counterparts, was perhaps the result of the more reserved attitudes of the Louisiana clients or the limited availability of qualified local sculptors. New Orleans, however, compensated with its ornamental ironwork. There are a few sarcophagus-type tombs by New Orleans craftsmen that reveal varying degrees of decorative ornamentation. The VanBenthauysen monument in Lafayette No. 1, James Hagan builder, has a flamboyantly carved pediment, acroteria, and family name (fig. 24). The tomb erected by Joseph Barelli in memory of his son is surmounted by five praying angels; the narrative low-relief panel on the façade describes the draped spirit of the Barelli boy lifted into a sky filled with cherubs. Below the heaven-bound figures is the scene of the November, 1849, disaster that took the life of the boy and many fellow passengers—the explosion of the steamer *Louisiana* in the New Orleans harbor (fig. 25).

The double sarcophagus was another popular form used mainly for larger family tombs. Perhaps the most representative of this type is the McCall-Jones family tomb in St. Louis I (fig. 26), and the Durel family tomb in St. Louis II, Square 2 (fig. 28). The McCall-Jones tomb is attributed to de Pouilly and was erected by Monsseaux in 1857. The prototype for the latter (fig. 27) was a tomb from a book J. N. B. de Pouilly brought from Paris, *Le Père La Chaise ou recueil de dessins aux traits et dans leurs juste proportions des principaux monumens de ce cimitière.* Compare also figure 20, lower right.

Other notable sarcophagus designs in St. Louis II are the monuments of J. C. de St. Romes, J. Pierre Cazelar, the Felix Armas (d. 1839) tomb, and the Dupeire tomb, designed 1842 by de Pouilly (fig. 29). In St. Louis I, the Henry Dick tomb is an elegant example of the sarcophagus form.

The table tomb is often categorized under forms that relate to the classical sarcophagus. Originally an ancient Greek form, the table tomb gets its name from the low flat top that functioned as a support for vases and ceremonial libations used by the family to commemorate the deceased. The form of the table tomb was popular in the early nineteenth century and was briefly noted in the unit on early brick tombs. The basic table tomb in marble is best illustrated by the J. D. Roasenda tomb (d. 1846) in St. Louis II, signed H. Blakesley (fig. 30), which has pilaster strips for its only ornamentation. Stacked table tombs were constructed in St. Louis I and II, as seen in the Lange tomb, St. Louis I, and the Labatut tomb in St. Louis II. Other versions are found in the Canal Street and City Park Avenue cemeteries. The weathered monument in St. Louis I (fig. 31A), a ledger slab elevated by supports, is a table form; however, it was not designed to enclose a body. This form, which was seen in England as early as the seventeenth century, was known to Latrobe, who sketched the type in his *Impressions Respecting New Orleans* (fig. 31B). The tomb was probably made in Philadelphia and shipped to New Orleans.

Many varieties of marble and granite tombs were built in the second half of the nineteenth century using features of either or both the table and sarcophagus types. Some feature pedestals with vases or figures. Others feature the same basic foundation and structure but vary the decorations on the facade and entablature. A few of the more interesting or popularized forms are illustrated in figures 32, 33, and 34.

In the late nineteenth century and early twentieth century, particularly impressive

Fig. 27. Detail from *Le Père Lachaise* book owned by the de Pouillys. Prototype of the McCall-Jones tomb. Notice also the similarity in basic design with the lower right sarcophagus in figure 20.

Fig. 28. Durel tomb, St. Louis II, Sq. 2. Probably built by Monsseaux.

Fig. 29. J. B. Dupeire, St. Louis II, Sq. 2. Designed by J. N. B. de Pouilly. Sketch for tomb indicates date, 1842, and marble *blanc du nord.* P. H. Monsseaux builder. Width center front, 5 feet, length center side, 8 feet 4½ inches.

Fig. 30. J. D. Roasenda (d. 1846), St. Louis II, Sq. 2. Inscription plaque signed H. Blakesley.

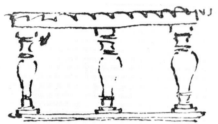

Fig. 31B. Latrobe sketch from *Impressions Respecting New Orleans.*

Fig. 31A. Table- or bench-type tomb, St. Louis I. Inscription badly weathered. Date of death, 1805 (?). This type was more common in the eastern United States, according to B. H. B. Latrobe's *Impressions Respecting New Orleans,* and was probably imported from Philadelphia. The type appears on advertisements from early city directories for tomb builders; however, this is the only monument of its kind in New Orleans today.

Fig. 32. Don José Javier de Olanzabal (d. 1832), St. Louis II, Sq. 2. Signed Kain and Stroud. An 1829 advertisement announced that James Kain of New York had arrived with a "large and elegant assortment" of monuments and tombs. Stroud was a local builder.

Fig. 33. Johnson and Walker tombs, Cypress Grove. Signed Reynolds, 1871.

Fig. 35. Emory Clapp (d. 1880), Metairie Cemetery. Base is Hollowell granite, sarcophagus in Italian marble.

Fig. 34. E. Schinkel (d. 1899), St. Louis II. Built by Birchmeir. A similar tomb is in Lafayette Cemetery No. 1.

Fig. 36. Delgado family tomb, Metairie Cemetery. Samuel Delgado (d. 1905). Also buried here is Isaac Delgado, a benefactor of the New Orleans Museum of Art. Built by Weiblen of Barre, Vermont, granite.

sarcophagi inspired from Roman designs were elevated in Metairie Cemetery. Of special interest are the Lacosst, Delgado, and Clapp monuments. The Emory Clapp (d. 1880) sarcophagus (fig. 35) is freestanding whereas the Eugene Lacosst (page 55, fig. 90) and Delgado sarcophagi (fig. 36) are enshrined in superstructures. The Delgado family tomb (early twentieth century) employs a columned canopy over the symbolic sarcophagus. The Lacosst sarcophagus is monumentalized within an apselike niche in a classical structure reminiscent of a Roman triumphal arch. All three of the sarcophagi are oval, ornately carved, and rest on clawed feet. The Ward sarcophagus designed by Albert R. Huber, in St. John Cemetery, is a copy of the Napoleon sarcophagus (page 48, fig. 75).

The Classical Temple

Many tombs that may be interpreted as sarcophageal in design have strong architectural elements, scale, and a frontality that is more reminiscent of a classical building. These structures resemble a temple without a portico and usually have pilasters on the four corners. The Dusuau tomb by de Pouilly and the Foudriat and Puig family tombs are examples of this type in stone (fig. 37). The design was also frequently built in plastered brick. Large pilastered brick tombs such as the Cazadores de Orleans Society tomb employs the pilaster motif. This type of tomb, *i.e.*, brick with pilasters, may be traced back to ancient Roman tomb designs.

A most impressive classical monument for family or society burials is a structure that emulates a small columned temple. De Pouilly helped bring about its popularity in the 1840s and the temple mausoleum continued to be a favorite funerary form. In the mid-nineteenth century the most conventional temple tomb, as reflected by de Pouilly's designs, was prostyle (a temple with columns supporting a front portico) elevated by a low podium with steps leading to a shallow portico. The pedimented roof is supported by columns, usually two, of the classical order, while the main structure of the tomb may or may not have a shallow *chapelle* preceding the vaults. Whenever the front chamber was employed, iron or bronze doors close the entrance. De Pouilly's most notable temple designs are the Peniston (1842), Plauche (1845), Lacoste (1849), and Miltenberger (1850) in St. Louis II and the Maunsel White (1869) tomb in Cypress Grove (color plate 5 and figs. 38–41C). De Pouilly also sketched restoration designs for the Blineau and Carriere tomb, constructed 1845; the monument is an interesting prostyle temple tomb with cast iron columns supporting the portico (fig. 42). De Pouilly achieves variation within the style, and the effect of his designs is grand without being ostentatious. He modifies and freely interprets the classical orders. The Doric order dominates; although the fluting on several of the columns is more akin to the Ionic, and the entablature does not always correspond to the rules of the order.

In the age of elegance at the end of the nineteenth century and in the early decades of the twentieth century, classical temple tombs of numerous designs and plans were constructed. There are so great a number of elegant examples in Metairie Cemetery that the few illustrations included here represent only a small percentage of the total. The Chapman H. Hyams tomb was inspired by the peripteral temple, that is, a temple of Greek origin that has freestanding columns on all four sides (fig. 43). The interior of this lovely mausoleum contains a stained glass window illuminating a marble angel that mourns over a classical altar. Temples with columns *in antis* reminiscent

Fig. 37. Dusuau family tomb, St. Louis II, Sq. 2. Designed by de Pouilly. P. H. Monsseaux builder. Built 1846. Original sketch indicates marble from ''Cap Girardon''—perhaps Cape Girardeau, Missouri, a small city on the Mississippi. The structure is constructed of sandstone.

Fig. 38A. Detail corner of Peniston and Duplantier mausoleum, 1842, St. Louis II, Sq. 2. Designed by de Pouilly. P. H. Monsseaux builder. See color plate 9.

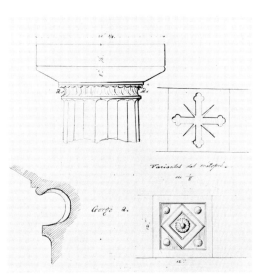

Fig. 38B. Peniston-Duplantier tomb, detail from de Pouilly sketchbook. (Courtesy Historic New Orleans Collection.)

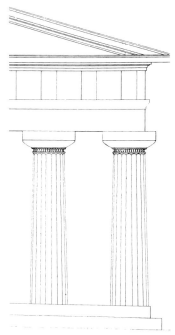

du Petit Temple de Paestum.

Fig. 38C. Detail, archaic Greek temple at Paestum, from Durand's *Recueil et paralléle des édifices.* The necking of the capital probably inspired de Pouilly's design for the Peniston column.

Fig. 39. Lacoste family tomb, St. Louis II, Sq. 2, 1849. Granite. Designed by de Pouilly. Newton Richards, builder. The design is based on a prostyle Greek Doric temple. This tomb, unlike the Peniston, has no shallow front chapel. Width 6 feet, length 10 feet 4 inches.

Fig. 40A. Jean-Baptiste Plauché tomb, St. Louis II, Sq. 2. General Jean-Baptiste Plauché commanded the Orleans Battalion at the Battle of New Orleans. He died in 1860; however, de Pouilly designed the tomb in 1845. P. H. Monsseaux, builder. *"Marbre blanc du nord,"* noted on sketch. Width 7 feet 4 inches, length 11 feet 9 inches.

Fig. 40B. Sketch for the Plauché tomb. (Courtesy Historic New Orleans Collection.)

Fig. 41A. Miltenberger family tomb, St. Louis II, Sq. 2. Granite. Designed 1850 by de Pouilly. Built by Newton Richards. Width 9 feet 1 inch, length 9 feet 10 inches.

Fig. 41B. Original design, Miltenberger tomb, from de Pouilly sketchbook. (Courtesy Historic New Orleans Collection.)

Fig. 41C. Detail, Miltenberger tomb.

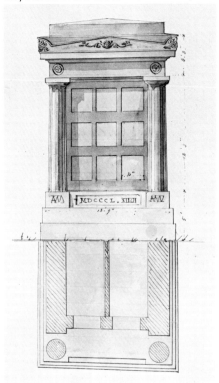

of the Athenian Treasury at Delphi are also prevalent. Among the various tombs that employ this motif are the Bruning, Buck, S. D'Antoni, and Vatter family tombs (figs. 44, 45). Prostyle temple tombs with four columns supporting the portico were also popular. Built in the mid-twentieth century, the William G. Helis mausoleum is an impressive reproduction of the Temple to Nike Apteros, an amphiprostyle temple on the Acropolis, Athens (fig. 46).

Other family mausoleums, like the William Syer tomb, are patterned after Roman rectangular temples in the tradition of the Maison Careé, Nimes (fig. 47). The Tuscan order is employed on the Walmsley family tomb, a textured and polished Quincy granite temple tomb designed and executed by Charles Orleans in 1905–1906 (fig. 48). The portico is compressed and the columns more ornamental than functional. A similar compression of the portico is seen in the John Dibert (d. 1912) family mausoleum, designed by Jean Duffy (color plate 7). Of polished Quincy granite, the tomb uniquely includes cast bronze ornamental decorations on the Ionic capital volute, the base of the column shaft, and the front and back pediments. The steps are flanked by large draped urns also in bronze. Another unique feature of the Dibert tomb is the combination of pediment and acroteria with a centalizing monolithic dome.

Fig. 42. Oliver Blineau and Antoine Carriere mausoleum, St. Louis II, Sq. 2. Built 1845. De Pouilly proposed a design for renovating the center vaulted chapel.

Fig. 43. Chapman Hyams family mausoleum, Metairie Cemetery. Built in early twentieth century by Weiblen. Freestanding Ionic columns are placed on all four sides. The classical acroteria on the roof are ornamented by the anthemion motif. Interior illustrated, page 129, figure 132.

Fig. 44. Vatter family mausoleum, Metairie Cemetery. Built *ca.* 1919 by Victor Huber.

Fig. 45. Buck family mausoleum, Metairie Cemetery. Built in the early twentieth century by Weiblen. The carvings of the basket and globes atop the columns are especially impressive. The globes are banded by the signs of the zodiac.

Fig. 46. William G. Helis mausoleum. Built in the mid-twentieth century by Weiblen. The design is especially suitable for Mr. Helis, who was born in Greece. It represents a scale copy of the classical Temple of Athena Nikè (Nikè Apteros) on the Acropolis, Athens. Helis' casket rests on soil brought from his native Greece.

Fig. 47. William Syer mausoleum, Metairie Cemetery.

Fig. 48. Walmsley mausoleum, Metairie Cemetery. Granite. Built by Charles Orleans. It contains an especially lovely stained glass window.

The circular or central motif, based on Greek and Roman tholos temples, creates an elegant ciborium effect over the Story and Spofford monuments (figs. 49, 50). Although it is not topped by a dome, the Story monument elegantly encircles a symbolic pedestaled urn. The sculptural details and decorations, based on classical motifs, are intricately carved with consummate skill. The Henry M. Spofford memorial, a cenotaph, enshrines a seated angel. A similar structure tops the Perseverance Fire Company No. 13 tomb designed by John Barnett in Cypress Grove. An octagonal enclosed central plan employing pilasters is the Luca Vaccaro (d. 1936) mausoleum (fig. 51). The motif above the doorway, carved in low relief, features two kneeling figures on either side of a classical stele, or gravemarker. Angels and other symbolical figures ornament the remaining sides. The monument was adapted by Albert Weiblen from the Hellenistic Tower of the Winds, Athens. The sculpture was executed by Albert Rieker. The Lawrence Fabacher tomb employs a similar design, but with unequal sides.

Other impressive tombs in Metairie Cemetery inspired by the Greek Revival are the W. H. B. Brook (d. 1912) tomb (fig. 52), the Hewes tomb, and the Penick-Miller tomb.

Fig. 49. Story Monument, Benjamin Saxon Story (d. 1901), Metairie Cemetery. Built by Weiblen and inspired by the Roman circular temple such as the Temple of Vesta. The carvings on the pedestal contain a family coat of arms, and scenes of "Civil War memories" and "the day's work is done."

Fig. 52. Family mausoleum of William Henry Dark Brook (d. 1912), Metairie Cemetery. A variation on the Greek Doric temple.

Fig. 50. Spofford cenotaph. Metairie Cemetery. Erected by Ophelia Martin Spofford in memory of her husband.

Fig. 51. Lucca Vaccaro mausoleum, Metairie Cemetery. Built in the 1930s by Weiblen. Inspired by Hellenistic Tower of the Winds. The relief carvings were executed by a local sculptor, Albert Rieker. Henri Gandolfo, who worked for many years with Weiblen and is a major source of information on Metairie Cemetery, posed for one of the panels.

The Classical Column

The freestanding classical column, usually elevated by a pedestal and terminated by a symbolic or decorative motif, makes an impressive commemorative marker. The column was popular for war memorials especially when topped by an honored soldier; such a memorial recalls the Roman columns of Trajan and Marcus Aurelius. Also popular is the broken column, which is often used on graves of men who died tragically or in early manhood. Both types retain an elegance and monumentality even though the scale is greatly modified. De Pouilly sketched several columns; the A. D. Crossman (d. 1859) monument in Greenwood is a product of his design (fig. 54). The John Oliver Locke memorial column in Greenwood, a cenotaph, was elevated to the memory of a young man who was killed during the Civil War in Marietta, Georgia, in 1864. The column by Newton Richards is topped by a capital ornamented with the oak tree and acorn motif symbols of eternity, virtue, and strength (figs. 55A, B). The Holcombe-Aiken column in Metairie Cemetery, carved by Daniel Warburg, has an unfluted shaft entwined by morning glory vines and blossoms that symbolize, among other things, the Resurrection, and bonds of love (figs. 56A, B). The festooned capital is topped by the anchor of hope and the cross of faith linked by morning glory vines. Warburg, an exceptional sculptor and marble cutter, was known for his morning glory motif. He was one of several children born to a Jewish émigre from Hamburg, Germany, and Marie-Rose, a Cuban Negro slave.

De Pouilly is credited with the Irad Ferry monument in Cypress Grove. The fluted broken shaft commemorates the death of a volunteer fireman who met his death in 1837 in the line of duty. The broken shaft with its three and a fraction drums, supposedly symbolizing the age of Ferry, is planted atop the classical sarcophagus

Fig. 53. Commemorative column from de Pouilly sketchbook. (Courtesy Historic New Orleans Collection.)

Fig. 54. A. D. Crossman monument, Granite. Greenwood Cemetery. Built 1863. Possibly designed by de Pouilly. Crossman was mayor of New Orleans from 1846 to 1854.

Fig. 55A. Locke family monument, Greenwood Cemetery. The column was erected to the memory of John Oliver Locke who died in the Civil War at Marietta, Georgia, 1864. He is buried in the neighboring Samuel Locke family tomb. Newton Richards, builder.

Fig. 55B. Detail, capital of Locke column

Fig. 56A. Holcombe-Aiken monument, Metairie Cemetery. The column was carved by Daniel Warburg, Jr. Ensign Aiken died in Italy in 1904 aboard an American battleship.

Fig. 56B. Detail, Holcombe-Aiken column.

Fig. 57. Broken column to the memory of Captain Charles W. McLellan, "Killed in defense of Richmond, Va., June 1, 1864. He fell without fear as many loved ones fell in defense of our rights." Built by Newton Richards on elevated family plot.

Fig. 58. David C. Hennessy monument, Metairie Cemetery. Designed and built by Albert Weiblen. Unveiled May 29, 1893. Shaft of Hollowell granite, 26 feet high. The broken shaft is covered by a pall over which hangs a police belt and club. The classical base is ornamented with acroteria, crosses, and the egg-and-dart motif.

(page 27, fig. 36). The sarcophagus still retains a crisp relief of a nineteenth-century fire engine. In Lafayette Cemetery No. 1 stands a broken Tuscan shaft on an elevated plot. The work, by Newton Richards, commemorates Capt. Charles W. McLellan who died June 1, 1864, "in defense of Richmond, Virginia" in the C.S.A., 15th Regiment (fig. 57). The Hennessy Monument in Metairie Cemetery is erected to the memory of the Irish police superintendent, David C. Hennessy, who met his death at the hands of gangland violence in 1890. The structure, designed and executed by Albert Weiblen, after winning a competition and at a cost of $3,300, is an unfluted broken column covered by a heavy drape (fig. 58). The classical pedestal of contrasting polished and unpolished Hollowell Granite includes inscriptions honoring the sacrifice of Hennessy whose "Fidelity to Duty Was Sealed with His Death." Along with the drape that covers the broken shaft are relief emblems of the New Orleans Police Department, the star and crescent, the policeman's club, and at the base, the pelican, state bird of Louisiana.

Other Trends and Variations of Neoclassicism

Many of the tombs in the New Orleans cemeteries that employ classical decorative details are nevertheless too individualistic to be categorized as a typical type or form. Other tombs, created in the eastern United States and imported in New Orleans in the early nineteenth century, show varying degrees of neoclassical influence. The monument of Eliza Lewis, first wife of Louisiana's Governor William

C. C. Claiborne, and her brother, Micajah Lewis, was designed by Benjamin H. Latrobe (fig. 59A). It was carved by Franzoni, an Italian sculptor who came to the United States to work on the nation's capitol in Washington, D.C. In its square form, the structure recalls the antique classical altar. A sketch in Latrobe's *Impressions Respecting New Orleans* shows a similar design and its proposed vaulted foundation (fig. 59B), which, according to Latrobe, would insure the stability of the monument. The low-relief sculpture ornamenting the monument describes the mourning husband in classical drape kneeling at the bed of his deceased wife, a child across her body. The three-year-old daughter of Eliza died the same day as her mother. An angel above the bed holds the crown of immortality and motions heavenward, while at the head of the bed a fasces, an emblem of ancient Roman magistrates, symbolizes the governmental authority and rank of Claiborne. The monument was erected in New Orleans in 1811, and in the same year the monument to the second Mrs. Claiborne, Clarisse Duralde, was elevated a few feet away (fig. 60). The second monument, supposedly made in Philadelphia, is asymmetrical and more in the style of early stepped-top brick tombs. An inscribed marble pedestal that sits atop the structure was designed for elevating a vase.

The Garibaldi Italian Benevolent Association tomb and the Columbus Society tomb in Metairie Cemetery are also classical in design (figs. 61, 62). However, rather than drawing inspiration directly from antique prototypes, these monuments along with neighboring tombs show strong allegiance to the teachings of Renaissance-type classicism particularly of theorists such as Palladio. His classicistic teachings called

Fig. 59B. Drawing from Latrobe's *Impressions Respecting New Orleans*.

Fig. 59A. Monument of Eliza Lewis, first wife of Governor William C. C. Claiborne, their daughter, and Micajah Lewis, brother of Eliza. St. Louis I. The square monument recalls antique commemorative altars. Benjamin H. Latrobe designer, 1811. Made in Philadelphia and sculptured by Franzoni.

Fig. 60. Back view of the tomb of Clarisse Duralde, second wife of Governor Claiborne, St. Louis I. The basic monument, despite the asymmetrical appearance, is in keeping with the early stepped-top tombs. The heavy pedestal, however, is an added feature.

Fig. 61. Garibaldi Society Italian Benevolent Association tomb, 1906, Metairie Cemetery.

Fig. 62. Columbus Society monument, Metairie Cemetery.

for the free use of motif, such as the classical orders, columns, arches or pilasters, taken from antiquity and applied to designs that theoretically embody noble, balanced proportions and serene grandeur. This classicistic trend, which denies actual copying of the antique, is a strong factor in many neoclassical designs, and most of the important tomb architects adhered to these influences.

Baroque Trends

Baroque ornamentation is occasionally combined with neoclassical designs, and "baroque classicism" could describe, with few reservations, the use of baroque design elements in New Orleans cemeteries. One motif that recurs is the decorative curving spiral found on late Renaissance and baroque architecture. This spiral, supporting engaged half vases, ornaments the Delachaise-Livaudais monument in St. Louis II, and the Gallier cenotaph in St. Louis III, both of which structures also have strong classical features (figs. 63, 64). The Delachaise-Livaudais families' tomb is adorned with delicate low-relief scroll work that frames the inscription plaque. On the cornice small curving braces create an ornate molding in the baroque manner. The Gallier monument, designed by James Gallier, Jr., employs baroque motifs similar to those of the Delachaise-Livaudais tomb; for example the flanking ornamental spirals, the half vases, and the curving brackets. The Gallier monument is dedicated to the memory of James Gallier, Sr., a prominent New Orleans architect, and his wife who lost their lives when the steamer *Evening Star* sank on a voyage from New York to New Orleans, October 3, 1866. The design of the Gallier monument is twice repeated, with minor variations, in Metairie Cemetery. The monument of the Choppin family (Samuel Choppin, d. 1880) was inspired by the Gallier design.

Fig. 63. Delachaise-Livaudais tomb, St. Louis II, Sq. 2.

Fig. 64. Gallier cenotaph, St. Louis III. Designed by James Gallier, Jr.

Perhaps the only tomb that approaches baroque form with a play of concave and convex movement is the New Orleans Italian Mutual Benevolent Society tomb erected in 1857. The design by architect Pietro Gauldi is circular with two concave niches containing sculpted images of Italia and Charity.

The Egyptian Revival

Egypt has long been associated with the timeless pyramids and the grandeur of exotic tombs. Egyptian designs and decorations were known in Europe long before the nineteenth century. Fanciful Egyptianisms inspired Piranesi in his *Cammini* prints, published in 1769. It was the Napoleonic expedition to Egypt in 1798–1799, however, that gave the public a renewed interest in Egyptology. Although many academically minded architects looked on the Egyptian Revival style as ugly, heavy, and monotonous, other designers welcomed the Egyptian architectural vocabulary with the same gusto as the classical and Gothic. Significant architects such as Maximilian Godefroy, Robert Mills, and John Haviland employed Egyptian Revival forms in American architecture. R. G. Hatfeld in an 1844 publication, *American House Carpenter,* said of the order, "The general appearance of the Egyptian style of architecture is that of solemn grandeur amounting sometimes to sepulchral gloom. For this reason it is appropriate for cemeteries, prisons, and c[*sic*]; and being adopted for these purposes, it is gradually gaining favor."

Fig. 65. Cypress Grove Cemetery entrance. Designed by Frederick Wilkinson, 1840. (Photograph by Guy F. Bernard.)

Egyptian forms offered the obelisk, the pyramid, and the pylon as basic structural types and the battered wall (thick at the base with an incline toward the top) and the cavetto (concave) cornice as structural motifs. These types and motifs were well adapted to nineteenth-century cemetery design. The pylon was especially suitable for entrance gates and was employed, often with an imaginative flair, in nineteenth-century American cemetery portals. Robert Cary Long, Jr., designed an Egyptian gateway for Greenmount Cemetery in Baltimore, Maryland; however, his Gothic design was preferred and built. Henry Austin created a pylon entrance for Grove Street Cemetery in New Haven, Connecticut, 1845, and Isaiah Rogers built an Egyptianized gateway to the Old Granary Burying Ground in Boston in 1840. In New Orleans in the same year, 1840, Frederick Wilkinson designed the Egyptian entrance for Cypress Grove Cemetery (fig. 65). A small print in Norman's *Guide to New Orleans,* 1845, imaginatively illustrates the Cypress Grove gate with a heavy cavetto lintel supported by twin piers, whereas a later print, 1895, from the *History of the Fire Department of New Orleans,* edited by Thomas O'Connor, shows the entrance as it appears today.

The pyramid on the Varney tomb is the dominant monument in an 1834 watercolor of St. Louis I by John H. B. Latrobe (color plate 1). Today the Varney tomb, recently renovated, has lost much of the original effect of the earlier setting (fig. 66). The tomb, crowded by other monuments and a tree, has much of the original foundation covered. Only the stepped base of the brick pyramid appears at ground level. Splendor and romantic nostalgia describe the Brunswig (Lucien M. Brunswig, d. 1892) pyramid in Metairie Cemetery (fig. 67A). The structure has an Egyptianized pylon entrance closed by a bronze door. The door opens into a central hall with crypts on either side. A monumental female figure motions sadly toward the family name while a sphinx silently guards the entrance (figs. 67B, C). The urn is ornamented with the lotus plant motif and the cavetto cornice is carved with the

Fig. 66. Varney monument, St. Louis I.

Fig. 67B. Detail, Brunswig tomb, figure.

Fig. 67C. Detail, Brunswig tomb, sphinx.

Fig. 67A. Lucien Brunswig tomb (d. 1892), Metairie Cemetery.

winged sun disc that, according to the Egyptians, was a symbol of divine protection. The tomb was supposedly inspired by an original German design, and was built by Weiblen in the early twentieth century.

The most often duplicated Egyptian tomb is a simple design with one or two chambers covered by battered walls and a cavetto cornice. The design is occasionally constructed in brick, (the John David [d. 1839] tomb in St. Louis II), and in granite, (the Edward Duncan [d. 1858] tomb, fig. 68). By no means a local invention, the basic shape was known to French cemetery design in the early nineteenth century as illustrated by a print of a Montmartre tomb dated 1812 (fig. 69). Granite tombs in this style abound and must have been a basic model available to New Orleanians on a mass-production level. An impressive variation in Cypress Grove, the Hohn family (Henry Hohn d. 1854) tomb, includes an obelisk atop the monument (fig. 70). A sketch in the Historic New Orleans Collection illustrates a similar design by Gallier, dated 1841 (fig. 71). This type, topped by cavetto cornice and obelisk, was also frequently constructed in the now demolished Girod Street Cemetery.

The obelisk, like the column, has universally become associated with commemoration. It can be successfully varied in scale and combined with other structures. In some instances the obelisk is combined with styles other than Egyptian. Perhaps the most important obelisk for historical reasons is that of François Xavier Martin (d. 1846), one of the most profound jurists of his time. The granite monument,

Fig. 69. Print of 1812 tomb built in Montmartre Cemetery, Paris, from J. Marty *Promenades pittoresques aux cimetières*.

Fig. 68. Edward Duncan (d. 1858) tomb, St. Louis II, Sq. 1. Newton Richards, builder.

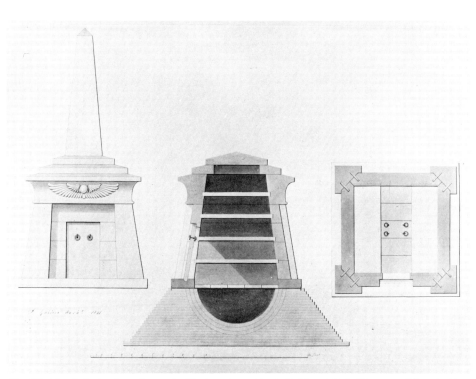

Fig. 71. Tomb in the Egyptian style. Design signed by J. Gallier, 1841. (Courtesy Historic New Orleans Collection.)

Fig. 70. Henry Hohn mausoleum (d. 1854), Cypress Grove Cemetery.

about twenty-seven feet tall, was erected by Newton Richards in 1847 (fig. 72). A more traditional obelisk is elevated on the Langles plot, Metairie (page 59, fig. 99). A rusticated obelisk tops the Spanish Cervantes Mutual Benevolent Society (founded 1887) tomb in St. Louis I (fig. 73). The obelisk is combined with the classicized design of the J. H. Keller family tomb (1881) in Metairie Cemetery, and with a Gothicized pedestal on the DeVilla monument in St. Louis III (figs. 74, 75). Although the top is not terminated by the traditional pyramidal point, the square shaft tapering toward the top is basically associated with the obelisk. This variation on the obelisk is evident in the Milne monument, St. Louis II, and the Moriarty monument in Metairie. The monument to the philanthropist Alexander Milne (d. 1838) employs a neo-classical cornice, pediment, and acroteria atop the tapering square shaft (fig. 76). Milne's will, in which he bequeaths much of his fortune to establish an orphanage, is enscribed on the heavy granite foundation. The structure is signed by Newton Richards. The Moriarty monument, built in the early twentieth century, towers over the surrounding landscape in Metairie Cemetery (fig. 77). The granite shaft, with beveled edges creating an eight-sided effect, is elevated by an impressive multistage pedestal with foliated columns on the four corners. Above the columns, at the base of the shaft are four female figures; one holds the anchor of faith, one the cross of hope, and the other a cornucopia, probably symbolizing charity. The fourth figure holds a wreath, a symbol of mourning and memory as well as immortality. The shaft is topped by a cross.

Fig. 72. François Xavier Martin monument (d. 1846), St. Louis II, Sq. 2. Erected by Newton Richards, 1847.

Fig. 73. Spanish Cervantes Mutual Benevolent Society tomb, St. Louis I. Founded 1887.

Fig. 74. J. H. Keller tomb, 1881, Metairie Cemetery.

Fig. 75. DeVilla monument, St. Louis III.

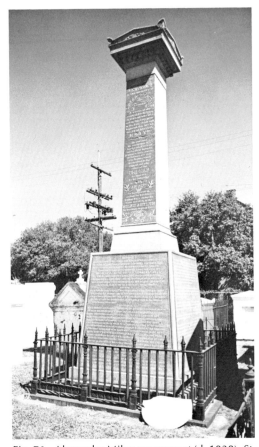

Fig. 76. Alexander Milne monument (d. 1838), St. Louis II, Sq. 2. Erected by Newton Richards.

Fig. 77. Moriarty monument, Metairie Cemetery. See also page 55, figures 91, 92.

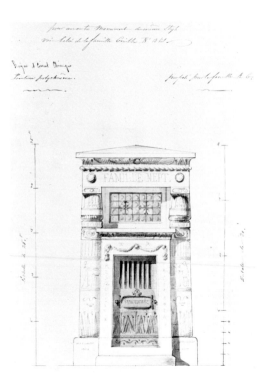

Fig. 78B. Egyptianized chapel tomb designed by de Pouilly for Grailhe but rejected in favor of the existing mausoleum. (Courtesy Historic New Orleans Collection.)

Fig. 78A. Grailhe tomb, 1850. St. Louis II, Sq. 2. Designed by de Pouilly. Built by Monsseaux. Width 8 feet, length 11 feet 6 inches.

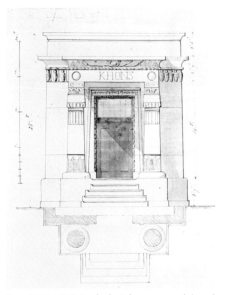

Fig. 79B. Original sketch proposed by de Pouilly for the Kohn tomb. (Courtesy Historic New Orleans Collection.)

Fig. 79A. Kohn family tomb, Cypress Grove Cemetery. Designed by de Pouilly.

The Graihle family tomb (1850), St. Louis II, and the Kohn family tomb, Cypress Grove, are examples of de Pouilly's interpretation of the Egyptian style applied to the chapel tomb. His sketchbook design for the Graihle tomb, without some of the ornate details, is a fairly faithful rendering in marble (fig. 78A). A second design, also Egyptian, was proposed for the Graihle family. De Pouilly's rejected sketch indicated that the structure was to be cemented brick with polychrome decorations, materials that would not have lasted in the New Orleans climate (fig. 78B).

The Kohn family tomb is more austere, less ornate than de Pouilly's original sketchbook design. The tomb in the sketchbook reads *Khons* rather than *Kohn*. De Pouilly read a relationship between the family name and the Khons of the Theban trinity. He noted this on the design page (figs. 79A, B).

The Egyptian Revival style remained popular into the twentieth century. An exceptionally impressive chapel tomb is the Frank Williams tomb in Metairie Cemetery (fig. 80). Two ornate columns with bell capitals based on the papyrus plant flank the Egyptianized bronze doors. The ornamentation, rendered in crisp details by the hands of a skilled stonecarver, follows traditional Egyptian inspirations. Also of interest in this style is the A. J. Fabacher (d. 1947) tomb in Metairie. Egyptian decorative motifs are also occasionally found on tablet or slab inscriptions in the twentieth century.

The Gothic Revival

In the middle ages it was a common practice to bury notable parishioners in the church, and this practice continued through the nineteenth century in many areas of

Fig. 80. Frank B. Williams family mausoleum, Metairie Cemetery. Designed by Favrot and Livaudais and built by Albert Weiblen in the early 1920s. The carving was executed at Weiblen's Stone Mountain, Georgia, quarry. Buried in this tomb is Marguerite Clark, a Hollywood movie queen famous in her day, and other notable members of the Williams family including General L. Kemper Williams and his wife Leila, benefactors of the Historic New Orleans Collection.

the world. The medieval church was associated with the Kingdom of God and the heavenly environment; and the Romanesque and Gothic churches understandably inspired designers of tombs. The Gothic Revival style, born in the late eighteenth and early nineteenth centuries, gave impetus to the application of medieval design to architecture. The Gothic Revival vies with the classical in cemetery design. Romanticists equated the middle ages with a period of spiritual enlightenment divorced from pursuits of the worldly and the industrial, and although Gothic Revival architecture was never favored as much as the neoclassical in France, it found a welcome place within the precincts of the cemeteries. Gothic tombs with spired canopies, pointed arches, high pitched roofs, and medieval decorative patterns stand beside Greek temples along the avenues of Père Lachaise and in Montmartre Cemetery. Perhaps the most famous neo-Gothic tomb is that of Heloise and Abelard reconstructed in Père Lachaise in 1817 (fig. 81).

In New Orleans, de Pouilly was among the first architects to employ the Gothic style in cemetery design. He proved his versatility by producing designs in the classical and Gothic styles for the consideration of the J. W. Caballero family who chose one of the Gothic designs. The tomb, built by Monsseaux (figs. 82A, B) in 1860, exhibits one of de Pouilly's decorative sketchbook designs. Although many of

Fig. 81. Heloise and Abelard tomb. Père Lachaise Cemetery, Paris. (Photograph courtesy Professor John Tice.)

Fig. 82A. Back view J. M. Caballero tomb, St. Louis II, Sq. 2. Designed in 1860 by de Pouilly. Width 5 feet 9 inches, length 11 feet 2 inches.

Fig. 82B. Original sketch for Caballero tomb, J. N. B. de Pouilly.

de Pouilly's original designs included ornate sculptural details, they were often destined to remain on paper. The Samuel Stewart tomb, signed "Monsseaux, 1857," now in Metairie Cemetery, employs the same delicate Gothic features as the de Pouilly designs. The inscription on the tomb is of historic interest; Samuel Stewart lost his life in a tragic disaster, a hurricane that befell Last Island on August 10, 1856 (fig. 83).

The basic sarcophagus is occasionally Gothicized by the additions of pointed arches and ornate rib and flambeau moldings on the façade such as those seen in the Antoine Abat family tomb signed by Florville Foy, 1854, and the nearby Victor Dejan family tomb, also signed Foy, 1854, in St. Louis II (fig. 84).

The neo-Gothic style became increasingly popular in the late nineteenth century in Cypress Grove, Greenwood, and Metairie cemeteries. In Greenwood Cemetery the family tomb of A. and W. J. Thomson employs steep gables, pointed and foliated arches, and narrow spires topped by flamboyant finials across the façade (fig. 85). In Cypress Grove the Slark and Letchford family monuments are the most dramatic examples of the medieval revival styles (fig. 86). The year on the inscriptions is 1868; however, the heavy style is reminiscent of monuments built in the late nineteenth century. Romanesque and Gothic revival styles were popular in the early years of Metairie Cemetery. Among the most romantic and charming neo-Gothic designs is the Bentinck Egan tomb (d. 1881) in Metairie Cemetery (fig. 87). The tomb is a small twin-towered Gothic chapel constructed in ruins. Great care has been taken to create

Fig. 83. Samuel Stewart tomb. Signed Monsseaux, 1857. Now in Metairie Cemetery.

Fig. 84. Antoine Abat family tomb, St. Louis II, Sq. 2. Signed Florville Foy, 1854.

Fig. 85. A. and W. J. Thomson family tomb, Greenwood. Built probably in the 1860s.

Fig. 86. Slark and Letchford tombs. Robert Slark (d. 1868), Sarah Augusta Slark, wife of W. H. Letchford (d. 1868), Cypress Grove.

Fig. 87. Bentinck Egan family tomb, Metairie Cemetery. Probably built in the late nineteenth century.

the poetic effect of broken stone, cracked marble, and crumbling inscriptions. The design was supposedly inspired by the chapel on the Egan estate in Ireland. Charles Orleans, who built many of the major tombs in the late nineteenth century in Metairie, especially favored medieval motifs. However, Orleans did not sign his tombs; consequently without further research and documentation, it is difficult to specify exactly which tombs were designed and built by his firm.

Among the more notable tombs in the medieval revival styles attributed to Orleans are the monuments of Charles Howard, J. Hernandez, Joseph A. Walker, and David C. McCann in Metairie and the Firemen's Monument in Greenwood. The McCann family tomb is dominated by a monumental Gothic spire over crossed pitched roofs (fig. 88). The exterior of this impressive mausoleum is of light gray granite with polished details and pink granite inlay. The style is reminiscent of the High Victorian Gothic. Like many other family mausoleums in Metairie, the McCann tomb has a stained glass window that illuminates the vaulted chamber. The lovely, rich colors of the window are visible through an iron gate personalized by the David C. McCann initials. The pointed arch of the door, supported by columns, is ornamented by delicate grape and vine motifs, symbols of Christ and the Eucharist. The entrance is flanked by freestanding draped urns and mourning figures. Finials top the four end gables of the roof and the spire. Near the McCann family tomb are several other Gothicized monuments (fig. 89). Two of these designs, the family tombs of W. B. Schmidt (d. 1901) and F. M. Ziegler (d. 1901), are identical and employ Gothic

Fig. 88. David C. McCann mausoleum, Metairie Cemetery. Attributed to Charles Orleans.

Fig. 89. Right, W. B. Schmidt (d. 1901); center, F. M. Ziegler (d. 1901); left, Nelson McStea (d. 1888), Metairie Cemetery.

motifs such as stained glass windows, pointed arches, flamboyant finials, and towers over the crossed high pitched roofs. The third, the McStea (Nelson McStea, d. 1888) family tomb is similar except for a dome-covered gabled roof. It is similar to the Slark monument in Cypress Grove; see figure 86. Nearby, the Agar family tomb, with a freestanding pointed arcade encircling the burial vaults, is unique (fig. 90). Built by Albert Weiblen of French Caen stone, with Gothic pointed arches and flambeau crocket ornamentation, it is nevertheless treated with a classical restraint that does not sacrifice grandeur. A similar effect is evident in the Perfect Union Lodge mausoleum in the Masonic Cemetery. Here, however, the arcade is not freestanding and crenelations ornament the roof (fig. 91).

Charles T. Howard was one of the original founders of Metairie Cemetery. The Howard family tomb, designed and built by Orleans, employs Gothic motifs in the portal (fig. 92). The hipped roof is surmounted by a classical figure, and seated inside is a marble figure of Silence that looks much like a classical philosopher.

Fig. 92. Charles T. Howard mausoleum, Metairie Cemetery. Built by Charles Orleans.

Fig. 90. Agar family tomb, Metairie Cemetery.

Fig. 91. Perfect Union Lodge mausoleum, Masonic Cemetery.

The Joseph A. Walker (d. 1893) and J. Hernandez (d. 1893) family tombs, both attributed to Orleans, are more Romanesque than Gothic. The portals of both tombs employ small columns supporting rounded arches. The Walker monument is ornamented by rusticated stone contrasted with smooth arcaded moldings and four miniature towers. The high pitched roof is mounted with a Gothicized pedestal and cross (fig. 93). The Hernandez monument is visually lighter in weight but no less grand. The center aisle with crypts on either side is barrel vaulted and opened at either end; iron gates allow the viewer to look through. The gable is topped by the cross and crown, symbols of Christ's sovereignty (fig. 94).

Among the many other monuments in Metairie that are notable for the use of medieval motifs are the Delafield monument and the Monteleone family mausoleum. The monument to Melinda Delafield (d. 1891) was designed and built by Albert Weiblen (fig. 95) and is dominated by a canopied Gothic spire. A small monument, the Delafield tomb has a delicacy and intimacy often lost in larger structures. The Anthony Monteleone (d. 1913) tomb, a miniature Gothic church, is topped by a small canopied spire.

The Gothic canopy is employed in the historically significant Fireman's monument

Fig. 93. Joseph A. Walker tomb (d. 1893), Metairie Cemetery. Attributed to Charles Orleans.

Fig. 94. J. Hernandez tomb (d. 1893), Metairie Cemetery. Attributed to Charles Orleans.

in Greenwood Cemetery. The monument, finished in 1887, is dedicated to the firemen who lost their lives in the line of duty (fig. 96A). According to a newspaper article of October 24, 1887, Charles Orleans was commissioned to design and construct the main body of the monument while the marble sculpture was created in Italy by Nicoli from a model by Alexander Doyle (fig. 96B). The monument proper is of Hollowell, Maine, granite. Charles Orleans was for many years the New Orleans representative for Hollowell granite and most of his designs were built in this light grey material.

Near Eastern Architecture

The category of Near Eastern architecture contains a conglomeration of styles associated with numerous cultures. This extensive grouping is dominated by non-Western cultures that profess to the Islamic faith. Early contact and diffusion between Moslems and Christian Europeans occurred during the Moorish occupation of Spain in the eighth century and during the height of the Byzantine empire between the sixth and ninth centuries. The style is called by various names including Islamic, Muslim, Moorish, and by the name of the related countries such as Turkish, Arabian, Persian, and Indian. Egypt is also occasionally included.

The Bernau (Elizabeth Hale Bernau, d. 1891) tomb exhibits a Byzantine quality in the use of the Greek cross floor plan, the small domed bell tower above the crossing, and the interior ornate altar (fig. 97). The lengthy epitaph on the exterior was taken from an oration delivered by Augustus Bernau at the dedication of the entrance lodge

Fig. 95. Melinda Delafield monument (d. 1891), Metairie Cemetery.

Fig. 96A. Firemen's Charitable Association monument, Greenwood, completed 1887 at a cost of approximately $14,000. Structure is by Charles Orleans. Figure is by Alexander Doyle, sculptor.

Fig. 96B. Detail of Firemen's monument.

Fig. 98. Charles A. Larendon tomb (d. 1888), Metairie Cemetery.

Fig. 97. Bernau tomb, (Elizabeth Hale Bernau, d. 1891), Metairie Cemetery.

Fig. 99B. Cason tomb detail, entrance.

Fig. 99A. Benton W. Cason tomb, Metairie Cemetery. Designed and built by Weiblen.

at Metairie cemetery. The structure is simple in its ornamentation and design when compared to the more exotic styles of fully realized Islamic-inspired designs.

The Charles A. Larendon (d. 1888) tomb has a portico topped by a modified dome (fig. 98). A cross of the Eastern Church stands on the apex. The cusped horseshoe arch and the repeated patterns sculptured to contrast lacy designs of lights against darks like the dome, are traditional Islamic Revival motifs. The circular stained glass window was picturesquely integrated into the design.

Islamic Revival motifs appeared late in funerary architecture in New Orleans. The style, seen primarily in Metairie Cemetery, flourished from 1890 to 1940. Albert Weiblen's designs for the Benton W. Cason family tomb and the Arthur Barba, Sr., tomb are excellent proof of the elegance and charm of this exotic style (figs. 99A, B, 100). The exterior carvings of the Cason tomb are executed with a feeling for the ornate character of Moslem decorative design. The cast bronze door, signed by J. C. Loester, Sr., features a mezzo relief of a draped female mourner. Other interesting examples of the style are the R. T. O'Dwyer (d. 1940) family tomb and the H. and B. Beer family tomb (fig. 101) in Metairie Cemetery. The drawing and elevation from Weiblen (figs. 102A, B) illustrate the basic tomb in this style.

Fig. 100. Arthur Barba, Sr., mausoleum, Metairie Cemetery. Built in the early twentieth century by Weiblen.

Fig. 101. H. and B. Beer mausoleum, Metairie Cemetery. Built in the early twentieth century, ca. 1920, by Weiblen.

Fig. 102A. A basic Moorish, Near Eastern Revival tomb by Albert Weiblen. (Photograph courtesy LSUNO Library archives.)

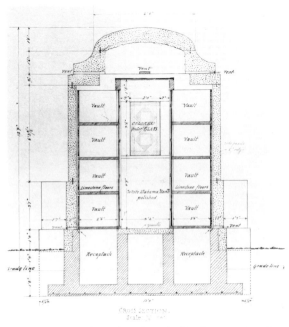

Fig. 102B. Interior elevation indicating construction details. (Courtesy LSUNO Library archives.)

Design and Style Variations

The tumulus form, crypts covered by earthern mounds, inspired a number of designs in Metairie and Greenwood cemeteries. The New Orleans versions of this ancient burial structure are usually surmounted by a figure, representing the sponsoring organization or society. Access may or may not be available to the crypts within the artificial mound. Among the military monuments that employ the tumulus concept are those of the Army of Tennessee, Louisiana Division, and the Army of Northern Virginia, Louisiana Division, in Metairie Cemetery, and the Confederate Soldiers' monument in Greenwood. The Benevolent and Protective Order of the Elks tomb in Greenwood employs a tumulus mound topped by a large bronze elk (p. 40,

Fig. 103. Fitzpatrick family tomb, Greenwood Cemetery. Victor Huber, builder. John Fitzpatrick (d. 1919) was president of the Firemen's Charitable and Benevolent Association for twenty-seven years.

fig. 63). The Fitzpatrick family tomb in Greenwood, built by Victor Huber, uses a smaller version of the tumulus (fig. 103).

The Benevolent Association of the Army of Tennessee, Louisiana Division, laid the cornerstone of their monument on March 31, 1883 (figs. 104A–E). The celebration was typical of the unveiling or dedication ceremonies for most large benevolent association tombs. A group of about three hundred Confederate States of America Veterans met at the Army of Tennessee headquarters and marched to the Canal Street train and were delivered to the precincts of the cemetery where they again marched, preceded by a band, to the lot set aside for the Army of Tennessee tomb, at that time located to the right of the main entrance. There the veterans met with other gentlemen and ladies to participate in the formal ceremonies of the laying of the cornerstone. A newspaper article of April 1, 1883, describes with much detail the contents of the speeches and the history of the speechmakers. Among the more interesting participants were Charles E. Hooker, general of the C.S.A., and Jefferson Davis, who delivered a tribute to Albert Sidney Johnston. The occasion was highlighted by the cornerstone ceremony. The engineer, John Glenn, and builder, Pierre Casse, were asked to affirm the perfection of the granite cornerstone. Casse remarked "I have given it my care — the square and the plumb — and I find no defects. It is indeed worthy to become the cornerstone of your great edifice." Contained in the center of the stone in a copper casket are articles and mementos of the Confederate States of America. The monument was completed during 1886–1887.

The mound is elevated about thirty feet upon a lot sixty feet in diameter. At the top sits General Albert Sidney Johnston on horseback. The bronze figure and the marble

Fig. 104A. Benevolent Association of the Army of Tennessee, Louisiana Division, Metairie Cemetery.

Fig. 104B. Interior of Army of Tennessee tomb.

Fig. 104C. Detail, bronze equestrian statue of General Albert Sidney Johnston, by Alexander Doyle. Compare page 54, figure 88. In the background are the Moriarty and Lacosst monuments. (Photograph by G. E. Arnold; courtesy Leonard V. Huber Collection.)

Fig. 104D. Detail, Army of Tennessee monument. Marble orderly with roll. By Alexander Doyle.

Fig. 104E. Bronze insignia of Army of Tennessee above door to vaults. Achille Perelli, sculptor.

orderly sergeant who stands at the base with the roll of the honored dead are from designs of Alexander Doyle (figs. 104A, B, C, D, E) who was paid $12,000 for them. The model of the horse was selected from the same bloodline as the general's horse, Fire Eater, and the statue represents the moment before Fire Eater rode to his death at the Battle of Shiloh. A sculptor of national renown, Alexander Doyle was born in Ohio in 1857 and was educated at the national academies at Cararra and Florence, Italy. Doyle was a visitor to New Orleans in the 1880s and is also credited with the sculpture of the fireman for the Firemen's Monument in Greenwood (fig. 96B), the Margaret statue, and those of General P. G. T. Beauregard and General Robert E. Lee.

Achille Perelli created the bronze insignia above the entrance to the crypts of the Tennessee monument (fig. 104E). Perelli also sculptured the eight-foot nine-inch figure of General Stonewall Jackson that stands atop the thirty-eight foot granite column on the mound of the Louisiana Division, Army of Northern Virginia (fig. 105). The design for the monument was executed by Charles Orleans. (See also page 61, figs. 106, 107.)

A low mound forms the burial site for approximately six hundred soldiers of the C.S.A. in the Confederate Soldiers' Monument in Greenwood Cemetery (fig. 106). The mound, surmounted by a structure of white Cararra marble and granite, was built through the efforts of the Ladies' Benevolent Association of Louisiana at a cost of approximately $12,000. The main part of the monument was carved in Italy and features a life-sized Confederate infantryman leaning on his rifle. On the marble shaft that is approximately nine feet tall, are life-sized busts of Stonewall Jackson, Robert E. Lee, Leonidas Polk, and Albert Sidney Johnston (pages 61-62, figs. 106, 107, 108). The steps and the platform base are of granite. Benjamin Harrod, architect, and George Stroud, builder, collaborated on the monument, which was unveiled in 1874 with a grand ceremony.

The Washington Artillery Monument in Metairie Cemetery, designed by Charles Orleans, was unveiled and dedicated on February 22, 1880 (fig. 107A). Although it

Fig. 105. General Stonewall Jackson atop the tomb of the Army of Northern Virginia, Louisiana Division, Metairie Cemetery. Achille Perelli, sculptor. See also page 56, figure 94.

Fig. 106. Confederate Soldiers' monument, Greenwood Cemetery. See also page 37, figure 59.

Fig. 107B. Detail figure atop Washington Artillery monument. The face has a portrait likeness—probably of Colonel J. B. Walton, although this is sometimes questioned.

Fig. 107A. Washington Artillery monument, Metairie Cemetery.

cannot be classified as a tumulus because the structure is a memorial cenotaph, it is similar in design to the Confederate Monument in Greenwood and elevated by a low hill. An article in the February 15, 1880, *Daily Picayune* describes the monument as being "of granite, eight feet four inches at the base and twenty-three feet high; it stands on a mound nine feet high." The plot of ground surrounding it is 45 feet square enclosed with granite posts resembling cannon linked by galvanized chain. A similar fence motif was used in the Orleans Artillery Battalion tomb, attributed to de Pouilly, in St. Louis I. A print, cut from a nineteenth-century publication and pasted in de Pouilly's sketchbook, illustrates a similar use of cannon and chain. At the top of the Washington Artillery Monument stands a statue in granite, eight feet high, of an artillery soldier leaning on a "sponge staff." The figure is attributed to George Doyle.

Fig. 108B. Detail of De George and Guendanon tomb, St. Louis III. (Photograph by Guy F. Bernard.)

Fig. 108A. Row of precast concrete tombs, St. Louis III.

(George Doyle, locally, is listed as a painter in the city directory.) Coleman states in his 1885 *Historical Sketch Book and Guide to New Orleans* that the figure is the commander of the Washington Artillery Unit, Colonel J. B. Walton (fig. 107B).

Not all the nineteenth-century tombs can be catagorized in the styles and idioms of the romantic revival. Many tombs are exceptionally modest, purely functional and, literally, without style. Other tombs are individualistic and not significantly inspired by the architectural vocabulary of the romantic revival.

Two types of tombs, one exceptionally rusticated and the other exceptionally ornate in exterior wall treatment, were briefly popular in the late nineteenth century. The former type is recognized mainly by the use of rubble work. The walls are created from rusticated granite, occasionally with smooth convex mortar joints between the granite spalls. This type of work appeared in the mid-nineteenth century and reached a peak of popularity in the last decades of the century. The second type, built of precast concrete, has walls covered with units of decorative low relief patterns (figs. 108A, B). The overall effect may be described as a concrete version of gingerbread gothic. This type of family tomb is seen in limited number in several of the local cemeteries and especially in St. Louis III, Greenwood, and Odd Fellows cemeteries.

Among the more interesting tombs that have not been categorized under the styles of the romantic revival are the Morales family tomb and the Bobet family tomb, both in Metairie Cemetery.

The J. A. Morales tomb is usually called the Josie Arlington tomb because the structure was originally built for this colorful "madam" of a Storyville establishment (color plate 8). It was later purchased by Mr. Morales and the remains of Josie were removed from the crypt. Aside from the legends associated with the original owner, the tomb of Stoney Creek (New Hampshire) pink granite is appealing. The basic design by Weiblen is simple; the façade is created by posts and a lintel that frame an austere bronze double crypt door. Atop the lintel are two carved square vessels which serve as terminals to the posts and have large flames illusionistically blown by the wind. The vessel with flame symbolizing the eternal flame of life is a persistent motif on tomb design and is found on a large percentage of nineteenth-century monuments. A series of steps leads up to the Morales tomb and on the top step to the right of the door stands a life-sized bronze maiden. The sculpture, signed "F. Bagdon, 1911," was executed at the Dusseldorf, Germany, bronze works (fig. 109).

The cross is a motif that repeatedly recurs in Christian funerary art. The traditional symbolism of the cross, faith, and the resurrection, is especially appropriate to cemetery iconography. It appears in ironworks and in freestanding and relief sculptural ornamentation. Charles Lawhon, a native of Tennessee who was active in New Orleans around 1910–1925, employed the cross motif on the Edward Bobet family tomb (fig. 110A). This cross continues from the front to the back of the monument and is articulated by relief details and by texture contrasts. The metal door is ornamented with a palm branch, which in funerary art symbolizes spiritual peace and victory, and with a commemorative wreath. A stained glass window in a cruciform pattern is opposite the door at the end of the center aisle. The cross on the façade is decorated with convex molding carved with the grape and vine motif. In relief above the door hangs a festoon of flowers and a draped fabric. The cloth possibly represents the traditional black crepe of mourning; however, on the face of the fabric are the initials and crown of thorns of Christ. The design, therefore, may

Fig. 109. Detail figure and door of Josie Arlington tomb, today called the Morales tomb, Metairie Cemetery.

Fig. 110A. Edward Bobet family tomb, Metairie Cemetery. Designed by Charles Lawhon.

Fig. 110B. Sketch variation on Bobet design, by Charles Lawhon. (Courtesy LSUNO Library Archives.)

have been inspired by St. Veronica's kerchief. The sketch (fig. 110B) is a variation on the design.

The cross is also popular for tombstone markers. The Celtic cross frequently appears in St. Patrick's Cemetery; however, the most impressive and monumental version is in Metairie Cemetery. Charles Lawhon, one of the designers of the Brewster family cross, was careful to preserve the antique Celtic character and ornamental style (page 57, fig. 59). The carving was executed by Charles Dodd.

SCULPTURAL ORNAMENTATION AND SYMBOLISM: FURTHER OBSERVATIONS ON ARTISTS AND ARTISANS

Researchers face a dilemma in gathering historical data on the numerous brick masons, stonecutters, sculptors, and architects who worked in the early cemeteries. Often the only available information is a name inscribed on a tomb and a listing or an advertisement in the city directories. With few exceptions, even the more significant and productive artisans and designers left little personal history behind them.

Many of the tombs are not signed. Etienne Courcelle was probably responsible for constructing and designing a number of tombs in St. Louis I. He was listed in the 1853 *City Directory* as an architect and keeper of the Old Catholic Cemetery, who "respectfully informs his friends and the public that he still continues construction of tombs and vaults in granite or marble, inscriptions and railings at the lowest price and shortest notice." Tombs designed by Courcelle, however, are not identified.

When signatures do occur, several interpretations of the names are possible. Signatures on the lower right corner of inscription slabs do not necessarily identify the designer or builder of the entire tomb. A few craftsmen specialized in the lettering and ornamentation of inscription plaques, and these signatures are the most numerous and varied. Signatures on the tomb proper, on the lower right front, or more recently on the cement sidewalks, may indicate the builder who was responsible for construction of the tomb or the name of the owner of the marble firm supplying the materials. The builder or owner of the marble business is not necessarily the designer of the tomb. Several of de Pouilly's designs are inscribed with both the name of the builder and the architect; for example, the Graihle tomb and the Iberia Society tomb. However, the majority of his designs are only signed by the builder.

The following list of marble workers and tomb builders was compiled from a survey of Gardner's *New Orleans Directory,* Cohen's *New Orleans Directory,* and Soard's *New Orleans Directory* from 1853–1905 at three-to-five-year intervals. The list is supplemented with names of known marble workers. The dates indicate the decades in which directory listing occurred or the artist is known to have worked.

Victor Azereto, 1866.
J. Balony, 1859.
Peter Barr, 1868–85; sexton, Girod St. Cemetery.
Anthony Barrett, 1853–74.
Barret Brothers, 1885–92.
Charles Barret, 1880.
Frederick Barrett, 1875–81; sexton, Greenwood Cemetery.
Birchmeir & Simpson, 1866.
Frederick J. Birchmeir, agent of Washington

Marble Works 1870–77, independent directory listings, 1878–1902.
Horace Blakesley, sexton, Girod St. Cemetery before Civil War, ca. 1840–60.
Horace Blakesley, Jr., 1866.
S. Blakesley, 1866.
C. J. Boisseau.
René Bonné, 1900–30.
Pierre Bonnor, 1853.
D. & J. Boyer.
Frederick Bradley, 1876–80.

Fig. 111. Detail, corner of society Fleur de Marie, established 1850s, St. Louis II, Sq. 3. Cement plaster over brick. The motif on the acroteria was inspired by the anthemion design.

Fig. 112. Detail corner granite acroteria ornamented with face, unidentified tomb, Cypress Grove.

Fig. 136. Manuel Fernandez tomb, St. Louis II, Sq. 2, by Florville Foy. Note the broken flower, connoting life terminated. The two flower designs on the right probably represent lilies of the valley, symbols of purity and humility. The center daisy is a symbol of innocence.

Fig. 137. Our Angel Myrthee, detail from the D. R. Godwin tomb, Lafayette No. 1. Unsigned by sculptor.

Fig. 138. Peter Smith (d. 1907), St. Vincent de Paul I. Signed by Suarez.

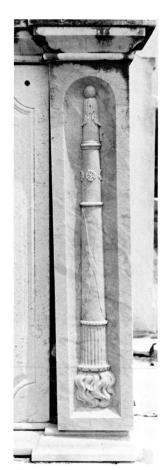

Fig. 134A. Detail Fouché tomb, St. Louis II, Sq. 1. Monsseaux builder.

Fig. 134B. Detail Robertson tomb, Cypress Grove. Signed Newton Richards.

Fig. 134C. Detail Aspill tomb, St. Patrick No. 1.

Fig. 135. Jean Baptiste Bozart tomb, St. Louis I. Signed Florville Foy. The pansy symbolizes remembrance and humility.

screw that locks the plaque to the tomb front. In the mid-nineteenth century, an architectural frame enclosing a marble inscription plaque was popular on wall vaults. The carving often included classical features and religious imagery (figs. 139, 140, 141).

Images on inscription plaques and tombstones are usually iconographical. Time is often symbolically represented by the winged hourglass with motifs of the Grim Reaper and salvation by Faith (fig. 142). The relief on the D'Aquin tomb, St. Louis II, Square 1, cut in the 1830s by Viau, is one of the more ornate inscription plaques in

Fig. 141. I. Celeste Peñavar (d. 1849) wall vault, St. Louis II, Sq. 2. The winged hourglass, symbol of passage of time, is placed in the center pediment.

Fig. 142. Henry Young (d. 1832), vault slab signed H. Blakesley. Now in St. John Cemetery. Formerly in Girod Street Cemetery.

Fig. 139. Clark vault, St. Louis II, Sq. 2. A mourner sits beneath weeping willows in the apex of the pediment. The classical sarcophagus format is copied in the wall vault design. Probably carved by Monsseaux.

Fig. 140. John Lawless (d. 1850) wall vault, St. Louis II, Sq. 2. An olive wreath, symbol of peace, ornaments the pediment. Anthemions ornament the corner triangular acroteria. Monsseaux sculptor.

Fig. 143. D'Aquin tomb tablet, St. Louis II, Sq. 1. Signed by Viau.

Fig. 144. Tombstone of Michael O'Hara, St. Louis II, Sq. 2. The sun symbolizes the dawn of life, the willows are a favored symbol of sorrow, and the cross symbolizes resurrection through faith. This tombstone is unique because it is the only one of its kind still standing in St. Louis II.

Fig. 145. Tombstone of the Edward Nester family, St. Patrick, No. 2. Monumental slab, over seven feet tall, was cut in the 1860s and employs traditional motifs—willow, lamb, kneeling mourner, and crosses—that are repeated with minor variations on numerous other gravestones.

the nineteenth-century cemeteries (fig. 143). An angel carries two infants into the heavens while an owl, an ancient symbol of death, spreads its wings behind the trio. Two other owls adorn the foliated border. The angel and babies are repeated in Lafayette No. 1, in a later period by another sculpture. Copying was common and continued to be common into the twentieth century. Other motifs of salvation, mourning, and commemoration, especially the weeping willow, the pedestaled urn, the cross, the lamb, the tombstone, and the mourning figure, become more stereotyped by the early twentieth century. Figures 144 through 150 represent a few examples of relief sculpture found on tomb inscription plaques and on tombstones.

Much can be said about funerary iconography and imagery. The few brief notes made here are from observations of the more obvious trends in sculptural design found in the local cemeteries. Other notes concerning specific details of designs and iconography are found throughout the book.

Fig. 146. Peralta inscription plaque, St. Louis II, Sq. 2. This is an early example, 1834, of the motifs of weeping willow, shrine, and in the background, tombstones.

Fig. 147. The Reverend Adolphe X. Chapuis, curé St. Vincent de Paul Church (d. 1892), St. Vincent de Paul I. The willow represents mourning; the broken column represents life cut short, and the cross, faith.

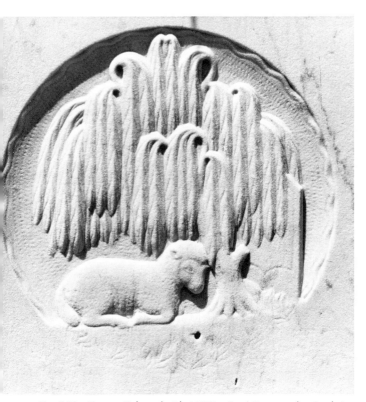

Fig. 148. Georg Schenck (d. 1903), St. Vincent de Paul I. Carving on inscription plaque. The lamb, Christ, rests beneath the willow. To the right is a tombstone. This design and the next figure are frequently duplicated.

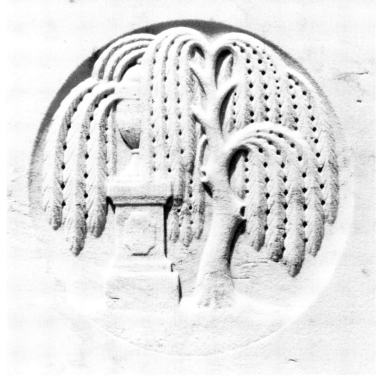

Fig. 149. Charles Frantz (d. 1887), St. Vincent de Paul I. This design, like many of the others found on inscription slabs, is also seen on memorial prints and death notices. Signed V. Suarez.

Fig. 150. Jacques Nicolas Bussiere de Pouilly reveals his versatile creative ability in his designs for the family tombs of Ursin Bouligny, Jr. (left) and J. M. Caballero (right). St. Louis II, Sq. 2. See also figures 82 A and B, page 105. (Photograph by Mike Posey.)

Jacques Nicolas Bussiere de Pouilly

EDITH ELLIOTT LONG

In 1833, when twenty-eight-year-old Jacques Nicolas Bussiere de Pouilly came to New Orleans with his wife, Laurence, and infant daughter, Lucienne, he brought along his own sketchbook of measured drawings of the finest tombs recently done in Père Lachaise cemetery in Paris. These plans were to influence cemetery architecture in New Orleans for years to come, and de Pouilly was to be a leading mausoleum designer.

But he was much more than that. In his heyday he was one of the most important — certainly he was one of the most creative — architects practicing in New Orleans in the nineteenth century. At one time the stamp of his genius could be seen throughout the Creole section of the city. Unfortunately, nearly all his major buildings have disappeared. In his own time he was never published. And his carefully collected plans, business papers, even scale models of his public buildings, his entire *oeuvre* was destroyed, by mischance, early in the 1900s. His name might well have vanished from the lists had not the memory of his achievements, the charm and élan of his buildings, lingered in the public mind, in contemporary travel books, and in reviews by the press.

Today a few of his buildings still stand, though modified, along the banquettes of the Vieux Carré and in Faubourg Tremé. Detailed drawings and specifications for a number of buildings exist in the New Orleans Notarial Archives. Quite possibly more of these will come to light as researchers comb the acts of notaries who flourished during de Pouilly's most productive years. His skill as a draftsman and watercolorist can be judged by some 228 Plan Book drawings also contained in the Notarial Archives.

Housed in the Historic New Orleans Collection, there is a sketchbook in which de Pouilly apparently fantasized his commissions, presenting buildings as he originally designed them, as he was uniquely trained to create them — though he had learned that the limited means of building available in New Orleans and his conservative Creole clientele would reduce them to provincial simplicities in the end. This sketch book contains a large number of tombs. The Iberia Society Tomb sketch less the corner torches and garlands, indicates the quality of the designs and the character of the constructed tomb (figs. 1,2).

De Pouilly came to New Orleans well born and well schooled for this career. His birthplace, in 1804, was Chatel-Censoir, on the Yonne, France. Extant family records, articles of the time, his own scant notices and letters all bespeak good breeding and a gentle background. He was a Beaux-Arts man, Paris-trained at this great national school of the fine arts at a time when its influence was predominant.

Fig. 1. De Pouilly sketchbook design of the Iberia Society tomb. The design also was offered to the Cazadores Voluntes.

Fig. 2. Iberia Society tomb, St. Louis II, Sq. 2, built by Monsseaux in the 1890s. Jacques de Pouilly designed the palatial St. Louis Hotel on the site of the present Royal Orleans Hotel and the St. Louis Cathedral on Jackson Square. He also designed the most notable of the tombs in St. Louis Cemetery II that were built in this era. In the middle square of this cemetery tombs of the Delachaise-Livaudais, Plauche, Peniston-Duplantier, Bouligny, and Caballero families testify to his skill. He did not confine himself to the St. Louis Cemetery but designed impressive tombs in other cemeteries such as the New Lusitanos Society tomb in the Girod Street Cemetery (now demolished), the Irad Ferry tomb in Cypress Grove Cemetery and others.

Fig. 3. Jacques Nicolas Bussiere de Pouilly in his later years. (Courtesy Mrs. Sidney Azby Stewart.)

Since the days of Louis XIV, French artistic supremacy had been acknowledged all over Europe. The French system of architectural education was no exception. It lapsed during the Revolution, but was restored and given fresh impetus by Napoleon, who revived the Ecole des Beaux-Arts and established a great engineering school, Ecole Polytechnique.

A distinguished professor of architecture at the Polytechnique, J.-N.-L. Durand, between 1802 and 1805, synthesized the new romantic classicism of the day in a landmark work, *Précis des leçons d'architecture données á l'Ecole Polytechnique*. This and the books of Krafft and Ransonette were basic texts at the time of de Pouilly's training and profoundly influenced his later work. He emerged from this discipline an architect of the French neogreque school, versed in engineering, imaginative, progressive, years ahead of his time for the tastes and techniques available in his chosen city.

No records of de Pouilly's first buildings in the city have turned up. But he must have had a measure of success, for the next year he was joined by his younger brother, Joseph Isidore de Pouilly, who is also reputed to have been a Beaux-Arts graduate in architecture. Together they must have made an effective firm. Jacques Nicolas was its head and chief designer. Joseph Isidore seems to have handled most of the business details. His name is on a number of contracts with which they were both associated, and he managed several of their sideline operations. Yet his influence and reputation pale before those of his older brother. Perhaps it is because he put down few roots in New Orleans. He never married, left no heirs, and the partnership was dissolved some years before his death in 1866. At the height of the de Pouilly career, however, they were together, and any study of de Pouilly achievements must take Joseph Isidore into account.

Opportunity and fame came early in New Orleans to de Pouilly *freres*. A mounting city need and their unique talents met at a moment of portent to them both. Unlike most creative artists, de Pouilly did not work up to the apotheosis of his career. He began at the top. It is not fair to assume that the rest of his career went gently downgrade, though indeed, such spectacular commissions seldom came his way again. The truth is more nearly that the Creole portion of the city, with which he was allied, exhausted itself in one great outburst of public building and civic betterment in the 1830s. From then on it was a struggle to keep these enterprises afloat in the boom-and-bust economy that followed.

In his autobiography, James Gallier, a prominent architect who was a contemporary of de Pouilly, commented on the difficulty of securing timber and other materials in boom-time New Orleans. The de Pouillys undoubtedly faced the same problems, and like Gallier they coped by organizing sideline operations. The brothers set up a steam mill to produce the plaster from which cornices and medallions of their own designs could be made as well as all kinds of stucco work. They invented a machine to "plane boards from half to three inches in thickness and from three to ten inches in breadth."

When some marble was required, Joseph went north to superintend its selection and cutting. In 1837, needing more, the firm advertised in the *Courier* that he would undertake similar commissions for others wanting granite, stone, and marble while he was there.

In 1853 the educator, Simon Rouen, who had married Lucienne de Pouilly, founded Audubon College, a boys' school at the corner of Dumaine and Burgundy streets. For many years de Pouilly taught "linear drawing as applied to buildings, machinery, surveying with landscape and perspective" at this institution (fig. 3). He entered competitions as they occurred and continued scholarly pursuits. As late as 1869 he made the winning plan for "Best Drawing in Water Colors for an Auctioneer's Exchange" offered by the Third Grand Mechanics and Agricultural Fair.

De Pouilly practiced almost to the end of his life, maintaining offices, until 1873, at old number 56 Exchange Passage. Becoming ill, he retired to his home at old 179 St. Ann, where he died Sunday, February 21, 1875 (fig. 4). This last home was in Faubourg Tremé, just across from the open area now called Beauregard Square. Though this whole portion of Tremé has been razed for the new theater and park, the gaunt and neglected raised dwelling at 179, and later 1125 St. Ann, stood in the schoolyard beside McDonogh 35.

Only the French-language newspaper, *L'Abeille de la Nouvelle-Orleans,* noted his passing with an appreciative obituary in the February 23 issue. It cited his most important work as the Cathedral, the Citizens' Bank, St. Augustin, and the St. Louis Hotel, *"le plus beau monument san contradit de la Nouvelle-Orleans."* Seemingly these were the buildings closest to his heart. He was described as the leading architect in the city, and his great talent, his dignity, and deep modesty were mentioned with respect and regard.

He was buried unpretentiously in a small wall vault in St. Louis Cemetery II surrounded by many of the imposing tombs of his own design (fig. 5). His grandson, the well-known historian and notary, Bussiere Rouen, who remembered him well, described him as "a scholar, an architect, and a born artist inspired by the very highest ideals; notwithstanding his noble ancestry, he was very modest and on account he was beloved by all who knew him."

Vous êtes prié d'assister au Convoi et à l'Enterrement de feu

J. N. De POUILLY,

Décédé ce matin à 5 heures,

A l'âge de 70 ans

L'enterrement aura lieu demain LUNDI, à 9 heures précises du Matin.

Le corps est exposé rue Ste. Anne entre Remparts et St. Claude.

De la part des Familles :

DE POUILLY,

Et de ses Gendres S. ROUEN,

C. BABLED.

Nlle-Orleans 21 *Février* 1875.

A vendre par J. Bonnel, No. 1 rue Ste. Anne, entre Chartres et Royale.

Fig. 4. Death notice of J. N. B. de Pouilly; typical of those posted on street-corner poles and prominent buildings. (Courtesy Mrs. Sidney Azby Stewart.)

Fig. 5. Tomb of J. N. B. de Pouilly, St. Louis II, Sq. 1.

Typical round picket and projectile point front enclosure, St. Louis I.

Cemetery Ironwork

MARY LOUISE CHRISTOVICH

New Orleans cemetery ironwork, both wrought and cast, reflects a continuous sequence of decorative patterns favored by the city's nineteenth-century citizens. It is a visual exposition of individual tastes equal to those of tomb and sculptural designs. The text and photographs in this volume are intended as avenues of miscellaneous imagery, to aid the uninitiated in an appreciation of a long-neglected art form. The ironworker, be he the artistic blacksmith, the inventive fabricator, or the leading founder, has provided us an opportunity to examine a cultural expression in great quantities and varieties.

These men who created designs or assembled stock patterns into hundreds of small front tomb enclosures and full fence enclosures have left their works unsigned and undated. It was only in the latter part of the nineteenth century that companies began to cast their names into the posts or attach nameplates. Building contracts for tombs, though often available, fail to mention ironwork, indicating that the owners dealt separately with the builder, designer, and the ironworker or even that the tomb may predate the enclosure. Notable exceptions are the outstanding tombs of J. N. B. de Pouilly, for which he designed his own bronze or iron doors and enclosures. Thus we must evaluate the artistry, technical expertise, and ingenuity of these unknown men through their works, without benefit of attribution.

A century of blacksmith accomplishments preceded this outburst of decorative ironwork. Some of the earliest known pieces of ironwork were financed from the French and Spanish kings' treasury. A wrought iron transom on the House of the Director (fig. 1) and an elaborate gate bearing the king's arms designed by Ignace Broutin (fig. 2), neither of which still exists, were more than likely the handicraft of local smiths. The railings of the Cabildo (1795) and of Le Petit Théâtre du Vieux Carré, as well as those moved to Correjolles House, 715 Governor Nicholls Street, have been attributed to Spanish ironworker Marcellino Hernandez, who worked here for several years. Hernandez came to New Orleans from the Canary Islands and left at the end of the Spanish period. The stair railing from the original Ursuline Convent, built in 1734, is the only known extant iron from the first half of the eighteenth century; it retains the exquisite balance of function and materials indicating the practical rendering by the colonies' inchoate blacksmiths.

The names of these first smiths were recorded as early as the census of 1726, and a hundred years later their roles swelled to ten times, then forty times, the original list of three. Mathieu Roy is the first mentioned, then Etienne Barrosson and Julien Binard, who had been called LaForge by Le Sieur Diron in 1721. Numerous gun and locksmiths and several makers of nails were a part of this census; a year later seven

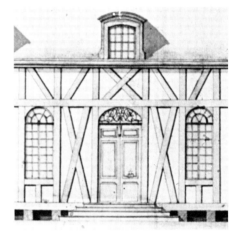

Fig. 1. Wrought iron transom on Bienville's home. (Courtesy Samuel Wilson, Jr.)

Fig. 2. Gate cresting by Ignace Broutin, 1832, for *Powder Magazine*. (Courtesy Samuel Wilson, Jr.)

more blacksmiths were included. Joseph Moreau lived with his three children on Rue de Conde and Gilles Avat on Rue St. Louis, while François Brunet and Nicolas Humbert lived on Toulouse. That same year, 1727, Jean Melain(*dit* D'Orange), Pierre Cleron and Claude Bedeson were listed on Rue St. Anne.

By 1731 Brunet appears again, and LaRoche Castel and Daublin are added to the rolls. The Flannery Census of 1805 records four blacksmiths: William Malus, Jaque Rouly, Pierre Hurteebise and Joachim Courcelle. The "first directory" of 1807, along with the *Annuaire Louisianais* (1809), both reprinted in a local publication called *Le Diamant* (1887), were compiled and published by surveyor–ironmaster Barthelemy Lafon. It reveals that William Malus, "Rouli," and "Urtubuise" were joined in their trades by Jean Baptiste Wiltz and Devault. The tangible work of these men remains unknown to us, yet their traditional practices swept well into the nineteenth century as evidenced by the longevity of the Malus and Hurtubise names on the blacksmith roster. Along with thirty-two blacksmiths counted in the *New Orleans Directory* of 1822 are A. Malus and Pierre Hurtubise; five iron foundries "lately established" were reported also but were actually identified as brass foundries. The Joachim Courcelle family continued in the iron business through the activities of Etienne Courcelle into the twentieth century.

Skilled slaves and free men of color commanded an important position in the production of New Orleans ironwork from the colonial period forward. Marcus Christian's *Negro Ironworkers of Louisiana, 1718–1900* is a superb statement on the interdependence of the races in the ironworking field. This treatise leaves no doubt that Negro laborers, trained by the French and the Spanish, provided strength and artistry and were highly valued for their work.

The predominance of these laborers within skilled trades was seriously threatened by the influx of German and Irish immigrants during the early nineteenth century. Names such as Anheiser, Isnehart, and Garner identify blacksmiths in the city directory of 1822. Soon German and English names appeared as proprietors and workers, and remained in the directory throughout the nineteenth century.

It is not surprising that many of the Germans coming to New Orleans gravitated toward ironworking. For many centuries Germany had produced skilled workers. Before the Napoleonic period German iron artisans became proficient in cast iron because of its lower cost. There were hundreds of foundries in Germany by 1800, and those who immigrated to the United States were often trained men, well acquainted with the iron trade.

The English also were quite at home within decorative iron, for their country bloomed under the creative genius of Jean Tijou, a seventeenth-century blacksmith who fled to England from France to escape religious persecution. Tijou transformed iron into flamboyant designs and imbued generations of ironworkers with a professional standard of elegance. Although nothing in New Orleans ironwork has ever reached the height of Tijou's wrought iron, his publication *A New Book of Drawings* (1693) influenced the entire field in Europe and, eventually, America.

Englishman Henry Cort in 1784 discovered a method of changing pig iron into wrought iron by refining it in a puddling furnace (molten metal stirred constantly with a long bar bent at the end). Cort also invented a method to roll iron bars. Both of these improvements increased the usability of iron for ornamentation and provided a ready supply for export from England and Germany to the United States, thus bringing New Orleans closer to architectural, ornamental, and production influences of these two countries.

Whereas New Orleans was manufacturing wrought iron at a minimal rate of $10,000 per annum during this period, it is interesting to note that bar and pig iron were being shipped into New Orleans in large quantities, and that as early as 1806 John McMillan & Company was exporting from Liverpool to Robert Dyson in New Orleans casks containing cast iron balconies. The commerce lists have this same company and consignee sending cast iron, wrought iron, and materials for balconies in four separate shipments during 1821. By 1822 cast iron balconies represented the major shipments by McMillan, whereas Ashton Finlay and Company exported from the same port to New Orleans to consignee A. Lockhart and Company wrought iron sugar pans, cooper pans, and material for hydraulic presses. Flat, round, and square iron bars, as well as gates, pillars, pilasters, bundles of steel, and sheets of lead were imported also through Liverpool by the New Orleans company Tayleur and Bates in 1823. As the decade wore on, thousands of bars of Swedish iron were sent from Göteborg through the local company of William Alderson.

Throughout 1828–1831 huge cargoes of iron in every form arrived from Boston, New York, Liverpool, and Göteborg. Gordon Forstall, R. D. Shepherd, and Benjamin Slark imported the metal to fill the rising appetite for iron ornamentation. One of the fascinating entries in a ship's list is that appearing June, 1830. On the *General Putnam* out of Liverpool, W. & I. Brown sent to Puech, Bein and Company 1,012 iron molds. No further description is given as to the design nature of these molds. They could have been for plows, gates or rails. Puech, Bein & Company evolved into the equivalent of a modern-day wholesaler and became Priestly and Bein, still supplying all needs to the iron industry in New Orleans as late as 1857 (fig. 3).

Fig. 3. Advertisement in the *Louisiana Courier,* 1830s. (Courtesy New Orleans Public Library.)

WROUGHT IRON AND CAST IRON

Wrought iron is "worked" iron. It is one of the oldest methods of shaping iron and a technique that has varied little for centuries. It is fibrous in structure, light gray in color, and when cold or hot can be hammered, twisted and stretched. The more it is worked, the more dense, brittle and hard it becomes, but it can always be brought back to a malleable state by reheating and cooling slowly. Iron will burn at temperatures beyond white heat or welding heat. (*Wrought Iron in Architecture,* by Gerald Geerlings).

The well-equipped blacksmith's shop with forge and bellows may contain as many as thirty or more tools, the most important of which are hammers, anvils, tongs, and chisels. By means of these mechanical aids the blacksmith can produce simple or complex designs. He joins wrought sections by welding (a point reached at highest temperatures) or by riveting with cotterpin intersections. The latter method is often disguised with ornament attachments or by a banding piece called a collar. His versatility can expand from fashioning motifs of the Greek orders to scrolls, volutes, petals, diamonds, flame shapes, and monograms, all executed with incredible plasticity.

Cast iron, on the other hand, is brittle, not workable, and must be poured into molds in a molten state. This art form involves many skills, including those of carver, patternmaker, founder, and iron finisher. In order to provide accuracy of form from a master pattern of wood, allowance must be made for double shrinkage between the pouring of the metal pattern and the final casting. Any imitation or duplication of this pattern is readily revealed by additional shrinkage.

Many nineteenth-century architects and tomb owners required that the original pattern be destroyed after a design was executed. Most patterns, however, were designed in large foundries of New York, Boston, Chicago, and Philadelphia, although a thorough investigation could reveal original New Orleans patterns by artists of unquestionable talents. Several writers on the subject of cast ironwork in New Orleans have implied that some New Orleans designs are repeated often in this city but are not found elsewhere. Mystery also clouds the identity of the carvers of these lovely patterns, and there is within the trade little protection by copyright for any original designs.

A monthly journal published by the famous Chicago firm Winslow Brothers Company in 1893 described the "lifting" practice by a competing St. Louis firm of iron and wire workers: "The best designs in the entire group were taken—to use a mild term—from a catalogue published three years ago by the Winslow Brothers Company; others had appeared in current publications duly credited to the originators, and others have no known parentage, as the publishers very carefully refrain from any word on the subject." The article followed with a detailed list of twenty-six designs original to the Chicago company, which were "borrowed," and further stated it would be possible to extend this list but that there was ample material with which to "point a moral and adorn a tale." The New Orleans manufacturers' agents of Winslow Brothers were Bowles and Dearborn, located at 189 Gravier in 1894. In 1880 Winslow Brothers executed the gilt bronze St. Joseph chapel altar in the Church of the Immaculate Conception (Jesuit) for $10,000 and in 1890 the Chapel for the Blessed Sacrament.

EARLY FOUNDRIES AND IRONWORKERS

The successful operation of a foundry required that a measurable tonnage of iron be melted in the cupolas or furnaces every day. The amount necessary for ornamental iron was insufficient to justify the concentrative efforts of the large foundries. Therefore, ornamental pieces were cast from extra molten metal during the daily operation of the large industrial plants. Advertisements clearly stated that sugar mills, steam engines, centrifugal machines, and other heavy equipment were their primary concern, although they often mentioned "ironwork of any kind."

The ornamental ironwork shops were fabricators, i.e., shops where original patterns could be ordered and the finished product assembled, but usually not where the iron was actually cast. The employment in these shops rarely exceeded five or ten persons, whereas the foundries had hundreds of employees, including patternmakers, blacksmiths, turners and molders. The small shops registered their patterns with one or more foundry, placed orders, and fabricated the castings received.

The oldest of the large New Orleans foundries was started in 1823 with C. C. Whiteman & Company. Two years later Jedediah Leeds became a one-third owner. By the following year he was sole owner. This business remained a successful operation until the 1900s. The *Louisiana Advertiser* on August 16, 1830, reported that Leeds had established his foundry on the upper part of Faubourg St. Mary, near the river, in a brick building 120 by 140 feet (fig. 4). Within this building four-hundred tons of Tennessee pig iron and two hundred tons of old iron were consumed annually. "There are eight lathes, from the largest to the smallest size, for

Fig. 4. Leeds Foundry, from a lithograph by B. Simon. (Courtesy Historic New Orleans Collection.)

turning and boring of every description in iron and brass, which are propelled by steam, the *Advertiser* further noted. ''The furnaces consist of two Blast, and one Air.'' The whole concern, including the lot and slaves, was valued at more than $175,000.

Leeds associated his nephew, John Leeds, with him in the early years, and when he died in 1844 his two sons, Charles J. and Thomas L., became partners, together with their cousin Edward Grinnell. Charles Leeds, the founder's son, was mayor of New Orleans in 1875–1876.

Joseph A. Shakspeare, another son of a founding ironmonger, also became mayor of New Orleans in 1880. The firm established in 1838 by Samuel Shakspeare was first a blacksmith's shop. In 1849 it became the company of Wheeler and Shakspeare, progressing to Geddes and Shakspeare, then Shakspeare and Smith, and finally to Julian Swoop, Shakspeare and Swoop Company. For two years, 1856–1857, before entering his father's business, Joseph A. Shakspeare acquired a thorough knowledge of the iron industry through the New York Novelty Ironworks Co. Shakspeare manufactured heavy iron, steel, and brass equipment and continued operation into the twentieth century.

Daniel Edwards, a native of England, was brought up in the foundry business of Liverpool and founded his own firm in New Orleans in 1846. By 1894 this firm employed 250 skilled laborers and shipped sugar machinery to Mexico, Cuba, and Central America. Railings were a minor part of their operation (fig. 5).

Smaller firms such as Nuttall & James (fig. 6) on Lafayette Street near Camp actively sought cemetery ironwork in 1850, as did another concern, that of Julian Murray, who advertised in 1858 to furnish tomb grilles. Luther Holmes (fig. 7) and Benjamin T. K. Bennett were active in the ornamental ironwork field, and it is believed that they employed some of the large local foundries to execute their castings. In 1857 Bennett was in partnership with Francis Lurges (fig. 8). This firm

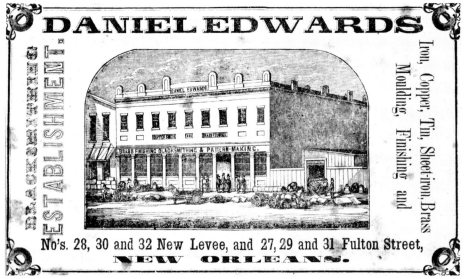

Fig. 5. Daniel Edwards Foundry, from *Brice Directory*, 1857. (Courtesy New Orleans Public Library.)

HOMES LUTHER, Foundry and ornamental iron works, Benton, c. Euphrosine sts; manufactures the latest and most approved patterns of railings, verandas, doors, shutters, vaults, bridges, straight and circular stairs, store fronts, capitals, and all other kinds of work used for building purposes. Railings, castings, guard boxes, sashweights and ventilators; 106 St. Charles, d. Hercules, n. Felicity

Fig. 7. Foundry catalog advertisement. (Courtesy Special Collections Division, Tulane University Library.)

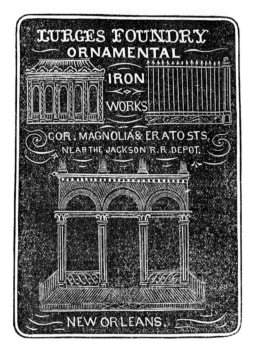

Fig. 6. Advertisement for James Nuttall, manufacturers of cemetery ironwork, from *Crescent City Business Directory*, 1858. (Courtesy New Orleans Public Library.)

Fig. 8. Foundry advertisement, from *Graham's Crescent City Directory*. (Courtesy Special Collections Division, Tulane University Library.)

furnished many iron columns and gates; one excellent example is the main gate of St. Louis III.

Before the Civil War, Wheeler and Forstall, successors to Long and Maglone, John Armstrong, Lud's, and the New Orleans Ornamental Ironworks had their businesses in the "American Sector." The war apparently put Cook and Fallon, owners of the Algiers Belleville Ironworks, out of business (fig. 9), for the New Orleans *Times* in a section called the "Looker-On" reported in 1865 that these imposing crenulated brick buildings were now deserted after having been occupied by soldiers for four years.

There was no dearth of foundries in that year and the next decade, however, even though a spokesman for McCan and Harrell, operating from a huge plant on Fulton near Notre Dame, complained of its inability to meet the cheap labor conditions of the North and East. He further stated that the pig iron being used was mainly brought from Scotland, with some from England and Pennsylvania, and a small amount from Tennessee.

Jacob Baumiller, John Christe, and Pierre Pelanne (fashioner of the fence at Jackson Square) were now listed as iron fence builders, but Wood & Miltenberger are recorded with the iron foundries. It is more than likely that the latter was an agent and shipped cast railing to New Orleans from Wood and Perot of Philadelphia.

The late 1860s and 1870s also saw the establishments of the Coleman, Johnson, and Reynolds foundries, respectively. C. C. Timpe worked for Reynolds (fig. 10) and invented and installed his elevator in prominent mercantile houses in the city, such as the Monteleone Building (known as Hotel Victor) and the Albert Baldwin Building at Camp and Common streets. One of Timpe's signed gates is in St. Louis III cemetery.

Joseph Sutton & Sons took over the firm of Mims & Cochran in 1886. The latter had been in business since before the war. Sutton advertised a vast amount of light ornamental ironwork for galleries, verandas, stairways, and tombs. J. L. O'Connor was the sole agent for the Champion Iron Fence Company and was "happy" to furnish architectural ironwork, railings, crests, or wire work.

This was also the era of Hammond & Spitz Company and the founding of the still famous Hinderer Ironworks. Frederick Hinderer came to New Orleans before 1880 and established himself in the iron business. His first directory listing is that of an iron furniture manufacturer in partnership with Frederich Daimler. Then, with Charles Pike, whose fences are quite common in the New Orleans Garden District, he was co-owner of the Novelty Iron and Wire Works at 304 Camp Street. Hinderer and William Spitz were associated as early as 1889, even though the latter was also a member of a company called Hammond, Timpe and Spitz in 1893. Spitz took over the Hinderer Ironworks after the founder's death. Spitz's sons continued the business and Henry Alcus, the present owner, became associated with the one surviving son, Joseph Spitz, in 1929. Their partnership ended in 1933 when Spitz retired. Henry Alcus operated Hinderer's until 1962, after which time it became increasingly difficult to find capable ironworkers or blacksmiths. Ernest Guerre, one of the last of the artistic blacksmiths, left Hinderer's in 1956 after working for half a century at his craft. Alcus has spread thousands of patterns around the country in selected foundries and still fills a few orders when pressed.

Numa J. Lorio established his first ironworks at 1053 Camp in 1905 after having been associated with Hinderer's for many years. His three sons operated the business on Gayoso Street. Numa H. Lorio, Jr., third generation, is now in charge and has recently moved to Laussat Street in Metairie. The company still furnishes original Lorio patterns and has all its foundry work executed in Birmingham, Alabama.

Few tradespeople or even large companies signed their work until trade plates became popular by the 1880s. Cast iron building pilasters, such as those on the Bon Ton Restaurant on Magazine Street, carry the name of the mid–nineteenth-century Julia Street Foundry, but few other foundries were signing their work even though they advertised prodigiously. Some of these trade plates or maker's marks from the Henry Alcus collection include the nineteenth-century companies of Hinderer, Spitz; Hammond & Spitz; C. Pike; and two twentieth-century concerns, Continental and Star Fence (figs. 11A, B, C, D, E, F). The Geddes-Shakspeare & Company plate

Fig. 9. Advertisement for Belleville Iron Works. (Courtesy Special Collections Division, Tulane University Library.)

Fig. 10. Foundry advertisement, 1881. (Courtesy New Orleans Public Library.)

Figs. 11A, B, C, D, E, F, G. Maker's marks. (Courtesy Henry Alcus Collection.)

Figs. 12, 13, 14, 15. Maker's marks.

(fig. 12) is from the Sebastian Swoop tomb in St. Patrick No. 2, as is the strange railing mark which appears on the John Bofill enclosure of 1865 (fig. 13). The Reynolds plate appears on both side panels of the family tomb in Metairie Cemetery (fig. 14). The Thomas B. Pearce plate (fig. 15) is on the Coliseum Street and Prytania Street gates of Lafayette Cemetery No. 1. There is no marker on the main Washington Street gate of this cemetery.

A vast network of artisans, fabricators, and importers has contributed a wide selection of iron components to this metropolitan area since the beginning of the nineteenth century. Most of the local iron companies have always imported cast projectile points, rosettes, or stamped ornaments. New York companies such as J. W. Fiske, Julius Blum, and J. G. Brown have been New Orleans' main suppliers of these adjunctive materials. J. G. Braun, representing fabricators in Germany, still has a nationwide distribution.

Smyser-Royer Company of Philadelphia in the late nineteenth and early twentieth centuries kept the New Orleans market filled with trellises and iron fence components, as did many metal fence companies from the midwest between Louisville and Cincinnati. All the companies considered herein supplied wrought and cast components to New Orleans cemeteries.

Ironwork is no longer demanded by New Orleanians in the quantities of the past. However, for over a century, until the late 1920s, New Orleanians continued the progression of fanciful ironwork in, on, and around their homes. The cemeteries mirror their ornamental preferences, for they enriched the homes of the dead coordinately with those of the living. Protection for the tombs could never have been a serious consideration for the railings are often low or easily scaled; the gates rarely have anything but the simplest latch. There is distinction throughout all of the cemeteries in the selection of ironwork: the crosses, crestings, and terminals of the early pieces are to be found in St. Louis I and II. The excitement of variety and design of the cast railings is experienced as well in most of the city's other cemeteries.

CROSSES — FORM, STYLE, AND SYMBOLISM

Crosses in the St. Louis cemeteries provide a pleasurable opportunity for viewing style changes of the Christian symbol as interpreted by the New Orleans iron artisan. All are wrought, from the earliest which are embedded in the low brick tombs to those mounted on high pediments or welded on the ornate gate crestings.

The crucifix forms bearing the figure of Christ or the Virgin Mary have vanished, yet photographs made as recently as the 1950s illustrated their existence in St. Louis I. These marker crosses are seen now in "country" cemeteries and are still ordered from local ironworkers.

F. R. Webber, in his book, *Church Symbolism,* states that there are over four hundred forms of the cross. Fifty are utilized within Christian symbolism and have their origin in heraldry. The terms *Latin cross* and *Greek cross* refer to the overall proportion of the vertical and horizontal members, further identification to stylistic interpretation of symbols.

Fig. 16. The cross above the Antoine Bonneval tomb, St. Louis I, defies the proper proportions of either a Latin or a Greek cross. The wider horizontal measurement of 27½ inches versus its heighth of 24 inches suggests the possibility that an extra row of bricks in which it now stands was added some years after its erection. If it had equal bar proportions, it would be classified as a Greek cross. Its style is of a Cross Fleurée with ends terminating in three petals. Incised with the name Antoine Bonneval, it contains the earliest inscribed death date, 1800.

Fig. 17. The Jean Marie cross surmounts a small brick tomb behind the J. B. Leseur tomb of 1815, St. Louis I. A marble slab by the early stone cutter, Isnard, is too faded to reveal a date, but it is quite possible that this cross could predate the tomb and be one of the earliest in the cemetery. The ends are chiseled out in a version of the Cross Botonnée, which in the Latin and the Greek design terminates in trefoils. This was a common style used by early stone cutters and ironworkers. It measures 21½ inches by 26½ inches and could be considered a Latin cross with an elongated vertical member.

Fig. 18. The Marie Felicié Comming cross of 1811 has two cross bars of equal proportions, St. Louis I. It is possible that the vertical has been further embedded in the tomb top than it was in the original installation. A Greek Fleurée cross, or one having the horizontal and vertical members of equal lengths, it has ends terminating in three petals. Incised is the name of the deceased, a baby girl who was born March 1, 1809, and died in 1811. A second cross, now bent and leaning, is of the same design. It marks the grave immediately next to the Comming site and is incised with the name Zenon.

Figs. 19A, B. The Gelpi and the LeBeau de la Barre crosses, St. Louis II, Sq. 2 are hammered from one piece of iron and not riveted by a center bolt. Both are Crosses Fleurée of Latin form. The Gelpi cross is painted silver and has a center rosette, whereas the LeBeau de la Barre is unpainted, and tenoned through a curved base above an early iron enclosure. This cross is in the rear section of a rare enclosure. The front cross has been broken off, as have many of the urn finials. Both the tomb and ironwork are mutilated, hardly fitting for the memory of Dr. J. LeBeau, scion of this family.

149

Fig. 20. The pediment cross of the Valentine tomb, St. Louis I, is a variation of the Anchor cross. This symbol, known from the first days of Christendom, was one of faith and hope. The cross is one solid piece of iron with no decorative marks other than the anchor flukes made by the ironmaster's sharp stroke when the ends were worked.

Fig. 21. The Joseph Enoul Degue Livaudais tomb, St. Louis I, is one of six vaults built of plastered bricks in the 1830s. Livaudais fought in the American Revolution and was an owner of vast lands throughout the state. The complete iron enclosure has double gates with round pickets, pierced through heavy horizontal bars. The spikes are forged tips, and the twelve standards or round posts have sphere finials (of which six are missing). The cross mounted between the gates has a Latin Fleurée style ornamented with graceful C scrolls above the transcept and extended lateral S scrolls below. The proportions of this solid, hammered cross to the tomb and enclosure and its strong but graceful ornamentation render it one of the finest in St. Louis I.

Fig. 22. The J. B. Labatut cross, 1838, St. Louis II, Sq. 2, a beautifully elongated Latin cross, is also in one piece, but the ends terminate in copper filigree work. A center rosette of cast lead blends well with the round nimbus with simple beaded rays. The small dolphin scrolls balance the cross on the wide, delicately designed enclosure crest.

Fig. 23. J. L. Pilié, one of New Orleans' leading nineteenth-century surveyors and architects, is buried in a high brick plastered tomb (1839) that is in an advanced stage of deterioration, St. Louis II, Sq. 2. A Latin cross adorned with wrought cast terminals in which small rosettes are riveted is well poised over a half oval forming a sunburst crest with twelve spikes. Vigorous dolphin scrolls attach at the lower section of the vertical and top horizontal enclosure of the rail. Excellent artistry in the scrollwork is repeated in the double-lyre motif gates.

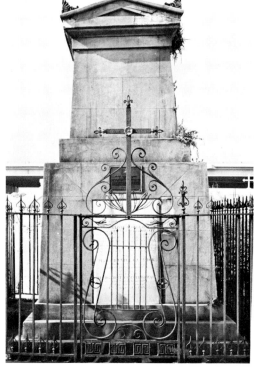

Fig. 24. Major Daniel Carmick, 1816, St. Louis II, Sq. 1, has one of the most outstanding iron enclosures, with a gate and crosses of superb workmanship. The elongated Latin cross is 40 inches high with a 30-inch horizontal spread. Composed from one iron bar, the cross ends terminate in wrought *fleur-de-lis* with rosettes; a center rosette is a five-petal rose variety. Dolphin scrolls offset the sides and add elegance and rhythm to the composition. From the base a cluster of lilies with iron stamen and delicate leaves attach to form a work of magnificent symmetry.

Fig. 25. The Lavigne-Courcelle tomb is a wide double-vault tomb with slate tablets. Located in St. Louis I, the tomb dates from the 1830s. Both the tomb and iron enclosure are crumbling, the former from engulfing vegetation, the latter from the loss of sections, thus weakening the whole. There is a marked resemblance in the ironwork treatment in this enclosure, which may have had lyre gates (both now missing) and the Pilié and Carmick ironwork. This cross, with large and small rosettes in the dolphin scrolls, is wider and thicker than the Carmick cross and lacks some of its fluency. The inverted C scrolls below the top rail and the Greek Key design bordering the bottom have the touch of an excellent craftsman.

Fig. 26. The Adolph W. Pichot cross, St. Louis II, Sq. 2, is formed by two intersecting square stock bars with the terminals split into a flamed figure eight. C scrolls form a center design.

Fig. 27. The Famille Dominguez cross, St. Louis II, Sq. 2, also an elongated passion style of the Latin cross, resembles the Pichot in that it is a square bar with flame-eight-shaped terminals. It, however, is elevated above the double gates on a second horizontal top bar, which at one time had finials and a border below. The front of this complete enclosure has three gates, the third having been added to service the sides and rear of the tomb.

Fig. 28. The Société de St. Louis de Gonzagues, 1900, St. Louis II, Sq. 3, is not unlike the Pichot and Dominguez crosses in feeling, although its elongated proportions are necessitated by the height of the eight-vaulted tomb over which it rises. The stylized dolphin scrolls dip attractively above the stone pedestal in which this cross is embedded.

Fig. 29. The Rivarde-Haydel tomb, 1836, St. Louis II, Sq. 2, is a high, truncated, table tomb having a square bar, complete enclosure. A cross within a cross, welded together with square iron separater, this Latin cross is well secured to the gate cresting. The border cross flares at the base in simulated geometric scroll form. The cresting, with modulated movement, is unlike the rather severe line of the cross and enclosure.

Fig. 31. In ruinous condition is the Victor Wiltz stepped tomb, St. Louis II, Sq. 1. The ironwork is of the finest quality; the enclosure is unusual, a high, narrow, long fence with an oval-heart monogram and one rams-ear scroll in the front. A Latin cross has feather terminals and a spiked nimbus around a plain circle rosette. The supporting scroll forms a horizontal base. The Wiltz family has given Louisiana a governor and outstanding leadership in the past.

Fig. 30. The Christine Ferry cross, 1840s, St. Louis II, Sq. 1, is a small cross within a cross. The center is welded to the outer cross by iron buttons and supported at the base with rivets and small vertical scrolls. The front enclosure has a variety of picket points and standard finials and is intact, except for three alternating spikes on the lower rail.

Fig. 32. Above the John Desir Maignan table tomb, 1835, St. Louis II, Sq. 1, is a cross with the most elaborate base scrolls in any of the city's cemeteries. Of exquisite grace and proportion, the scrolls support an elevated, tripart cross with delicate flame terminals. A heart rosette is in the center. The Maignan family were ironworkers, having been listed in New Orleans directories as early as 1822.

Fig. 33. The wreath cross on the St. Martin-Roumage family tomb, 1840s, St. Louis II, Sq. 1, is almost Greek in form, and utilizes tiny hearts as terminals. A lead casting of entwined bay leaves, signifying death, forms a partially broken, floral rosette. This cross stands above a gate cresting of swirling volutes on a complete enclosure of square pickets, spikes, and cast standard brackets. The gate is a mixture of heavy cast ornaments and square bars which somewhat negate the talent exhibited in the cresting volutes.

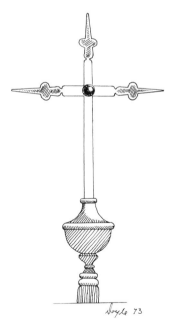

Fig. 34. Many solid iron crosses, seemingly alike, are quite different in skill and imagination when closely scrutinized. A Latin Botonnée cross stands above the large ornate enclosure of the Lanusse-McCarthy family tomb in St. Louis II, Sq. 1.

Fig. 35. Two crosses placed at the front and rear of the J. C. de St. Romes enclosure have file shaped ends that accentuate the crosses' simplicity. The enclosure and the tomb it surrounds are in excellent condition, in St. Louis II, Sq. 1. De St. Romes was the editor of the first New Orleans newspaper, Le Courier de la Louisiane.

Fig. 36. The Tricou cross is a split terminal cross on the Brown-Labranche-Fernandez enclosure in St. Louis I.

OPEN CROSSES

Open crosses, Crosses Voided, are perhaps the single most popular style throughout the cemeteries of New Orleans. They are found in every size from the smallest to the largest. The diversity of terminals, rosettes, and scroll bases seems infinite. Patterns of diamond and circle shapes are expertly placed inside the voids. Even quatrefoil, latticework, and monograms display extensive individuality as well as artistry. Most of these open crosses stand on small gates of front enclosures and often are continuous bent, flat bars forming cross and scroll base together. The J. B. Robert Armant, 1850s, is a flat bar open cross (fig. 37). A 4½ inch sunburst rosette in the Joachim Bermudez cross, 1830s, and the angel-face rosette cross with plume terminals of the James Desban, 1840s, provide enough variation in design technique to make the novice viewer overlook the standardization (figs. 38, 39). All three are in St. Louis I.

Fig. 37. Flat bar open cross on tomb of J. B. Robert Armant, St. Louis I.

Fig. 38. Open cross on Bermudez front enclosure, St. Louis I.

Fig. 39. Rosette on open cross, St. Louis I. (Photograph by Guy Bernard.)

Fig. 40A. Rouvelle flat bar open cross, St. Louis I; height 19¼ inches, width 32 inches.

Fig. 40B. D'Abernini open cross with rosette, St. Louis I; height 24¾ inches, width 22 inches.

Fig. 40C. Harris open cross, St. Louis II, Sq. 2; height 9¼ inches, width 6½ inches.

Fig. 40D. Vignaud open cross rests on a globe shape, simulating the "cross of triumph." St. Louis II, Sq. 2; height 40½ inches, width 38 inches.

Fig. 40E. Bergamini open cross varié with knob terminals, St. Louis I; height 20⅜ inches, width 12 inches.

Fig. 40F. Thomas-Leon family open cross with rosette and fleurée terminals, St. Louis II, Sq. 2; height 36 inches, width 33¼ inches.

Fig. 40G. Louis Colin open cross with rosette and Botonnée terminals, St. Louis I; height 28 inches, width 26¼ inches.

Fig. 41. The James Freret complete enclosure of square pickets and honeysuckle points alternating with sharp spikes is in excellent condition, as is the red brick tomb which it surrounds. St. Louis II, Sq. 1. There are several such tombs in St. Louis II and in the Protestant section of St. Louis I, although they are most prevalent in Cypress Grove. The bricks of the Freret tomb are beautifully molded in both the base and cornice. The side tablet dates from 1834. The open cross surmounts a sunburst gate cresting in beautifully executed scrolls within scrolls. Diamond and circle shapes are riveted within the cross bars with tiny pins and form a unified design.

Fig. 42. A similar cross and cresting may be found nearby on the complete enclosure of the Cazelar family. The copper terminals add a decoratively distinctive element. This magnificent granite tomb, because of the qualities of the material, does not yet show signs of its inevitable deterioration by neglect. The slate tablet is not in place, and the iron enclosure has lost most of its finials and should be reanchored to the coping.

Fig. 43. Open Latin cross with cast quartrefoil elements riveted within void. Two copper sphere terminals remain. This pediment cross adorns the tomb of the Ladies Progressive Friends B.M.A.A. The five-vault tomb was built in 1900 by A. J. Ossey. St. Louis II, Sq. 3.

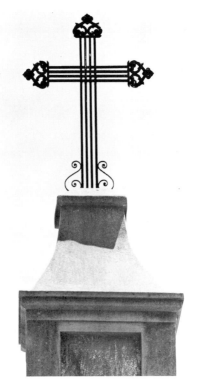

Fig. 44. Four interlaced bars form this pediment cross with heavy cast terminals above the Young Men of St. Michael's tomb built in 1909. St. Louis II, Sq. 3.

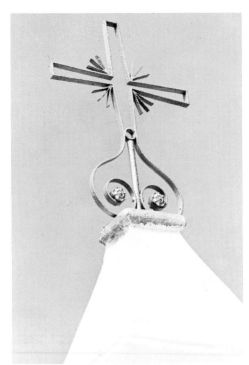

Fig. 45. The Wiltz-Vigné pediment cross is the same style as that on the gate of the Germain Musson enclosure in St. Louis I. Both are modest open crosses of plain execution.

GATES AND RAILINGS

Gates and railings to which these crosses are riveted range from the simplest round bar to the most ornate combination of wrought and cast elements. Most of these verticals were tenoned through the rails with molded projectile points being pressed on their tapered ends. The vast majority of these projectiles are lead castings with incurved modeling. These cast and wrought points are often called spikes, spearheads, picket tops, which are interchangeable terms used to afford variety. When the term *enclosure* is modified by the words *front* and *complete,* the reference is to the iron fence or railing. If the fence surrounds the site, it is complete; if restricted to the front, similar to a small window balcony, it is a front enclosure.

A survey count in St. Louis I reveals eighty-eight of the round picket projectile style, in front and complete enclosures: this style is by far the most popular in all the cemeteries. Some of these fences are in ruinous and rusted condition, while others, painted black, silver or white, are in fair to good condition (fig. 46). Other methods than painting should be employed for the protection of the iron for the beauty of its texture is lost under layers of paint. In the case of the lead points, paint is not required since the nature of the metal prevents its destruction from atmospheric conditions.

The round or square vertical bars and flat horizontals were part of the blacksmiths' iron stock. They are "merchant" bars milled at a foundry in fifteen- or twenty-foot lengths and standard size diameters. The smith cuts, assembles, and embellishes the enclosure according to the customer's orders, or simply supplies an enclosure like that of the tombs nearby. In this case it is ornamentation by analogy. On Alley 10 on the right side of St. Louis I (fig. 47) nine of these typical round picket with projectiles are used, providing an unusual row of tomb sentinels. Enclosures of this style span over a century of popularity in New Orleans.

It was often in gate forms that the local blacksmith had an opportunity for

Fig. 46. Round picket and projectile front enclosures far outnumber all other types in most New Orleans cemeteries.

flamboyant, artistic expression and it was here that he happily combined his gentle curves, inverted diamonds, and *S* and *C* scrolls into plain swirls and lyre and crossed arrow patterns. Two examples of the simple but effective wrought iron gate remain, broken from their enclosures. The first (fig. 48) leans near an unidentified tomb in St. Louis II between the Livaudais and Birot tombs. Another, in St. Louis I, belongs to the Sauvinet family (fig. 49) and the third gate, stolen before it could be photographed, was being used as a barricade for a condemned section of St. Louis I on the right side. It formerly was part of the Louis Marrec enclosure, 1853.

The lyre motif has for centuries been a favorite cemetery decoration, as has the crossed arrow and inverted torch. The latter is often attached to sheet iron panels on the corners of the railings (fig. 50), but its proliferation in iron never approaches its use in marble as tomb ornamentation; this also applies to the winged hourglass symbols (fig. 51). In New Orleans the inverted torch-within-gate design is noted in the last quarter of the nineteenth century in heavy cast iron patterns.

Fig. 47. Ironwork on Alley 10, St. Louis I.

Fig. 48. Wrought iron gate, St. Louis II, Sq. 1.

Fig. 49. Sauvinet wrought iron gate, St. Louis I.

Fig. 50. Cast iron inverted torch, St. Louis II, Sq. 1.

Fig. 51. Marie Aline Lange cast iron railing decoration, St. Louis II, Sq. 2.

Fig. 52. The lyre was a blacksmith's delight as so well illustrated in the Brown-LaBranche-Fernandez gates of the 1830s. The gates center a complete enclosure thirteen feet wide by eleven feet deep. Two large *S* scrolls, with forged split and curve volutes have as their centers the lyre pattern.

Fig. 54. The Carmick enclosure has delicate iron lilies repeating the cross base design. Its bottom gate panel features the wrought Greek Key. St. Louis II, Sq. 1.

Fig. 53. The Pilié and the Carmick enclosures represent some of the finest wrought iron to be seen in the city. Both in St. Louis II, Sq. 1, they resemble each other in technique and ornamentation. Pilié has a plain center picket gate and side panels in the wide lyre designs.

Fig. 55. The Alex Grima tomb, 1840, is enhanced with a wide gate and complete enclosure of outstanding wrought and cast elements. Again the *S* scrolls divided by three tapered verticals and a large chrysanthemum rosette give the illusion of a lyre motif. Alex Grima, a native of Malta, was an outstanding New Orleans merchant.

Fig. 56. The Louis Adam gate in St. Louis II, Sq. 2, includes a little of everything with the center section suggesting the lyre in contour with three bars. The winged hourglass and wreathed inverted torches add two death symbols. (Photograph by Guy Bernard.)

Fig. 57. The gate of Fourchy family in St. Louis III indicates the continued popularity of this motif with this late nineteenth century example by C. C. Timpe, ironmaker. Note ironmaker's mark under cross.

Fig. 58. The J. B. Labatut enclosure, St. Louis II, Sq. 2, has three gates in front with a plain diagonal bottom panel with rosettes. On either side of the middle gate is an elongated lyre, an inverted arrow piercing the center. The arrow has symbolized martyrdom, pestilence, persecution, or remorse.

Fig. 59. The beautiful arrow-lyre front panel of the Robert Avart enclosure in St. Louis II, Sq. 2, affords another example of this style. Three identical lyre designs are separated by panels of sheet iron, providing one of the most handsome interpretations of this motif.

Fig. 60. The Moquin-Perriliat tomb of 1829 has a front enclosure of round pickets, with pierced tulip points and a lovely gate with a well-modulated crossbow piercing an incurved center diamond with graceful volutes. All intersections are competently met with riveted rosettes, with three distinct rosette styles illustrated here. They and the lively curled iron feathers are cast iron; the curved bars are wrought. In St. Louis I.

Fig. 61. The Raymond Lacoul complete enclosure and gate differ only in dimension from the Moquin-Perriliat. In St. Louis I.

Fig. 62. Appolaire Perrault gate, 1865, illustrates another version of the crossbow, and there is an indulgence in decoration of rosettes, balls, plumes, and finial ornamentation. Flattened cast dahlias fill adjacent front panels, and the cast plume ornaments are repeated on the open cross. Two styles of foot pedestals complete this erstwhile simple front enclosure. In St. Louis I.

Fig. 63. The Cressione 37-inch front vault enclosure is of cross bar and plume design and one of the few pieces of vault ironwork in good condition. In St. Louis I.

Fig. 64. The James Desban gate, shown here in a photograph by Guy Bernard, is rich in cast elements indicating the extent one could decorate even a small front enclosure. In St. Louis I.

Fig. 65. The wreaths which form four panels in the gate before the Peniston-Duplantier tomb, designed by de Pouilly, St. Louis II, Sq. 2, repeat the motif in the lower panel of the bronze chapel doors. Superior, sophisticated workmanship is the hallmark of this entire enclosure.

Fig. 66. The Grailhe gates, also by de Pouilly, St. Louis II, Sq. 2, have strong handles and aureole designs repetitive of the bronze chapel gates and when viewed as a unit indicate the strong synthesis with Egyptian tomb design.

Fig. 67. The front enclosure of the Monrose tomb in St. Louis II, Sq. 2, is the only known design of this type. Completely cast, there is extraordinary floral detail entwining in this vertical pattern. The small Dantesque heads are perfect in feature rendering. A master carver would have required many months to carve this pattern.

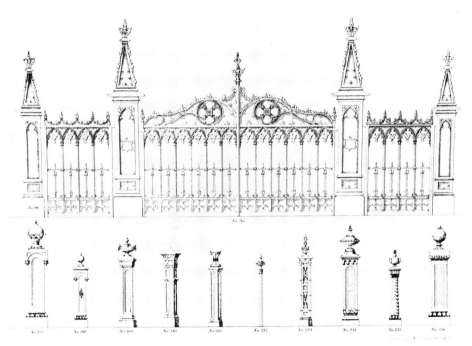

Fig. 69. Gates of the quality of the James H. Caldwell ironwork could be ordered by catalog number, as seen in this advertisement from Badger & Bogardus. (Courtesy Architectural Library, Tulane University.)

Figs. 68A, B. Superb cast work is to be seen in the James H. Caldwell gate, also in Cypress Grove. The heavy padlock securely fastens the gate and the dog-head latch handle remains operative. There is no need for the lock precaution for part of this marvelous half oval shaped enclosure is missing and there is easy entry to the tombs inside. James Caldwell was one of New Orleans most successful early nineteenth-century entrepreneurs.

Fig. 70. The Caballero enclosure of 1860 in St. Louis II, Sq. 2, exemplifies the Gothic interpretation with emphasis on the cast finials with detailed forms.

Fig. 71. The Benjamin Slark gate in Cypress Grove is identical t[o] of the Jacob Baumiller which once stood in the old Girod Cemetery. Baumiller was a manufacturer of iron railings, and was an iron importer and wholesaler.

Fig. 72. The Conery family was prominent in the factoring business and responsible for building many homes in the area known today as the Lower Garden District. Their tomb in St. Joseph No. 1 is a Doric temple with a heavy rusticated archway. A suggestion of Gothic design in the gate is repeated in the Gothic tracery inside the chapel. The quite ordinary household porcelain knobs indicate a further pot-pourri of detail.

Fig. 73. The weeping cherub or *putti* holds an inverted torch in his hand i[n] gate before the Smith L. Isard tomb, 1873, in Cypress Grove. The lotus dangle at the top of the castings around the figure and morning glory blos[soms] surround the bottom. Although these romantic Victorian gates have been us[ed in] gardens, their appropriateness remains funereal for their motifs pertain to [death] and resurrection.

Fig. 74. The Fitzwilliam-Kimball gate, St. Patrick No. 3 is part of a raised coping enclosure where there is no tomb, only a headstone. Burial is directly in the ground or vault below the ground. Most of the sites in the three St. Patrick cemeteries are of this type. Here the Victorian figure holds grape clusters and a wine jug. Interpreted with a death theme, one can associate the wine with Christ's blood shed for the redemption of man. This casting is one of interchangeable usage for it has little solemnity.

Fig. 75. The gate fragment is an example of the ever-popular bier and urn theme. Clarence Laughlin, author and photographer, once noted in a similar casting that the "angel kneeling before an incense altar is particularly interesting because of her disproportionate body, with tiny hands and feet." This plot in St. Patrick No. 2 is owned by a Fitzpatrick family.

Fig. 76. The name of E. Lacroix is barely visible on the nameplate in this gate cresting, which is dated 1858, in St. Louis III. The center of the gate features a weeping willow tree. An entire willow tree cult can be traced in New Orleans stone carvings on slabs and headstones; however, even though the tree was popular in New Orleans, it was not frequently utilized in iron castings.

SPIKES AND TERMINALS

Next to the F. Alex Grima tomb in St. Louis I is a tomb with no further identification than the inscription Tombé de Famille (fig. 77). Total neglect pervades the tomb and the beautiful wrought iron complete enclosure. Pickets and spike terminals of this enclosure resemble the Livaudais enclosure (fig. 21) and belong to the early examples of wrought craftsmanship. The elements were executed by a blacksmith

Fig. 77. Wrought iron picket and spiked terminals.

Fig. 78. The front enclosure of the Mamie Halphen tomb in St. Louis II, Sq. 2, is in poor condition, whereas the tomb is in a critical state of disrepair. The ironwork on this site is deceiving in its simplicity and is composed of very fine wrought elements. These terminals were forged on an anvil with a hammer by heating the iron, after first having upset the lower area which was swelled out to simulate a base to the javelin head. These points were made easily without the use of a die or mold because they are flat and so contoured that they could be hammered to exact dimensions by any skillful blacksmith.

Fig. 79. The Famille Durrive tomb, St. Louis I, is completely enshrouded within a huge ficus repens vine. The branches must be parted to reveal the early nineteenth-century tomb now broken and abandoned. Still another javelin style complete enclosure remains; it is very probable that these elements were wrought in the same manner as those on the Halphen ironwork. However, they may have been cast and swedged to the top of the round picket. Many of the pickets are missing in this enclosure, which is quite large, measuring eleven feet across the front by thirteen on the sides.

Fig. 80. The Christine Ferry enclosure, St. Louis II, Sq. 1, affords an excellent opportunity to observe the craftsman's welding ability in wrought iron. Both the picket and standard terminals were formed by the first terminal method discussed, the C scrolls and S scrolls were shaped separately, and the blacksmith weld was accomplished by laying the three pieces of iron together, heating them to the proper temperature, and beating them together until the iron blended into one element. The standard or post finial is again the same wrought terminal from a square bar rather than a round bar as in the case of the Livaudais and Halphen enclosures. To this bar two sets of C scrolls are welded, the tapered end is split and welded, and the S scroll is riveted by means of the cast rosette. In the hands of the skilled craftsman the work is not difficult and is performed with amazing speed.

Fig. 81. The Sociedad Ibera de Beneficence Muerta tomb, St. Louis II, Sq. 2, built by Monsseaux in 1843 was designed by J. N. B. de Pouilly. The exceptional quality of the cast spearheads on the wrought merchant bars is typical of the refined workmanship accompanying this architect's projects. At each corner eight feathered spearheads form a base to a rod shaft column four feet in height which terminates in a foliated flame-filled urn, nine inches high. The square enclosure is composed of five panels on each side, each panel consisting of nine round bar pickets. The panels are separated by square bar standards with small oval urn finials. Three of these finials are missing as are many of the beautiful spearheads. Still another cluster treatment of these spikes and columns is used at the gates. The enclosure is very like that around the Duncan Kenner tomb in Donaldsonville, Louisiana.

who heated a section of an iron bar to malleable heat, "upset" the end of it to increase the diameter where the design bulge was to be and tapered the tips as well as the two depressed areas below to approximate the design desired. An iron block, which contained an inlet of the terminal picket shape, was prepared in advance and served as a mold. The bar was then reheated and laid in the mold while the blacksmith turned and beat it until it fit the shape of the mold. This required frequent reheating and hammering. One element could be worked while another was heating, and thus a number of terminals that appeared almost identical in character and dimension could be quickly done.

According to the manuscript account book of John Mitchell, 1833–1840, (in the possession of Dr. Marcus Christian, historian and author), Daniel Dana, a Julia Street blacksmith, was paid "$7,500 to fashion a massive fence around the old United States Mint Building." The fence which surrounds this building, a design of the noted architect William Strickland, has excellent spearheads or projectile points.

Fig. 82. The projectile points of the Leeds family tomb in Cypress Grove could possibly have been inspired by de Pouilly. The quality, style, and execution resemble that of Sociedad Ibera.

Fig. 84. The front enclosure of the Germaine Musson tomb, St. Louis I, shows a very stylized cast urn finial and cast iron ornaments decorating a top border section.

Fig. 83. This urn belongs to the Grima enclosure and is very illustrative of the garland style, handled urn. It is riveted to a cast standard which has detailed paneling and egg-and-dart motif. Many examples of cast railings, spikes, and urn finials show the vast assortment of types available for enclosures. All iron enclosure urns observed throughout the cemeteries are hollow core castings. They are riveted to blocks or directly to railing standards. Some are plain spherical shapes simulating an urn; others are gadrooned, draped or garland wreathed, with handles and elaborate base designs. Most have a flame motif, symbolizing the soul's eternity.

Fig. 86. The fence of the Jefferson Fire Company No. 22 in Lafayette No. 1 was fabricated by Wood and Miltenberger of New Orleans. In this railing a pipe is run horizontally through the cast pickets and standards. This enormous enclosure and its many-vaulted tomb need immediate attention.

Fig. 85. A section of the James H. Caldwell enclosure in Cypress Grove. Everything here is cast, even the machine molding of the top railing.

Fig. 88. Illustrates a four-gated mold. (Courtesy Henry Alcus Collection.)

Figs. 87A, B, C. These three examples of picket tops are found in many cemeteries. These are cast iron malleable spearheads which were cast and heat treated to minimize brittleness. They were then driven on the round or square pickets and served as an inexpensive decorative ornament. There were as many as five hundred different designs of this type which could be cast in "gang or gate" molds four or twenty-four at a time.

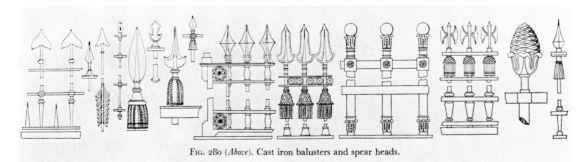

FIG. 280 (*Above*). Cast iron balusters and spear heads.

Fig. 89A. Catalog from L. N. Cottingham Company of England in the mid–nineteenth century. (Courtesy Architectural Library, Tulane University.)

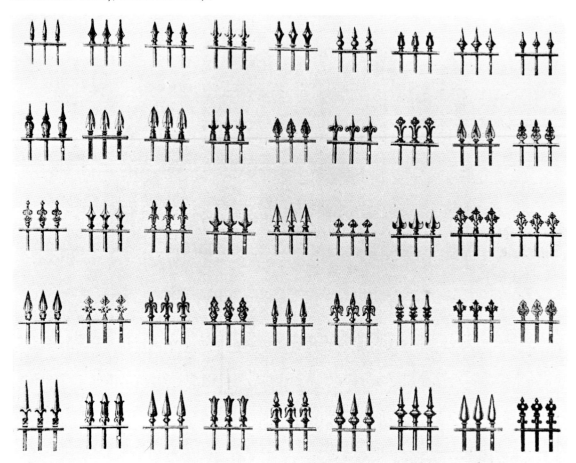

Fig. 89B. A range of spearheads for railing terminals. From a mid–nineteenth century Cottingham catalog. (Courtesy Architectural Library, Tulane University.)

Fig. 90. Gate crestings were prevalent from the 1830s through the 1900s. The Grima tomb forms a space for a nameplate which, if ever applied, has long since disappeared.

Fig. 91. In Lafayette No. 1 on the Joseph Portes Austen tomb of 1847 the cast cresting has the vining motif, utilized so frequently in interpretations of the rustic and pictur-esque. There is space here also for a nameplate.

Fig. 92. The Joseph Hays gate cresting in Cypress Grove carries the ironmaker's mark and retains a measure of individuality; there are few examples of this style.

Fig. 93. A gate cresting style frequently used appears on the Mark Thomas gate. The double dove gate cresting was also extremely popular and could be purchased from many of the late nineteenth-century ironworkers. In Cypress Grove.

RAILINGS

More round picket and cast projectile point enclosures are found in all the cemeteries; this design is followed closely by the single and double Gothic styles (fig. 94A).

Within these latter groups there are many variations but basic overall simplicity prevails. The restraint of a third design, which for purposes of this treatise has been called the diagonal cross bar, might lead one to the classification "modern." It is, however, one of the very early nineteenth-century designs as shown in 1847 lithographs (fig. 95). The incorporation of the diagonal in the early classic revival tomb sketches is clearly revealed. Early views of the St. Louis cemeteries also show both the diagonal and plain round bar with forged and cast points (page 11, fig. 12).

Fig. 94A. Cristoval Toledano tomb enclosure, a single Gothic, in Lafayette No. 1.

Fig. 95. Example of early nineteenth-century interest in diagonal railing.

Fig. 97. The Alexander Bergamini front enclosure exhibits a favorite pattern found in the St. Louis cemeteries but rarely any of the other city cemeteries. Again calling on creative privilege this style is dubbed ''basket reja'' for its similarity to the Spanish window rejas and grilles.

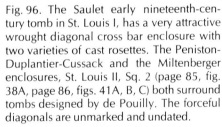

Fig. 96. The Saulet early nineteenth-century tomb in St. Louis I, has a very attractive wrought diagonal cross bar enclosure with two varieties of cast rosettes. The Peniston-Duplantier-Cussack and the Miltenberger enclosures, St. Louis II, Sq. 2 (page 85, fig. 38A, page 86, figs. 41A, B, C) both surround tombs designed by de Pouilly. The forceful diagonals are unmarked and undated.

Fig. 99. One side section of the Dubreuil front enclosure hangs onto the crumbling tomb in St. Louis I. Again the heart and diamond are combined in the wrought work, and lead balls and rosettes add a sad note of whimsy to the memory of one of Louisiana's earliest families. The Dubreuil family received one of the first plantation concessions for management in the 1720s.

Fig. 98. Only the side panels remain on this now unmarked gravesite in St. Louis II, Sq. 1, near the Lucien Delery plot. Both side panels and small front sections are gaudy with three styles of cast lead rosettes.

Fig. 100. One of the highest and most "protective" enclosures is that belonging to the Lanusse-McCarthy family in St. Louis II, Sq. 1. Here both cast and wrought elements are intermixed to provide a profusion of busy panels. It is sturdy and in good condition.

Fig. 101. The Laurent Millaudon complete enclosure on the left side of St. Louis I has a lovely "running" pattern cast in sections and fitted together with matching right and left pieces. One of the finer pointed oval loop styles, it is not commonly found in the local catalogs. The oval loop continued in variation from plain Gothic to the combined style with quatrefoils and foliation. The Catherine Williamson Peyton enclosure in St. Louis III, Sq. 1, is restrained, but the Patrick Comfort railing in St. Patrick No. 2 expands to a full Gothic expression.

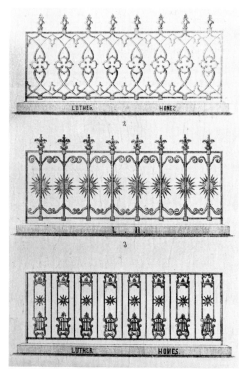

Fig. 102A. Luther Holmes catalog of Gothic and geometric styles. (Courtesy Special Collections Division, Tulane University Library.)

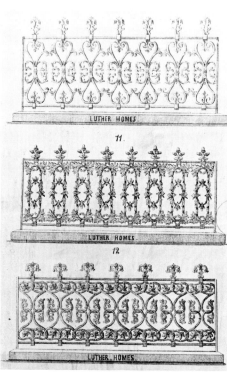

Fig. 102B. Variations in cast styles in Luther Holmes catalog. (Courtesy Special Collections Division, Tulane University Library.)

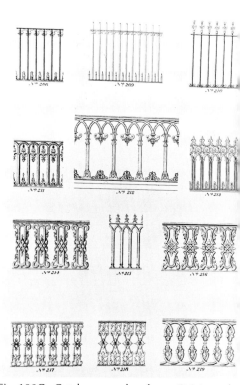

Fig. 102C. Catalog samples from *Origins of Cast Iron Architecture in America*, vol. 13. (Courtesy Architectural Library, Tulane University.)

172

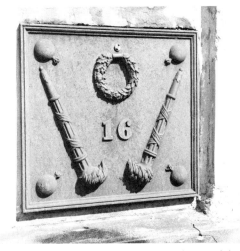

Figs. 103A, B, C, D, E. The New Orleans Battalion of Artillery sixteen-vault tomb, St. Louis I, was designed by J. N. B. de Pouilly. Inspired perhaps by relief plaques on family tombs in Pére Lachaise and Montmartre, the architect handsomely employed cannon balls in the iron vault slabs while yielding to the solemnity of death with inverted torches and beribboned wreaths. The military motif is poignantly apparent in the eight cannon posts chained together to form a complete enclosure. Only three lit cannon ball finials remain on these standards which are themselves askew or fallen. A picture found in the de Pouilly notebook owned by the Historic New Orleans Collection points directly to his utilization of European decorative ideas. One cannon standard is painted silver through the generosity of a neighboring tomb owner. The superior workmanship of the iron vault plate is readily discerned by contrasting it with that found in the Valence Street cemetery plate on the Odd Fellows Rest of Helvetia Lodge No. 44. This latter casting is later and is one reminiscent of stock fire-front plates.

Figs. 104A, B. Another "society" tomb is that of the Italian Society. Bronze lion heads link wreath handles and decorate each marble slab tablet; only two are missing. The handsome cast iron vault door is off its hinges and stands ajar revealing the inner receiving chamber. The iron railing is a special stylized design; the pattern is not repeated in the city's cemeteries. Heavy top railings are broken, yet most of the sections are in place. Vigorous and strong in detail, this enclosure survives as a superb product of Pietro Gauldi, the Italian architect hired by Joseph Barelli to design a baroque mausoleum for the society. Both men were themselves buried within this tomb.

Fig. 105. The Barelli enclosure in St. Louis II, Sq. 2, facing Priests Alley, is another very fine and individualized example of cast iron. The tomb, built for Joseph Barelli when his young son was killed, could well have been imported from Italy. The ironwork also could have come from abroad, but Barelli is known to have used the Jones, McElvain and Company foundry in Holly Springs, Mississippi, for the cast iron Moresque Building which stood on Camp, Poydras, North, and St. Charles streets. Again, this enclosure is unique within the city.

Fig. 106. The Dick tomb in St. Louis I has a complete enclosure of a geometric model with stylized dentils. This same design is used without the dentils and with a different species of top rail ornaments. The *fleur-de-lis* shown here were cast with the rail pattern. The sections, including the *fleur-de-lis* and the bottom loops were slipped onto the upper and lower rails.

174

Fig. 107A, B. The broken pieces of the Fassy-Sancho, St. Louis I, front enclosure shows the deterioration since 1947, when Guy Bernard photographed the same fence. Fragmented, peeling, and gateless, it is a testimony to vandals and neglect. This ironwork was a popular pattern and can still be seen intact on the E. E. and H. C. Parker tomb and in pieces on Les Dames du Progres vault in St. Louis II, Sq. 3.

Fig. 110. Louis R. Pierre tomb, St. Louis I.

Fig. 108. The varieties of geometrics, from the style of the P. A. Betat enclosure, St. Louis I, classified as "drip geometric," to the plain elongated oval known as the "widow's mite," could all be ordered from local ironworks catalogs. The "widow's mite" style was so called because it used much less iron and was "backed out," or hollow, with no back design. The Louis Pierre tomb (fig. 110) in St. Louis I has a widow's mite design complete enclosure.

Fig. 109. Another relatively simple and inexpensive enclosure is the Josephine Markey in St. Patrick No. 2. The six posts are formed by using a *T* iron bar with four other units. These were slipped through at least three ring forms, which in turn were attached to the rail or gate sections. A molded iron cap in which the *T* bar could be threaded is placed over these five pieces. Much less iron is used, thereby making available a less costly enclosure. Many examples of this style appear in St. Patrick, Greenwood, and St. Joseph cemeteries.

175

An architectural movement known as "Picturesque," along with the Gothic Revival, was popularized by New York architect, A. J. Davis, in the 1830s. Davis' close friend Andrew Jackson Downing, a landscape gardener and architectural critic, further spread interest in these styles by the publication *A Treatise on the Theory and Practice of Landscape Gardening Adapted in North America, 1841*. With these major influences, New York, Boston, and Philadelphia iron foundries began the production of "rustic" fences and iron furniture which sought to perpetuate nineteenth-century romanticism. Emphasis on naturalism was rendered in iron by simulating tree stumps and branches and entwining them with grape vines, oak, bay, or holly leaves.

Fig. 111. The picturesque style is illustrated in this enclosure in St. Patrick No. 2.

Fig. 112. The McIntosh fence in Cypress Grove is complete with arbor cresting above the gate.

Fig. 113. Local ironworks catalogs carried the vining style in the rose design seen rarely in the cemetery but used in St. Joseph No. 1 in front of the Jacob Lechner tomb.

Fig. 114. The Gothic Revival continues in the lovely bench of the 1840s seen on Alley 7 of St. Louis I.

Fig. 115. The bench within the Leeds family enclosure in Cypress Grove is copied from an English patent of 1846. The rococo style has scroll and leaf motifs, cabriole legs, and was characterized as a "Gothic settee" in both the Chase Brothers and Company of Boston and Vulcan Ironworks of New Boston, Illinois, catalogs. The arch patterns of the back must have been the inspiration for the latter identification.

IRON TOMBS AND TOWERS

The use of cast iron in the mid–nineteenth-century New Orleans cemeteries was not restricted to railings and rosettes. The interest in permanence and easy maintenance provoked to a limited degree the use of cast iron tombs. Historical reference to these has been sorely lacking, and few of the tombs are inscribed with anything but the family name; internment dates which often lead to clues of construction are only found on four of the sixteen known to exist.

One of the most unusual for classic simplicity and perfection of workmanship is the Leed's tomb (fig. 116A) in Cypress Grove. Dated 1844, it is an excellent example of a cast iron Greek Revival tomb complete with cast iron furniture within an exquisite complete iron enclosure. Urns (116B) and downspout grotesques (116C) decorate all sides which are rusticated under a heavy pitched pediment. Anthemions and wreaths and a large roof urn are of the finest quality. There is every reason to believe that all elements of this tomb and enclosure were cast in New Orleans at the Leeds foundry which at this period was one of the largest.

Fig. 116B. Pediment urn, Leeds tomb, Cypress Grove.

Fig. 116A. Leeds tomb, 1844, Cypress Grove.

Fig. 116C. Downspout grotesques, Leeds tomb, Cypress Grove.

The double Gothic tomb of James D. Edwards and B. T. K. Bennett, 1861 (fig. 117), in Greenwood is another example of individualization in cast iron. Each of these vaults has a chapel behind their ornate doors embellished with detailed tracery. Another set of iron doors leads into the tomb proper. The tomb and enclosure are beautifully preserved. Both the Edwards and the Bennett families owned foundries in New Orleans for over fifty years. (Photograph courtesy Leonard V. Huber Collection.)

The Karstendick tomb in Lafayette No. 1 (fig. 118) utilizes the Gothic style, although in a more restrained manner. Only the elaborate "pintelles" sweep along the roof with an air of flamboyant abandon. Otherwise, there is a severity in the paneling and a uniformity on all sides. There is neither a date nor maker's mark to aid in further identification.

Fig. 118. Karstendiek tomb, Lafayette No. 1.

The Miltenberger cast iron tomb (figs. 119 A, B, C, D) in Greenwood, however, is typical of those manufactured in Philadelphia and marketed in New Orleans by the firm Wood and Miltenberger. Vermiculated rustication on the corners and sides are characteristic of these stock patterns. Cornice medallions and anthemions were a part of the more fanciful enrichments as were Greek egg-and-dart and frieze embellishments. On the Miltenberger vault, side panels have inverted torches while the heavy hinged single door is adorned with a torch-bearing winged angel escorting the deceased soul, symbolized here by a handclasped, solemn female figure. The Pelton tomb, also in Greenwood, is exactly the same with the exception of a plain cornice and frieze motif. This latter tomb has the maker's mark (fig. 120) "Robert Wood & Co. Makers Phila." on the door. Note that even the doorknob has a classic

Fig. 117. Cast iron tomb, 1868, Greenwood Cemetery.

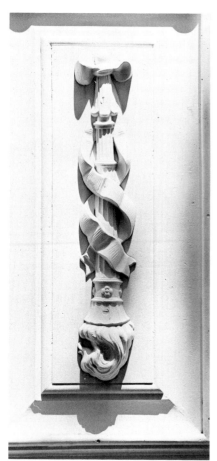

Fig. 119C. Miltenberger tomb, Green-wood.

Fig. 119A. Miltenberger tomb, Greenwood.

Fig. 119B. Miltenberger tomb, Greenwood.

Fig. 119D. Miltenberger tomb, Greenwood.

touch, that of a helmeted male surrounded by a festooned ridge. The Miltenberger tomb is painted white as are most of the cast iron tombs. The Pelton vault is, however, a bright glimmering silver.

Greenwood cemetery has at least three other stock cast tombs belonging to the H. M. Summers, the George Heaton, and the I. N. Marks families. The former was at one time surrounded by a cast iron enclosure of which only fragments remain. The enclosure resembled the single Gothic style of the Lunn tomb in the Masonic Cemetery. "Wood and Miltenberger, Makers, N. O." is stamped into the bottom of the paneled double doors.

The George Heaton vault is the same pattern tomb with conice decorations and a lovely iron roof angel (fig. 121). The rusticated enclosure has an arbor arch above the gate which is similar to the Austen gate in Lafayette No. 1. The I. N. Marks metal tomb is rusting away, yet its Gothic fence enclosure remains in good condition.

The N. M. Benachi family tomb stands in St. Louis III (fig. 122), and represents the same stock pattern with minor variations. A cross is riveted to the front cornice and the cast iron doors have been replaced with double marble slabs.

In Odd Fellows Cemetery two more of these cast iron tombs exist yet both have different door treatment. The E. H. Fairchild vault (fig. 123) has an open grille-work door now broken from its hinges and minus two of its Odd Fellow symbols. Pictures from the 1950s reveal this tomb intact with a large center medallion and castings above the cornice. There is a recessed chapel in which there is grim and sorrowful inscription.

Fig. 120. Cast iron doorway, J. M. Pelton tomb, Greenwood. (Photograph by Guy F. Bernard.)

Anson Ferauld Fairchild
(oldest son)

A member of Co. B. Crescent
Regiment La. Volunteers

Born 15 June 1843
Died 14 April 1862
18 years and 10 months

He fell exhausted on the Bloody Field
of Shiloh, Sunday 6, 1862
fighting for his country's liberty
and died in Corinth, Miss.
as recorded above.

Fig. 123. Fairchild tomb, Oddfellows Rest.

Fig. 122. Benachi tomb, St. Louis III.

Fig. 121. John George Heaton tomb, Greenwood.

The second cast tomb in Odd Fellows is the W. H. Foster one, red-leaded but otherwise exact in pattern to the Fairchild and Benachi styles. The door, completely broken, once had paneled, inverted, beribboned torches.

The Caufield-Armstrong is a six-vault brick-fronted cast iron tomb in St. Joseph No. 1 on Washington Avenue (fig. 124). Fluted iron Doric columns stand on iron steps, but the tomb rests on a brick chain wall. Its rusticated sides are peeling, and its century of age shows through lack of maintenance.

The Sebastian Swoop edifice (fig. 125) on the other hand is well preserved and may be difficult to identify as iron because of its fine finish. Honeysuckle "pintelles" decorate its roofline and somber wreaths its side panels. A "Geddes, Shakspeare & Co., 208 Girod Street, New Orleans, La." maker's mark is clearly stamped in the lower right corner.

The Reynolds tomb in Metairie Cemetery (fig. 126), painted a bright silver, incorporates a wide-edge iron coping with iron pedestal urns. Similar to the Wood and Miltenberger stock patterns, it differs in size and ornamentation. The iron door frames a marble slab on which the first internment date is 1877. The trademarks are placed on the right and left sides of the base. The Reynolds family were iron manufacturers from the 1860s. Both John and Louis Reynolds were leading architects in the city. The John Clark tomb is the second cast iron tomb in Metairie and is the same stock pattern as the Reynolds tomb although it does not have a maker's mark.

The Thompson hourglass obelisk (fig. 127) was photographed by Guy Bernard in 1957. Before that time photographs showed it with a large bowl-shaped urn at its peak. It is one of the many markers which have disappeared from Cypress Grove Cemetery but it did represent a nineteenth-century interest in this iron form.

Fig. 124. Caufield-Armstrong tomb, 1871, St. Joseph No. 1.

Fig. 126. Reynolds tomb of cast iron, painted silver, Metairie Cemetery.

Fig. 125. Sebastian Swoop tomb of cast iron, St. Patrick No. 2.

Fig. 127. Thomson cast iron obelisk, Cypress Grove. (Photograph by Guy F. Bernard.)

Fig. 128. Harriette Levi obelisk in white bronze, 1883, Hebrew Rest No. 1.

Fig. 129. Simon Weil obelisk in white bronze, 1884, Hebrew Rest No. 1.

In Hebrew's Rest No. 1 on Elysian Fields the obelisk serves as a marker for many sites. Particularly elaborate are the Harriet Levi (fig. 128) and Simon Weil (fig. 129) ones, cast in white bronze. On the former is a portrait over which is the poignant phrase "Absent Not Dead."

Coleman's White Bronze Works of New Orleans produced many of these works, and there is at least one example in Metairie Cemetery belonging to the Kurten and Grunewald families (fig. 130) which was made at the Monumental Bronze Company of Bridgeport, Connecticut.

In the Masonic Cemetery on City Park Avenue the Hotchkiss raised iron coping is rusticated with corner pilasters with large draped urns (fig. 131). The iron copings were also widely used on many of the iron fences in the three St. Patrick cemeteries.

On New Orleans streets throughout the nineteenth century it was necessary to place the wheel guards at the intersections and corners because of the deep ditches. Figure 132 from Greenwood is such a guard, and figure 133 is a pagoda style chain post, as well as wheel guard. The latter can still be found in Greenwood and Cypress Grove, a memory of an ordinary street component of the past century.

Fig. 131. Hotchkiss iron coping with cast, draped urns, Masonic Cemetery. (Photograph by Guy F. Bernard.)

Fig. 130. Kurten obelisk, by Monumental Bronze Company, Bridgeport, Connecticut; Metairie Cemetery.

Fig. 133. Wheel guard, Greenwood.

Fig. 132. Wheel guard made by Shakspeare and Geddes, Greenwood Cemetery.

IMMORTELLES

The desire to revere the dead reached a romantic phase in nineteenth-century cemeteries when relatives of the deceased adorned even the most sophisticated Greek Revival tombs with mementoes of ingenuity and variety. These immortelles, often imported from France prior to the mid–nineteenth century, were executed with skill and finesse by Vieux Carré artisans in the second half of the century.

In a *Picayune* article of March 17, 1846, it was reported: "Oldtimers here will tell you artificial All Saints' wreaths are staging a comeback. Beaded wreaths, also a New Orleans custom in former years, seem to have disappeared for good, as have the orphans who used to stand inside the cemetery gates with tin plates and tap for pennies from those who came to honor their dead."

Many memorial wreaths were made of black, white, and purple beads strung on pliant wires and garnished with delicately pale porcelain roses (fig. 134; color plate 5). Metal wreaths were cut from sheets of zinc to form garlands of ivy leaves which were painted black and speckled with glitter (fig. 135). More personalized, but never placed on tombs, were hair wreaths which combined innovative designs with beads, shells, small dolls, and strips of wool. The utilization of hair evolved into mourning articles of every description. Woven bracelets, necklaces and earrings were among the hair ornaments illustrated by F. Stubenrauch's advertisement in Gardner's *New Orleans Directory* of 1860 (fig. 136).

The hair wreaths, unlike immortelles, which remained on the tombs, were enshrined in glass-covered box frames. These were hung in family parlors along with small framed hair memorials executed on glass. The thematic content resembled that of memorial embroideries and watercolors. One of the traditional techniques of making hair memorials was painstakingly to lay strand by strand of hair on a sheet of waxed paper. When the sheet was filled, an unwaxed sheet was placed on top, and a

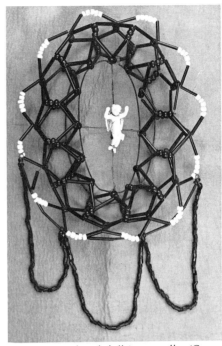

Fig. 134. Bead and doll immortelle. (Courtesy Historic New Orleans Collection.)

Fig. 135. Metal immortelle with glitter. (Courtesy Historic New Orleans Collection).

Fig. 136. Hair Works advertisement, Gardner's *New Orleans Directory*, 1860 (Courtesy New Orleans Public Library.)

Fig. 137. Hair immortelle. (Courtesy New Orleans Historic Collection.)

Fig. 138. Small metal stencilled immortelles. (Courtesy Historic New Orleans Collection.)

warm iron was used to melt the wax into the hair. The sheet of hair was then lightly lacquered and could be cut into any shape desired. These hair designs were glued to a painted glass, usually white in tone, and combined with drawings of personalized memorial monuments, all of which were allegories of death (fig. 137).

Immortelles stencilled in reverse on glass were another widely used memorial. Sealed with zinc disc backs, they were further weatherproofed with copper rim edges. Painted bright shades of blue and green, these memorials probably were imported from France with inscriptions—"To my brother," or sister, or husband—in both French and English (fig. 138).

When Mark Twain visited New Orleans in 1883, he characterized the practice of placing memorial wreaths on tomb fronts in a delightful manner, prophetically indicating a twentieth-century predilection to move rapidly away from the scene of grief: "The immortelle requires no attention; you just hang it up, and there you are; just leave it alone, it will take care of your grief for you and keep it in mind better than you can; stands weather first rate, and lasts like boiler iron."

Customs associated with death are as varied as the nationalities that formed the fabric of New Orleans Victorian society. Burials were expensive, although the frequency of yellow fever epidemics often forced a quick dispatch that allowed little time for grandiose funeral corteges. "Waking," reported to be of Irish origin, was adopted early by the Creoles who also affected the Victorian customs of stopping clocks in the home of the deceased, draping mirrors, and generally announcing the unhappy event through black-bordered street corner death notices. Mourning was "big business"; what one did not own or could not borrow was available from a local undertaker, who advertised such as early as 1831 (fig. 139).

Nor was the deceased forgotten during the years that followed entombment. All Saints' Day was but one day when all visited and refurbished tombs. For many, a visit to the cemetery was a commonplace Sunday outing. The cone-shaped metal containers that hung on either side of the tomb tablet were filled with fresh flowers, although, even then, artificial flowers were used occasionally. Anniversaries of death dates or recent entombments were sometimes observed by draping crape from the white porcelain knobs found in the upper corners of the tomb. These knobs, which resemble drawer pulls, are found in the St. Louis cemeteries and are most common to

Fig. 140. Twentieth-century immortelle made of plastic bottle holders and decorated with plastic flowers. The move from the metal age to the plastic age is complete, even within the older cemeteries.

JOSEPH FERNANDEZ, has the l onor of in-
forming the public, that he continues to
keep his establishment at No. 84 St. Ann, between Royal and Bourbon streets, for his sole
account, and without partnership with any one.
There will constantly be found at his store,
Coffins of all qualities and proportions, as well
as all sorts of funeral decorations, and from this
day forward his prices will be reduced as follows, to wit:

1st. For a simple coffin, linned with black
cotton, with ribbons and the small two
wheel hearse No. 1,......................$10
2d. For a coffin lined with velvet, with two
wheel hearse No. 2, decently ornamented
with plumes............................14
3d. For a coffin like the preceding one
with the four wheel hearse,.................20
4th. For a coffin lined with white satin,
and two wheel hearse No. 2, decently lined
in white with the necessary plumes........18
5th. Like the preceding one but with the
four wheel hearse,.....................22
6th. For a coffin lined with white cotton
cambric and two wheel hearse No. 1, decently lined,.............................14
7th. For Mahogany coffin and two wheel
hearse No. 2, well lined and ornamented
with plumes,..........................25
8th. Like the preceding one, but with the
four wheel hearse, complete lining & plumes, .30
9th. For a painted coffin, with hearse No 1, 6
10th. Like the preceding one, but with
hearse No. 2,.........................&

A diminution may be obtained according to
ircumstances.
For furnishing and putting up funeral decoration either black or white,...............10
Mr. Fernandez will also undertake to furnish,
cheaper than any one else, all articles used in funerals and funeral service, such as tapers of all
sizes, crape, scarfs, white or black gloves of all
qualities, funeral tickets, &c. &c. and also com-
munion tapers of all descriptions.
He will also undertake the furnishing of
Coaches, and the erection of TOMBS and
MONUMENTS of all descriptions. He will
have tombs opened and closed again when applied to. He will furnish all sorts of funeral
Marble and Tombstones, engraved, carved and
gilt, and finally will undertake the composition
of inscriptions and epitaphs, which will be made
by an able person.
Persons who will apply to him for every thing
they may want, will obtain tapers at the rate of
ten bitts to a dollar; and if they are desired to be
lined with paper, no more will be charged than
for those without lining. He will also furnish
stuff for mourning dresses, and those who may
not be able to pay in cash, will be allowed a rea-
sonable credit; and they will obtain gratis the
use of the necessary chandeliers and plate.
All persons in needy circumstances, who may
wish to have their friends decently buried, will
be charged only with the actual costs, without
any charge for work and labor.
The poor will be served without any remuner-
ation.
As to the mode of payment, Mr. Fernandez
will not do as is done in certain places, where
money is required forthwith, nay sometimes in
advance—but he will make arrangements according to the fortune and situation of his employers.
He will distress no one, and will send his bills to
be collected, only when the means of his cus-
tomers will allow them to pay them.   june 2

Fig. 139. Undertaker's advertisement, *Louisiana Courier*, June 2, 1831. (Courtesy Historic New Orleans Collection.)

Fig. 143. Carved marble portrait of a member of the Sciortino family attached to tomb pediment, St. Roch Cemetery.

Fig. 141. Carved marble portraiture of Maria Francesca Saltarelli, Metairie Cemetery.

Fig. 142. Bronze framed portrait on glass of Goldie Karnolsky imbedded in tomb tablet, Gates of Prayer.

St. Vincent de Paul. Some of the large vault society tombs in St. Louis II, Square 3, have large iron hooks, presumably for the same purpose.

The romantic gloom of the Victorian observation of death is no longer in vogue. Many of the cemeteries are scenes of vandalism and other crimes, and the new aesthetic of instant burial with commercialized, standardized procedures seriously jeopardizes the survival of nineteenth-century New Orleans cemeteries. In a manner similar to the buildings and homes bequeathed to us, they are key links between periods and are well-adapted to twentieth-century needs. Old New Orleans burial custom, as well as modern technology (cremation), provides the means whereby individual tombs may be used over and over, thus conserving valuable land and preserving architecturally valuable units with marble and iron decorative motifs unique to New Orleans.

Thoughts on New Orleans and Preservation: A Cemetery Elegy

BERNARD LEMANN

The truism that architecture conveys a message is almost universally accepted. Sometimes it is a concept or a symbolic meaning deliberately shaped into the object by the designer. Otherwise the message may be an implicit image or significance that develops cumulatively as the cultural expression of a people. All cemeteries of course are loaded with the first type, the overlay of symbolic suggestion. It is more to the point here to turn attention to the secondary effect: how our cemeteries tell us something of ourselves, or how, like all architecture, they play into the lives of the living.

There are many parallels between our old cemeteries and other aspects of New Orleans. For example, they figure prominently in the prevalent affairs of tourism. It is customary to stress the unique conditions of New Orleans even while recognizing how it falls in with the general trends of American or indeed all Western civilization. Still another circumstance whereby the cemeteries follow the city's consistency is the custom of burials above ground and the unusual walls of superimposed vaults, or "ovens": they too are almost, but not quite, a unique localism. While attracting the impersonal interest of transients, many New Orleans cemeteries still receive some attention from a citizenry that has always maintained a deep concern for its past. Here again they reiterate familiar thematic phases of community sentiment. As places of solace and ceremony they assume their role in the well-entrenched local mores, where drama and quiescence have commingled for generations. Finally, among the latest phases of expressive historic phenomena is the elevated speedway above the horizon of St. Louis Cemetery II, and the endless background hum of expressway traffic in others as well.

So, in one way or another, in her places of interment, the characteristic and varied charms of our dear old madam New Orleans can be recognized, sometimes trim and showy, here and there a little shapeless and deteriorated, and in other places excessively made up and refurbished. A few old-fashioned examples, such as St. Roch's, adopt the happy medium of continuous care and thereby avoid the extremes of neglect or stereotyped restoration. Here the effect of comfortable aging is aided by the local custom of annual small repairs and whitewashing in preparation for All Saints' Day (fig. 1). Increasingly, for an opportunity to observe some fairly sustained survival of indigenous folkway practices, it is necessary to go to an outlying area, such as the one-time remote and solitary villages in the Barataria area.

The accumulation of burials was a problem for cities centuries before the population pressures of modern times. In New Orleans, as in every other locality, the urban patterns of the last century have expanded beyond and surrounded the outlying burial grounds. Indeed, the earliest have long since disappeared, and

Fig. 1. "All-Saints Day in New Orleans—Decorating the Tombs..." from *Harper's Weekly*, November 7, 1885. Plant-life and weather intrude in the drama of the living and the dead. (Courtesy Historic New Orleans Collection.)

189

Fig. 2. The stubborn force of subtropical flora.

Fig. 3. Gaping crypt and cast iron casket.

subsequent notable examples of the 1820s also have been erased. Such was the fate of the Girod Street Cemetery, where now the Post Office is located, and Shanarai Chasset (Gates of Mercy) at Jackson Avenue and Saratoga Street, both of which were removed in 1957. One tends to think of the tomb's finality as the threshold into perpetuity, but the demands of city life and growth wipe away these supposedly last resting places.

Boston's Mount Auburn (1832) and Greenwood in New York (1842), spread out park-like in the romantic English landscape manner, expressed the city dweller's flight to suburban peace and greenery, and were actually used for family outings. They were modeled after Pére Lachaise which had been established several decades before (1804) when Menilmontant was still on the outskirts of Paris. Metairie, more or less New Orleans' own Pére Lachaise, once semi-rural as the name implies, was developed about two generations later than Mount Auburn or Greenwood in spite of Francophile preferences in other matters. In general the cemeteries of New Orleans have tended to have an urban character, their rows of tombs truly like streets of the dead, much in the ancient Roman manner (the Via Appia in Rome, or Aliscamps in Arles).

The cities that we presently inhabit often seem in the death throes. In vain we seek a sane solution for housing the impoverished, the mentally afflicted or incarcerated, not to mention the affluent, the powerful, and all the burgeoning in between. Certainly it is none too soon to give thought to the disposition of the mortal remains that also, as surely as fate, will continue to burgeon beyond measure. Already the statistics reveal how the debris from our active economy (junked cars, non-biodegradable trash bags, demolition residue) is acquiring a staggering bulk that, as planners suggest, threaten to crowd us off the planet. Though none too soon to consider, it may possibly be premature to make a firm decision about cemeteries, especially while concerns such as housing and transportation still hang in the balance.

Eventually, the problem should be one of the simplest of solution, once man has become impervious to shams and commercials. Much of our funerary practice is obsolescent, a long-delayed hangover from the superstitious age of Merlin or the Druids, or back into the halting infancy of precivilization. The funeral motorcades, a serious traffic hazard related to the illogical zoning of funeral homes, are no doubt carry-overs from the time when people felt that poor Tom somehow deserved a carved black vehicle drawn by plumed horses, and was somehow gratified by this special respect on his last ride. It was "as he would have wanted it." But the man on the street who paused and removed his hat as the hearse passed — he, too, has joined poor Tom of more than a generation ago.

It is entirely human that we drag along with us a few ancestral throwbacks. We are presently too dehumanized to shed these few quaint habits prior to moving into history's next phase. So much of the nineteenth century hovers in New Orleans, and its evocative flavor is a major factor that makes it livable and appealing to visitors.

As long as cemeteries are to be retained as part of the city plan, the question of their relation to the living community raises some mixed concerns. A policy of maintenance or restoration is a particularly complicated subject. Under general municipal or church control, individual plots are held under private title. Families disperse or dissipate, and the determination of ownership, and hence responsibility, often becomes an unsolvable matter.

On swampy soil (where they were usually located) tombs lean and tilt fantastically. Marble slabs curl out of line and inscriptions melt away. The soft mortar dusts away and frail brickwork splits open. Above all, the stubborn force of subtropical nature takes over (fig. 2). Innocent little seedlings become uncontrollable vines or trees with destructive roots.

Such signs of oblivion are of course symbolic messages, compelling enough to make Thomas Gray's early romantic *Elegy* seem like the neat little British ditty that it is. Here and there the anonymous, brick-cluttered foundation of a one-time tomb tells its own story, more historically revealing than any hypothetical restoration. Provided that the overwhelming vegetation can be modified to some extent, the weeds atop a wall or parapet, the wild, aggressive roots, and the dank, gaping crypt with a glimpse of an antique cast iron casket are appropriate complements to the homely inscriptions that feed the ruminative mood of the cemetery stroller (fig. 3). Interested and often entranced visitors, as opposed to persons attending a particular gravesite, are frequently to be observed in most of the older cemeteries.

The poetic and picturesque appeal of ruins and nature's processes have been deliberately recognized at least since the eighteenth century, and recently there have been various studies specifically directed to this topic.

Almost a century ago the melancholic atmosphere and dense, rich overgrowth of some local cemetery had evidently inspired Lafcadio Hearn to write one of his newspaper columns. The open crevice of a tomb and the vital force of creeping plants became the central theme of one of his most memorable and fantastic sketches entitled *L'amour après la mort (Times-Democrat,* April 6, 1884).

To judge by early descriptions, the city at large has almost from the outset been bathed in a moldering timelessness. To preserve the essence of the locale, the sense of an interplay of human effort and nature's forces would require the continuous application of a thoughtful, subtle, yet reasonably relaxed attitude. In matters relating to preservation, restoration, renewal and innovation, every instance is its own particular case, and is usually subject to more than one acceptable solution.

It has been customary to stabilize ruins, sometimes returning a few fallen parts to their original positions, and more particularly by introducing a protective fill or topping in order to stay the effects of continued decay. This has been done especially among ancient Roman ruins, and for archeological reasons this practice is often justifiable. But the essential appeal and meaningfulness of ruins can only be the vivid experience of the genuine condition, the apperception of them as part of a process. Any tampering merely creates an artificial intrusion. As a general rule some moderate or minimal measure is the best answer: curtail minimally the damaging plant growth, but leave the trees and roots in place wherever possible (figs. 4A, B). Best of all, of course, is the simple natural care of continued personal concern.

One outstanding example of misguided repairs can be cited: the striking pyramidal Varney monument, which today stands conspicuously at the entrance of New Orleans earliest surviving cemetery, St. Louis I. It appears in John H. B. Latrobe's watercolor of 1834 (see color plate 1), already at that time weathered and mellowed. Subsequently the original stucco was broken away, and now it has been "restored," without reference to the refinements of detail clearly documented in the Latrobe drawing, and with a hard modern cement, as crisp and sharp as the edges of One Shell Square. Both these landmarks will need at least two generations to settle into some future cityscape.

Figs. 4A, B. Before-and-after extremes bypass a moderate mean.

NEW ORLEANS CEMETERY LOCATIONS

St. Louis I . . . Basin and St. Louis Streets
St. Louis II . . . Claiborne Avenue, between St. Louis and Iberville
St. Louis III . . . 3421 Esplanade Avenue
St. Patrick No. 1, No. 2, No. 3 . . . 143 City Park Avenue
St. Roch No. 1, No. 2 . . . 1725 St. Roch Avenue
Lafayette No. 1 . . . 1427 Sixth Street
Lafayette No. 2 . . . Washington Avenue, between Loyola and Saratoga
St. Joseph No. 1, No. 2 . . . 2220 Washington Avenue
St. John . . . 4841 Canal Street
Metairie . . . 5100 Pontchartrain Boulevard
Cypress Grove . . . 120 City Park Avenue
Greenwood . . . 120 City Park Avenue
Odd Fellows Rest . . . 5055 Canal Street
St. Mary—Carrollton . . . Adams Street, between Spruce and Cohn
Carrollton . . . Adams Street, between Hickory and Birch
St. Bartholomew . . . Algiers
St. Mary . . . Algiers
Masonic . . . 400 City Park Avenue
Holt . . . 635 City Park Avenue
St. Vincent de Paul I, II, III . . . 1322 Louisa Street
Valence Street . . . Valence Street, between Daneel and Saratoga
St. Vincent—Soniat Street No. 1, No. 2 . . . 1950 Soniat Street
Gates of Prayer No. 1 (Beth Israel) . . . 4800 block Canal Street
Gates of Prayer No. 2 . . . Joseph Street, between Pitt and Garfield
Hebrew Rest . . . 2003 Pelopidas Street
Dispersed of Judah . . . 4901 Canal Street
Ahavas Sholem . . . Elysian Fields, Stephen Girard, Frenchmen, and Mandolin streets
Anshe Sfard . . . Elysian Fields, Frenchmen, Stephen Girard and Mandolin streets
Jewish Burial Rites . . . Elysian Fields, Frenchmen, Stephen Girard, and Mandolin streets
Charity Hospital . . . 5050 Canal Street
Mt. Olivet . . . 4000 Norman Mayer Avenue
Beth Israel . . . Stephen Girard, Elysian Fields, Frenchmen and Mandolin streets
Chivra Thilim (formerly Temmeme Derech) . . . South Anthony Street, near Canal

SELECTED BIBLIOGRAPHY

Appleton, Leroy H. *Symbolism in Liturgical Art.* New York: Scribner, 1959.

Bragg, Lillian Choplin. *Old Savannah Ironwork.* Savannah, Ga.: 1957.

Burgess, Frederick Bevan. *English Churchyard Memorials.* London: 1963.

Carey, Joseph S. *St. Louis Cemetery Number One.* New Orleans: 1948.

————. *Your Cemetery Plot and Title.*

Carter, Hodding, ed. *The Past as Prelude: New Orleans 1718–1968.* New Orleans: Pelican Publishing Co. for Tulane University, 1968.

Christian, Marcus. *Negro Ironworkers of Louisiana 1718–1900.* New Orleans: Pelican Publishing Co., 1972.

Crescent City Business Directory. New Orleans: Office of the Price-Current, 1858–59.

Crescent City Directory New Orleans. New Orleans: Graham Co., 1867.

Curl, James Stevens. *The Victorian Celebration of Death.* Detroit: Partridge Press, 1972.

De Pouilly, J. N. B. "3 Nouvelle, Orleans." Sketchbook, Historic New Orleans Collection.

Discovering Antiques, XII. New York: Greystone Press, 1973.

Durand, J. N. L. *Recueil et parallele des edifices de tout genre ancien et modern.* Paris: 1800–1801.

Eckels, Claire Wittler. "The Egyptian Revival in America." *Archaeology,* September, 1950.

Edgell, G. H. *American Architecture of Today.* New York, London: Charles Scribner's Sons, 1928.

Erskine. *Bent Iron Work.* New York: Scribner's Sons.

Federal Writers Project of the Works Progress Administration. *New Orleans City Guide.* Boston: Houghton, Mifflin Co., 1938.

Fletcher, Sir Banister. *A History of Architecture.* New York: Scribner's, 1961.

Fossier, Albert E. *New Orleans: The Glamour Period, 1800–1840.* New Orleans: Pelican Publishing Co., 1957.

Geerlings, Gerald K. *Wrought Iron in Architecture.* New York: Charles Scribner's Sons, 1972.

General Advertiser and Crescent City Directory. New Orleans: Gibson Ct., 1838.

Giedion, Sigfried. *Space, Time and Architecture.* Cambridge, Mass.: Harvard University Press, 1963.

Gowans, Alan. *Images of American Living.* New York: Lippincott, 1964.

Hamlin, Talbot F. *Benjamin Henry Latrobe.* New York: Oxford University Press, 1955.

————. *Greek Revival Architecture in America.* London: Oxford University Press, 1944.

Hatfield, R. G. *American House Carpenter.* New York: 1844.

Haviland, John. *Practical Builders Assistant.* Baltimore: 1830.

Herrin. *The Creole Aristocracy.* New York: 1952.

Hitchcock, Henry Russell. *Architecture: Nineteenth and Twentieth Century.* Baltimore: 1830.

Huber, Leonard V. *New Orleans, A Pictorial History.* New York: Crown Publishers, 1971.

————, and Guy F. Bernard. *To Glorious Immortality.* New Orleans: Alblen Books, 1961.

Korn, Bertram Wallace. *The Early Jews of New Orleans.* Waltham, Mass.: American Jewish Historical Society, 1969.

Lancaster, Clay. "Early Ironwork of Central Kentucky and Its Role in the Architectural Development." *Antiques* (May, 1948).

————. "Oriental Forms in American Architecture 1800–1870." *Art Bulletin* (September, 1947).

Latrobe, Benjamin Henry Boneval. *Impressions Respecting New Orleans.* Edited by Samuel Wilson. New York: Columbia University Press, 1951.

————. *Le père la chaise ou recueil de dessins aux traits et dans leurs Justes proportions des principaux monumens de ce cimetière.* Paris: Printed by Quaglia, n. d.

BIBLIOGRAPHY

Laughlin, C. "Architecture of New Orleans." *Architectural Review* (August, 1946).

Lichten, F. "Philadelphia's Ornamental Cast Iron . . . ."*Antiques* (August, 1953).

Martin, M. "Progress of Wrought Iron in America." *Arts and Decoration* (April, 1925.)

Marty, J. *Promenades pittoresques aux cimetierès du Père la Chaise, de Montmartre et autres.* Paris: 1844.

Memorial Symbolism, Epitaphs, and Design Types. Boston: American Monument Association, n.d.

Newhall, B. "Cast Iron Elegance." *American Magazine of Art* (December, 1936).

New Orleans City Directory. New Orleans: Polk Co., 1874–1900.

Polk Co., 1874–1900.

New Orleans *Courier,* 1833.

New Orleans *Daily Crescent,* March, 1848–November, 1869.

New Orleans. *Daily Item,* 1893–May, 1902.

New Orleans. *Daily Picayune,* 1837–April, 1914.

New Orleans. *Daily States,* January, 1880–March, 1918.

New Orleans *Times-Picayune,* May, 1914–1956.

New Orleans *Item,* May, 1902–September, 1958.

New Orleans Public Library. Photograph Files.

New Orleans *Times-Democrat,* December 1881–May 1914.

Norman, L. Aine. *Monuments funeraires.* Paris: 1847.

Orleans Parish Notorial Archives Records.

Pevsner, Nikolas, and S. Lang. "The Egyptian Revival." *Architectural Review* (May, 1956).

Plazcek, Adolf K. *The Origins of Cast Iron Architecture in America.* New York: Pa Capo Press Series, 1970.

Prospectus of the General Cemetery Company. London: 1830.

Rayner, Joan. "Pere-Lachaise." *Architectural Review* (October, 1939).

Records and Deliberations of the Cabildo, IV (September 19, 1800–July 17, 1802).

Records and Files of the Historic New Orleans Collection.

Reinders, Robert C. *End of an Era: New Orleans, 1850–1860.* New Orleans: Pelican Publishing Co., 1964.

Soards, L. *Soard's New Orleans City Directory.* New Orleans: Soard's Directory Co., 1870–1910.

Speltz, Alexander. *Styles of Ornament.* New York: Grosset and Dunlap.

Sweet, J., and G. Sweet. "Island Iron: Burial Plot Enclosures of Edgartown, Martha's Vineyard." *Magazine of Art* (March, 1945).

Weiblen Collection, Library Archives of Louisiana State University in New Orleans.

Wallace, Philip B. *Colonial Ironwork in Old Philadelphia.* New York: Dover Publications Inc., 1970.

Whittick, Arnold. *History of Cemetery Sculpture.* London: 1938.

Wilson, Samuel. *"New Orleans Ironwork."* *Magazine of Art* (October, 1948).

Wilson, Samuel, and Leonard Huber. *The St. Louis Cemeteries of New Orleans.* New Orleans: St. Louis Cathedral, 1968.

Works Progress Administration Records on New Orleans Artists. New Orleans Museum of Art.

INDEX

INDEX

196

INDEX

Chapel of St. Roch
New Orleans

Pen and ink sketch by Mrs. William
B. Gregory of St. Roch Cemetery Chapel
drawn to be reproduced on a post-
card, *circa* 1901. (Courtesy Leonard V.
Huber Collection.)